CONSTITUTIONAL DIALOGUE IN COMMON LAW ASIA

Constitutional Dialogue in Common Law Asia

PO JEN YAP
Associate Professor, Faculty of Law, The University of Hong Kong

OXFORD
UNIVERSITY PRESS

OXFORD
UNIVERSITY PRESS

Great Clarendon Street, Oxford, OX2 6DP,
United Kingdom

Oxford University Press is a department of the University of Oxford.
It furthers the University's objective of excellence in research, scholarship,
and education by publishing worldwide. Oxford is a registered trade mark of
Oxford University Press in the UK and in certain other countries

First Edition published in 2015
Impression: 1

Published in the United States of America by Oxford University Press
198 Madison Avenue, New York, NY 10016, United States of America

British Library Cataloguing in Publication Data
Data available

Library of Congress Control Number: 2015933286

ISBN 978–0–19–873637–0

Printed and bound by
CPI Group (UK) Ltd, Croydon, CR0 4YY

Foreword by the Honourable Chief Justice Geoffrey Ma

Professor Yap's highly stimulating book proceeds on the basis that the at times seemingly disparate and unconnected principles of constitutional law can be rationalized by a dialogic review approach adopted by the courts. This means that while the courts do strictly speaking, as is their constitutional mandate, interpret and apply the law, they do not in practice ignore the obvious fact that public law (especially constitutional law) in its societal context must also include the involvement of the executive and the legislature. It makes no sense in other words for courts to ignore the relevance of the role of the executive and the legislature. Thus, for example, concepts of the margin of appreciation come into play, and these are in truth convenient ways of recognizing the different roles that exist under any system having a separation of powers as a constitutional model. The courts of course interpret constitutions where they exist but owing to the broad words used in them, regard must be paid to the relevant context of any subject matter under scrutiny. This may involve looking into public policy considerations. Such matters are certainly within the province of the executive and the legislature's responsibilities.

This is a broad topic. Professor Yap studies the experience of three jurisdictions: Hong Kong, Malaysia, and Singapore. The dialogic review approach is tested the most in jurisdictions where the courts have the power to declare as void any legislation or act that is unconstitutional. For instance, in Hong Kong, the Basic Law effectively states this to be the position. This ability to strike down legislation or other acts as being void by reason of unconstitutionality is sometimes said to cause a tension between the judiciary and the other institutions of government. This is often misunderstood and exaggerated, particularly when one understands that the judiciary has no political role. However, it does mean that in the adjudication of particular public law cases, the courts do take into account realities and matters of public policy. How far these matters become decisive will depend on a variety of circumstances.

I commend this book to all serious students of and practitioners in constitutional law. It assists in the understanding of a complex subject, and a proper understanding of any legal subject is key to arriving at correct and just outcomes.

Geoffrey Ma
Chief Justice, Hong Kong Court of Final Appeal
20 December 2014

Acknowledgements

This book began as a doctoral dissertation, which I completed at the University of Cambridge. Needless to say, I owe a debt of gratitude to my supervisor, Christopher Forsyth, who meticulously commented on all the early drafts of this project. His insights have been pivotal in shaping the scope and substance of this project. I have also benefitted tremendously from the comments provided by my PhD examiners, Mark Elliott and Kent Roach. Their astute observations and attention to detail have made this book project far better than it could otherwise have been. Another mentor, Mark Tushnet, has also been exceedingly generous with his time and zealously read and commented on various drafts of this book.

This book was completed back in Hong Kong where I teach at the Faculty of Law in The University of Hong Kong. I am very grateful to Albert Chen, Cora Chan, Johannes Chan, Ernest Lim, Michael Hor, and Simon Young, all of whom have commented on different parts of this project in various forms. Michael Hor was the first person to introduce me to public law when I was a law undergraduate; he was generous with his time when he was my teacher and equally generous now as my colleague. Albert Chen has been my informal teacher on Hong Kong Constitutional Law, and I have had the privilege and pleasure of co-teaching Hong Kong Constitutional Law with him for many years.

I am also grateful to all the participants of the Comparative Constitutional Law Colloquium organized by the University of Washington in 2014. I have benefitted greatly from the feedback I have received, especially those provided by Stephen Gardbaum, Clark Lombardi, and Victor Ramraj.

Special thanks must also go to Eileen Lou, Sophie Mayatt-Simmons, Gilbert Mok, and Sally Wong, all of whom had fervently proof-read a series of drafts and had provided invaluable technical support. They have been indispensable.

A modified version of Chapter 2 was published as 'Defending Dialogue' in [2012] *Public Law* 527. A modified version of Chapter 5 was published as 'Dialogue and Subconstitutional Doctrines in Common Law Asia' in [2013] *Public Law* 779.

This research project has also been generously supported by a grant I received from the Hong Kong Research Grants Council's General Research Fund.

Above all, I dedicate this book to my family, who have always indulged my weakness for good food.

Contents

Table of Cases xi
Table of Legislation xvii

1. Introduction 1

2. Defending Dialogue 7
I. Legislative Supremacy and its Critics 8
II. Judicial Supremacy and its Critics 16
III. Dialogic Judicial Review and its Critics 22
IV. Conclusion 27

3. Overview of the Constitutional Systems 31
I. Hong Kong 31
II. Malaysia 40
III. Singapore 48

4. Judicial Crises 57
I. Judicial Crisis in Hong Kong 58
II. Judicial Crisis in Malaysia 66
III. Judicial Crisis in Singapore 73
IV. Conclusion 77

5. Dialogue and Sub-Constitutional Doctrines 79
I. Sub-Constitutionalism and its Discontents 80
II. Sub-Constitutional Doctrines in Common Law Asia 86
III. Conclusion 103

6. Freedom of Expression 107
I. Defamation 110
II. Contempt by Scandalizing the Judiciary 122
III. Regulatory Restrictions on Public Assemblies 128
IV. Conclusion 135

7. Freedom of Religion 139
I. Overview of the Three Models of Religious Liberty 141
II. Evaluating the Three Models 144

III. Dialogic Tools to Implementing the Balancing Model of Religious Freedom 152
IV. Conclusion 158

8. Right to Equality 161
I. Overview of the Four Models of Equality 163
II. Evaluating the Four Models 169
III. Justifying Equality Infringements 180
IV. Conclusion 192

9. Right to Due Process 195
I. Overview of the Four Models of Due Process 197
II. Evaluating the Four Models 204
III. Dialogic Tools to Implementing Substantive Due Process 213
IV. Conclusion 220

10. Conclusion 223

Bibliography 229
Index 241

Table of Cases

Australia

Lange v ABC (1997) 189 CLR 520 (High Court of Australia) 113, 114, 115

Canada

Andrews v Law Society of British Columbia [1989] 56 DLR 1 (Supreme Court of Canada). . . . 171
Eldridge v British Columbia [1997] SCR 624 (Supreme Court of Canada). 168
Multani v Commission scolaire Marguerite-Bourgeoys [2006] 1 SCR 256
(Supreme Court of Canada). 147
R v Oakes [1986] 3 SCR 103 (Supreme Court of Canada) 181
Vriend v Alberta [1998]1 SCR 493 (Supreme Court of Canada). 174
Withler v Canada [2011] 1 SCR 396 (Supreme Court of Canada) 161, 167, 175

Europe

Clift v UK [2010] ECHR 1106 (European Court of Human Rights). 175
Eskelinen v Finland (2007) 45 EHRR 43 (European Court of Human Rights) 95
Lingens v Austria (1986) 8 EHRR 407 (European Court of Human Rights) 115, 117
Sunday Times v UK (1979–1980) 2 EHRR 245 (European Court of Human Rights) 181

Hong Kong

Blakeney-Williams v Cathay Pacific Airways [2011] 1 HKLRD 901
(Hong Kong Court of Appeal). 111
Catholic Diocese of Hong Kong v *Secretary of Justice* (2011) 14 HKCFAR 754
(Hong Kong Court of Final Appeal) 140, 142, 145, 146, 147
Ch'ng Poh v Chief Executive [2003] HKEC 1441 (Hong Kong Court of First Instance) 90
Chan Kam Nga v Director of Immigration [1999] 1 HKLRD 304
(Hong Kong Court of Final Appeal) 62, 63, 64
Chan Kin Sum v Secretary of Justice [2008] HKEC 2077, [2009] 2 HKLRD 166
(Hong Kong Court of First Instance) 102, 103
Chan Kin Sum Simon v Secretary of Justice [2009] HKEC 393
(Hong Kong Court of First Instance) 102, 103
Cheng v Tse Wai Chun [2000] 3 HKLRD 418 (Hong Kong
Court of Final Appeal). 94, 112, 113
Democratic Republic of the Congo v FG Hemisphere Associates LLC (No. 1) (2011)
14 HKCFAR 95 (Hong Kong Court of Final Appeal). 88
Democratic Republic of the Congo v FG Hemisphere Associates LLC (No. 2) (2011)
14 HKCFAR 395 (Hong Kong Court of Final Appeal) 88
Director of Immigration v Lau Kong Yung (1999) 2 HKCFAR 300,
[1999] 3 HKLRD 778 (Hong Kong Court of Final Appeal) 64, 65
Fok Chun Wa v Hospital Authority (2012) 15 HKCFAR 409 (Hong Kong Court
of Final Appeal). 100, 162, 168, 175, 176, 188, 189
HKSAR v Hung Chan Wa (2006) 9 HKCFAR 614 (Hong Kong Court of Final Appeal). 211
HKSAR v So Wai Lun [2005] 1 HKLRD 443 (Hong Kong Court of Appeal) 216
Kong Yun Ming v Director of Social Welfare [2012] HKEC 229
(Hong Kong Court of Appeal). 189

Koo Sze Yiu v Chief Executive of Hong Kong (2006) 9 HKCFAR 441 (Hong Kong Court of Final Appeal) 101, 102, 218
Koon Wing Yee v Insider Dealing Tribunal (2008) 11 HKCFAR 170 (Hong Kong Court of Final Appeal) 96
Kulemesin v HKSAR (2013) 16 HKCFAR 195 (Hong Kong Court of Final Appeal) 217
Lam Siu Po v Commissioner of Police (2009) 12 HKCFAR 237 (Hong Kong Court of Final Appeal) 95, 96
Lau Cheong v *HKSAR* (2002) 5 HKCFAR 415 (Hong Kong Court of Final Appeal). 196, 203, 211
Lau Tat Wai v Yip Lai Kuen Joey [2013] 2 HKLRD 1197 (Hong Kong Court of First Instance) 94
Leung v Secretary of Justice [2006] 4 HKLRD 211 (Hong Kong Court of Appeal). 168
Leung Kwok Hung v HKSAR (2005) 8 HKCFAR 229, [2005] 3 HKLRD 164 (Hong Kong Court of Final Appeal) 98, 131, 132, 134
Leung Kwok Hung v Chief Executive of Hong Kong [2006] HKEC 816 (Hong Kong Court of Appeal). 101
Ng Ka Ling v Director of Immigration (1999) 2 HKCFAR 4, [1999] 1 HKLRD 315 (Hong Kong Court of Final Appeal). 57, 58, 59, 60, 61, 62, 63, 64, 66
Ng Ka Ling v Director of Immigration (No. 2) (1999) 2 HKCFAR 141, [1999] 1 HKLRD 577 (Hong Kong Court of Final Appeal). 63
Secretary for Justice v Choy Bing Wing [2005] HKEC 1971 (Hong Kong Court of First Instance) 125
Secretary for Justice v Choy Bing Wing [2011] HKEC 63 (Hong Kong Court of First Instance) 125
Secretary of Justice v *Yau Yuk Lung* (2007) 10 HKCFAR 335, [2007] 3 HKLRD 903 (Hong Kong Court of Final Appeal) 162, 167, 176, 181, 188
Shum Kwok Sher v Secretary of Justice (2002) 5 HKCFAR 381 (Hong Kong Court of Final Appeal). 98
So Wai Lun v *HKSAR* (2006) 9 HKCFAR 530 (Hong Kong Court of Final Appeal) 196, 203, 204, 211, 212, 216
Solicitor v Law Society (2003) 6 HKCFAR 570 (Hong Kong Court of Final Appeal) 214, 215
W v Registrar of Marriages (2013) 16 HKCFAR 112 (Hong Kong Court of Final Appeal). 103
Wong Yeung Ng v Secretary of Justice [1999] 2 HKLRD 293 (Hong Kong Court of Appeal). 124, 125, 126, 127

Malaysia

Abdul Kahar bin Ahmad v Kerajaan Negeri Selangor [2008] 3 MLJ 617 (Federal Court of Malaysia). 154
AG v Manjeet Singh Dhillon [1991] 1 MLJ 167 (Supreme Court of Malaysia) 126
Anwar v *The New Straits Times* [2010] 2 MLJ 492 (High Court of Malaysia) 114
Anwar bin Ibrahim v Mahathir bin Mohamad [1999] 4 MLJ 58 (High Court of Malaysia) 113
Anwar bin Ibrahim v *Mahathir bin Mohamad* [2001] 1 MLJ 305 (Malaysia Court of Appeal) 114
Anwar bin Ibrahim v *Mahathir bin Mohamad* [2001] 2 MLJ 65 (Federal Court of Malaysia). 114
Ayer Molek Rubber v Insas Bhd [1995] 2 MLJ 734 (High Court of Malaysia) 72
Ayer Molek Rubber v Insas Bhd [1995] 2 MLJ 833 (Federal Court of Malaysia) 72
Berthelsen v Director General of Information (1987) 1 MLJ 134 (Supreme Court of Malaysia). 67

Danaharta Urus v *Kekatong* [2004] 2 MLJ 257 (Federal Court of Malaysia) . . . 162, 164, 170, 190
Dato' v Kanagalingam v David Samuels [2006] 6 MLJ 521 (High Court of Malaysia) . . . 72
Dato' Seri Anwar bin Ibrahim v PP [2013] 3 MLJ 103 (High Court of Malaysia) . . . 133
Datuk Haji bin Harun Idris v *PP* [1977] 2 MLJ 155 (Federal Court of Malaysia) . . . 162
Dr Mohd Nasir Hashim v Menteri Dalam Negiri Malaysia [2006] 6 MLJ 213 (Malaysia Court of Appeal) . . . 132
Hong Leong Equipment v Liew Fook Chuan [1996] 1 MLJ 481 (Malaysia Court of Appeal) . . . 91
Latifah bte Mat Zin v Roasmawati [2007] 5 MLJ 101 (Federal Court of Malaysia) . . . 154
Lee Kwan Woh v PP (2009) 5 MLJ 301 (Federal Court of Malaysia) . . . 97, 196, 201, 202, 209, 214, 226
Lina Joy v Federal Territory Islamic Council & Director-General of the National Registration Department (2007) 4 MLJ 585 (Federal Court of Malaysia) . . . 150, 151, 152, 153, 154, 155
Mat Shuhaimi bin Shafiei v PP [2014] 2 MLJ 145 (Malaysia Court of Appeal) . . . 133
Meor Atiqulrahman bin Ishak v Fatimah Bte Sihi [2006] 4 MLJ 605 (Federal Court of Malaysia) . . . 143, 150, 152, 155
Menteri Dalam Negeri v Titular Roman Catholic Archbishop of Kuala Lumpur [2013] 6 MLJ 468 (Malaysia Court of Appeal) . . . 143, 144
Minister for Home Affairs v *Jamaluddin bin Othman* (1989) 1 MLJ 418 (Supreme Court of Malaysia) . . . 143
Mohd Noor Bin Othman v Mohd Yusof Jaafar (1988) 2 MLJ 129 (High Court of Malaysia) . . . 67, 68
Muhammad Hilman v Kerajaan Malaysia (2011) 6 MLJ 507 (Malaysia Court of Appeal) . . . 133
Nik Nazmi bin Nik Ahmad v PP [2014] 4 MLJ 157 (Malaysia Court of Appeal) . . . 133
Palm Oil Research & Development Board Malaysia v Premium Vegetable Oils [2005] 3 MLJ 97 (Federal Court of Malaysia) . . . 92
Pihak Berkuasa Negeri Sabah v *Sugumar Balakrishnan* [2002] 3 MLJ 72 (Federal Court of Malaysia) . . . 196, 198, 204, 214
PP v Dato' Yap Peng (1987) 2 MLJ 311 (Supreme Court of Malaysia) . . . 67
PP v *Harmenderpall Singh* [2007] 3 MLJ 433 (Malaysia Court of Appeal) . . . 162, 165, 190
PP v Khong Teng Khen [1976] 2 MLJ 166 (Federal Court of Malaysia) . . . 162
PP v The Straits Times [1949] MLJ 81 (Federal Court of Malaysia) . . . 126
Shamim Reza bin Abdul Samad v *PP* [2011] 1 MLJ 471 (Federal Court of Malaysia) . . . 196, 202, 209
Sivabalan a/L P. Asapathy v *The New Straits Times Press* [2010] 9 MLJ 320 (High Court of Malaysia) . . . 114, 119
Sivarasa Rasiah v Badan Peguam Malaysia [2010] 2 MLJ 333 (Federal Court of Malaysia) . . . 73, 132, 133, 162, 168, 169, 180, 190
The Government of the State of Kelantan v The Government of the Federation of Malaya (1963) 29 MLJ 355 (Federal Court of Malaysia) . . . 42
Titular Roman Catholic Archbishop of Kuala Lumpur v Menteri Dalam Negeri [2014] 4 MLJ 765 (Federal Court of Malaysia) . . . 144
YB Hj Khalid bin Abdul Samad v *Datuk Aziz bin Isham* [2012] 7 MLJ 301 (High Court of Malaysia) . . . 114, 119

New Zealand

Lange v Atkinson [1988] 3 NZLR 424 (High Court of New Zealand) 113, 114
Solicitor General v Radio Avon [1978] 1 NZLR 225 (New Zealand Court of Appeal) 125

Singapore

AG v Hertzberg Daniel [2009] 1 SLR 1103 (High Court of Singapore) 123
AG v Lingle [1995] 1 SLR 199 (High Court of Singapore) 123
AG v Shadrake [2011] 2 SLR 506 (High Court of Singapore) 124
AG v Wain Barry [1991] 1 SLR 85 (High Court of Singapore) 123, 124
Chan Hiang Leng Colin v Minister for Information and the Arts [1996] 1 SLR 294 (Singapore Court of Appeal) 133, 157, 158
Chan Hiang Leng Colin v *PP* [1994] 3 SLR 662 (High Court of Singapore). . . . 140, 141, 144, 145
Chee Siok Chin v Minister for Home Affairs [2006] 1 SLR 582 (High Court of Singapore). 129, 130, 132
Chee Soon Juan v PP [2011] 3 SLR 50 (High Court of Singapore) 130
Chng Suan Tze v Minister of Home Affairs [1988] 2 SLR 132, [1988] 1 MLJ 133, (1989) MLJ 69 (Singapore Court of Appeal). 54, 58, 74, 75, 76, 77
Constitutional Reference No 1 of 1995 [1995] 1 SLR 803 (Singapore Constitutional Reference Tribunal) 87
Goh Chok Tong v *JBJ* [1997] 3 SLR 46 (High Court of Singapore). 120
Jeyaretnam Joshua Benjamin v Lee Kuan Yew [1992] 1 SLR 791 (Singapore Court of Appeal) 115, 116, 117, 120
Lee Mau Seng v Minister of Home Affairs [1971–1973] SLR(R) 135 (High Court of Singapore). 74, 75, 76
Lim Eng Hock v Lin Jian Wei [2010] 4 SLR 357 (Singapore Court of Appeal) 117, 118
Lim Meng Suang v AG [2014] SGCA 53 (Singapore Court of Appeal) 166, 173, 174, 178, 199
M V Balakrishnan v PP [1998] SGHC 416 (High Court of Singapore) 216
Malcomson Nicholas Hugh Bertram v Naresh Kumar Mehta [2001] 4 SLR 454 (High Court of Singapore). 93
Mohammad Faizal bin Sabtu v *PP* [2012] SGHC 163 (High Court of Singapore) 196, 198, 199, 205
Nappalli Peter Williams v *Institute of Technical Education* [1999] 2 SLR 569 (Singapore Court of Appeal) 140, 142, 145, 146, 157, 158
Nguyen Tuong Van v *PP* [2004] SGCA 47 (Singapore Court of Appeal) 166
Ong Ah Chuan v PP [1979–1980] SLR 710 (Privy Council of Singapore) 205
PP v Chong Kai Xiong [2010] 3 SLR 355 (High Court of Singapore) 130
PP v *Taw Cheng Kong* [1998] 2 SLR 410 (Singapore Court of Appeal). 99, 100, 162, 165, 190
Ramalingam Ravinthran v AG [2012] SGCA 2 (Singapore Court of Appeal). 91
Review Publishing Co v Lee Hsien Loong [2010] 1 SLR 52 (Singapore Court of Appeal) 115, 116, 117, 118, 119, 120
Shadrake Alan v AG [2011] 3 SLR 778 (Singapore Court of Appeal) 122, 123, 127
Tan Khee Wan Iris v *PP* [1995] 2 SLR 63 (High Court of Singapore). 216
Taw Cheng Kong v PP [1998] 1 SLR 78 (High Court of Singapore) 172
Teo Soh Lung v Minister for Home Affairs (1989) 1 SLR 461 (High Court of Singapore) 76
Teo Soh Lung v Minister of Home Affairs [1990] 1 SLR(R) 347 (Singapore Court of Appeal) 75, 76, 77
Yap Keng Ho v PP [2011] 3 SLR 32 (High Court of Singapore) 130
Yong Vui Kong v *PP* [2010] SGCA 20, [2010] 3 SLR 489 (Singapore Court of Appeal) 162, 166, 190, 196, 199, 200, 201, 206, 207, 218, 219, 220, 226
Yong Vui Kong v AG [2011] 2 SLR 1189 (Singapore Court of Appeal) 89, 90

South Africa

Prince v *President of the Law Society of the Cape of Good Hope* 2002(2) 794 SA (South African Constitutional Court) 147
S v Mamabolo 2001 (3) SA 409 (South African Constitutional Court) 128

United Kingdom

Ahmed & Ors v HM Treasury (No 2) [2010] 2 AC 534 (Supreme Court) 218
Ahnee v DPP [1999] 2 AC 294 (Privy Council) 125
Associated Provincial Picture Houses Limited v Wednesbury Corporation [1948] 1 KB 223 (Court of Appeal) 135, 158, 225
Branson v Bower (No 2) [2002] 2 WLR 452 (Queen's Bench) 112
Carson v Secretary of State for Work and Pensions [2006] 1 AC 173 (House of Lords) 161, 167, 175, 188
Clift v Secretary of State for the Home Department [2007] 1 AC 484 (House of Lords) 175
Fox v Queen [2002] 2 AC 284 (Privy Council) 200
Ghaidan v Godin-Mendoza [2004] 2 AC 557 (House of Lords) 188
Huang v Secretary of State for the Home Department [2007] UKHL 11 (House of Lords) 181
Jameel v Wall Street Journal Europe [2007] 1 AC 359 (House of Lords) 111, 122
R v A (No. 2) [2002] 1 AC 45 (House of Lords) 14
R v Gray [1900] 2 QB 36 (Queen's Bench) 122, 126
R v *Hughes* (2002) 2 AC 259 (Privy Council) 200
R v Secretary of State for the Home Department (Ex parte Simms) [2000] 2 AC 115 (House of Lords) 26
Reyes v *The Queen* [2002] 2 AC 235 (Privy Council) 200
Reynolds v Times Newspapers [2001] 2 AC 127 (House of Lords) 110, 111, 112, 114, 115, 116, 117, 118, 119, 120, 121, 122, 225
Seaga v Harper [2008] 3 WLR 478 (Privy Council of Jamaica) 111
Secretary of State for Defence v Guardian Newspaper [1985] AC 339 (House of Lords) 127
Treacy v DPP [1971] AC 537 (House of Lords) 561 100

United States of America

Abrams v United States 250 US 616 (1919) (United States Supreme Court) 107
Adarand Constructors, Inc. v Peña 515 US 200 (1995) (United States Supreme Court) 188
Bivens v Six Unknown Named Agents of the Federal Bureau of Narcotics 403 US 388 (1971) (United States Supreme Court) 80
Dred Scott v Sandford 60 US 393 (1856) (United States Supreme Court) 28
Employment Division v Smith 494 US 872 (1990) (United States Supreme Court) 149
Korematsu v United States 323 US 214 (1944) (United States Supreme Court) 28
Marbury v Madison 5 US 137 (1803) (United States Supreme Court) 79, 83
Miranda v Arizona 384 US 436 (1966) (United States Supreme Court) 80
New York Times v Sullivan (1964) 376 US 254 (United States Supreme Court) 115, 117
Police Department v Mosley 408 US 92 (1972) (United States Supreme Court) 179
Romer v Evans 517 US 620 (1996) (United States Supreme Court) 188
United States v Virginia 518 US 515 (1996) (United States Supreme Court) 161, 188

Table of Legislation

CANADA

Canadian Charter of Rights and Freedoms 7, 9, 28
Supreme Court Act. 86

CHINA

Interim Measures for the Control of Chinese Citizens Travelling on Private Business to and from Regions of Hong Kong and Macao 61

EUROPE

European Convention on Human Rights 95, 119, 200
European Economic Treaty 65

HONG KONG

Basic Law of the Hong Kong Special Administrative Region of the People's Republic of China
Interpretation of art 22(4) and 24(2)(3) by the SCNPC on 26 June 1999. . . . . 63, 64
art 4 90
art 5 33
art 8 38
art 12 33
art 15 37
art 18 33
art 19 88
art 21 33
art 22 . . . . 61, 62
art 24 . . . . 58, 61, 62, 64
art 25 163
art 28 . . . . 39, 197, 203, 211
art 30 40
art 32 139
art 37 103
art 39 . . . . 38, 39, 97, 178
art 43 63
art 45 37
art 46 37
art 48 . . . . 37, 63
art 54 38
art 55 38
art 68 36
art 74 36
art 82 38
art 88 38
art 141 . . . . 139, 142
art 158 . . . . 38, 60, 61, 63, 64, 65, 88
art 159 . . . . 40, 59, 60, 63
Annex I 37
Annex II 36
Annex III 33
Crimes Ordinance (Cap 200) 216
Hong Kong Bill of Rights Ordinance (Cap 383). 39, 94, 95, 96, 167, 168, 177, 185
Immigration Ordinance (Cap 115) 62, 64, 65
Legal Practitioners Ordinance (Cap 159) 214
Letters Patent of 1843 . . . . 32, 39
Public Order Ordinance (Cap 245). 131
Registration of Local Newspapers Ordinance (Cap 268). 118
Sex Discrimination Ordinance (Cap 480). 185
Shipping and Port Control Ordinance (Cap 313) 217

MALAYSIA

Malaysia Constitution
art 3 . . . . 46, 139
art 5 . . . . 91, 97, 197, 198, 202, 214, 226
art 8 . . . . 163, 177, 185
art 10 . . . . 46, 47, 48, 132

art 11 . . . 46, 139
art 12 . . . 177
art 38 . . . 44, 47
art 45 . . . 42, 43
art 55 . . . 42
art 68 . . . 43
art 70 . . . 47
art 121 . . . 44, 45, 46, 67, 139, 151, 152, 154, 155
art 122 . . . 45, 46, 72
art 122AB . . . 46
art 125 . . . 45, 68, 69, 70
art 128 . . . 44
art 130 . . . 45, 87
art 138 . . . 45
art 149 . . . 46, 47
art 150 . . . 47
art 152 . . . 47
art 153 . . . 46, 47, 177
art 159 . . . 43, 44, 47, 48
art 161E . . . 48
art 183 . . . 44
2nd Schedule . . . 48
3rd Schedule . . . 43
5th Schedule . . . 43
6th Schedule . . . 48
7th Schedule . . . 48
9th Schedule . . . 42, 153, 154
Criminal Procedure Code (Act 153) . . . 67
Immigration Act (Act 155) . . . 198, 204, 214, 215
Internal Security Act (Act 82) . . . 47, 143
Peaceful Assembly Act (Act 736) . . . 132, 133
Printing Presses and Publications Act (Act 301) . . . 118
Road Transport Act (Act 333) . . . 165
Security Offences (Special Measures) Act (Act 747) . . . 47
Societies Act (Act 335) . . . 67

NEW ZEALAND

New Zealand Bill of Rights Act . . . 1, 4, 7

SINGAPORE

Singapore Constitution
art 2 . . . 205
art 4 . . . 53
art 5 . . . 55, 87
art 5A . . . 55
art 6 . . . 55
art 9 . . . 90, 197, 199, 200, 205, 219
art 12 . . . 163, 165, 177, 178, 185
art 14 . . . 115, 129, 130
art 15 . . . 139, 144, 145
art 18 . . . 52
art 19 . . . 52
art 21 . . . 52
art 22 . . . 52
art 22H . . . 87
art 22I . . . 52
art 37 . . . 52
art 39 . . . 51
art 44 . . . 208
art 46 . . . 51
art 65 . . . 50, 55, 208
art 66 . . . 55
art 76 . . . 54
art 77 . . . 54
art 78. . . . 54, 55
art 93 . . . 53, 58, 75
art 94 . . . 53
art 95 . . . 53
art 98 . . . 53
art 100 . . . 53, 55, 87
art 149 . . . 54, 58, 75
art 151 . . . 52
art 152 . . . 54
art 153 . . . 139
art 162 . . . 116
4th Schedule . . . 51
Administration of Muslim Law Act (Cap 3) . . . 139
Internal Security Act (Cap 143) . . . 52, 54, 58, 73, 74, 75
Maintenance of Religious Harmony Act (Cap 167A) . . . 52
Miscellaneous Offences (Public Order and Nuisance) Act (Cap 184) . . . 129, 130
Miscellaneous Offences (Public Order and Nuisance) (Assemblies and Processions) Rules . . . 130
Misuse of Drugs Act (Cap 185) . . . 199, 220
Newspaper and Printing Presses Act (Cap 206) . . . 118

Penal Code (Cap 224). 166, 191, 216
Prevention of Corruption
Act (Cap 241) 165
Public Order Act (Cap 257A) . . . 129, 133, 135
Republic of Singapore
Independence Act 50, 206

UNITED KINGDOM

Human Rights Act 1998 . . . . . . 1, 4, 7, 16, 86, 199, 205
State of Singapore Act 1958 49

1

Introduction

In the last decade, 'dialogue' has become a commonplace metaphor in constitutional discourse. This term was popularized by Peter Hogg and Allison Bushell[1] in a seminal article where they argued how Canadian judges are engaged in a collaborative conversation with the legislature over the optimum level of human rights protection within the constitutional state. The metaphor has however travelled across the oceans and has since entered the legal vernacular of other common law systems that have also adopted Bills of Rights under which legislatures are able to respond to, or reverse, judicial decisions, without resorting to constitutional amendments or popular referendums. In the United Kingdom, Tom Hickman and Alison Young have explored how the interplay of Sections 3 and 4 of the Human Rights Act 1998 (UKHRA) has allowed the English courts to forge a constitutional partnership with the legislature and the executive.[2] In the same vein, in New Zealand, Petra Butler has also discussed how its national courts can use the New Zealand Bill of Rights Act (NZBORA) to enhance the deliberative decision-making process of the legislature.[3] Although Australia does not have a federal Bill of Rights, Julie Debeljak[4] and Leighton McDonald[5]

[1] Peter Hogg & Allison Bushell, 'The Charter Dialogue Between the Courts and Legislatures (Or Perhaps the Charter of Rights Isn't Such a Bad Thing After All)' (1997) 35 *Osgoode Hall Law Journal* 75.

[2] Tom Hickman, *Public Law after the Human Rights Act* (Oxford, Hart Publishing 2010); Alison Young, *Parliamentary Sovereignty and the Human Rights Act* (Oxford, Hart Publishing 2009). See also Aileen Kavanagh, *Constitutional Review under the UK Human Rights Act* (Cambridge, Cambridge University Press 2009) though one must note that Kavanagh has reservations about the utility of this 'dialogue' metaphor.

[3] Petra Butler, 'Human Rights and Parliamentary Sovereignty in New Zealand' (2004) 35 *Victoria University Law Review* 341.

[4] Julie Debeljak, 'Parliamentary Sovereignty and Dialogue under the Victorian Charter of Human Rights and Responsibilities: Drawing the Line between Judicial Interpretation and Judicial Law-Making' (2007) 33 *Monash University Law Review* 9. See also R M W Masterman, 'Interpretations, Declarations and Dialogue: Rights protection under the Human Rights Act and Victorian Charter of Human Rights and Responsibilities' [2009] *Public Law* 112.

[5] Leighton McDonald, 'New Directions in the Australian Bill of Rights Debate' [2004] *Public Law* 22. See also Scott Stephenson, 'Constitutional Reengineering: Dialogue's Migration from Canada to Australia' (2013) 11 *International Journal of Constitutional Law* 870.

have explored how in those individual Australian states that have enacted state-level human rights instruments, that is Victoria and the Australian Capital Territory, the judiciary and their respective state governments can equally pursue this constitutional dialogue.

Common to these constitutional systems is the adoption of various creative structural mechanisms that expressly confer upon the respective national courts the right to interpret and apply fundamental human rights norms, while preserving the legislature's right to disagree with and/or reaffirm its views in the course of ordinary politics.

One must however note at the outset that while dialogic review is most commonly discussed in these common law systems where weak-form review[6] was first conceived, the existence of these structural mechanisms is not a prerequisite for a dialogic approach to constitutional discourse to occur. Even in constitutional systems, like the United States, where strong-form review is the norm, such that the courts are empowered to invalidate legislation and have the final word on constitutional understandings, its Supreme Court has exercised its 'passive virtues'[7] to abstain from constitutional controversies or has ruled in a minimalistic fashion so as to provide the legislative/executive branches with the constitutional space to disagree.[8] The spacious text in most Bills of Rights permits divergence on a litany of issues, and provides a framework for the political communities to disagree and struggle over the documents' meanings.[9] Where the judiciary facilitates but does not foreclose the constitutional debate for the electorate and its representatives, the processes of constitutional interpretation become more dynamic, and a dialogue between the judicial and political branches of government on constitutional meaning can ensue.

Notably too, discussions on dialogic review have primarily focussed on common law constitutional systems in the West. This book will thus seek to fill the lacuna in the literature by analysing three common law systems in Asia, that is Hong Kong, Malaysia, and Singapore. In particular, these three jurisdictions are former British colonies that continue to observe common law norms and traditions; their respective judiciaries are generally

[6] Weak-form review refers to a form of judicial review in which judges' rulings on constitutional questions are expressly open to legislative revision in the course of ordinary politics. See Mark Tushnet, 'Weak Form Judicial Review and "Core" Civil Liberties', (2006) 41 *Harvard Civil Rights-Civil Liberties Law Review* 1.

[7] Alexander Bickel, *The Least Dangerous Branch: The Supreme Court at the Bar of Politics* (2nd edn, New Haven, Yale University Press 1986) 115–98.

[8] Cass Sunstein, *One Case at A Time: Judicial Minimalism on the Supreme Court* (Cambridge, Harvard University Press 1999).

[9] Barry Friedman, 'Dialogue and Judicial Review' (1993) 91 *Michigan Law Review* 577, 654.

empowered under their written constitutions to invalidate legislation for perceived rights-violations, and their respective Constitutions also do not include any structural devices that enable the local legislatures to reverse or avoid a constitutional decision they disagree with, except via a constitutional amendment.

I argue that in the three common law Asian constitutional systems under study, that is Hong Kong, Malaysia, and Singapore, even though their respective Constitutions do not provide for structural devices that enable the local legislatures to reverse or avoid a constitutional decision they disagree with, the courts can still apply judicial techniques and canons of interpretation that foster a debate with the political branches of government on constitutional values.

In essence, constitutional dialogue is an observable practice of routine institutional interaction whereby the pursuit of legislative objectives can be 'constructively modified (from a rights perspective), but not impeded, by judicial input into the law-making process'.[10] This dialogue is sustained by a constitutional culture committed to instantiating a political order that negotiates the polarities of deference and disagreement.

Chapter 2 of this book will begin by explaining *why*, as a constitutional theory, dialogic review is normatively superior to the opposing alternatives of legislative or judicial supremacy. On one side, we can find judicial sceptics who champion legislative supremacy as they consider judicial review undemocratic.[11] At the other end of this constitutional continuum, we find legislative sceptics who argue in favour of judicial supremacy, as they doubt the capacity of the political branches of government to be sufficiently stable or impartial to serve as the ultimate arbiter of constitutional rights.[12] This chapter will seek to defend the normative value of dialogic judicial review against critics on both ends of this spectrum.

Chapter 3 will continue with a brief overview of the constitutional history in Hong Kong, Malaysia, and Singapore. The focus of this chapter will be on the constitutional structures and traditions the respective jurisdictions inherited from the British and the major constitutional developments since decolonization.

[10] McDonald (n 5) 28.

[11] Jeremy Waldron, *Law and Disagreement* (Oxford, Clarendon Press 1999); Adrian Vermeule, *Law and the Limits of Reason* (Oxford, Oxford University Press 2008).

[12] Larry Alexander & Fredrick Schauer, 'On Extrajudicial Constitutional Interpretation' (1997) 110 *Harvard Law Review* 1359; Trevor Allan, *Constitutional Justice: A Liberal Theory of the Rule of Law* (Oxford, Oxford University Press 2001); Jeffrey Jowell, 'Parliamentary Sovereignty under the New Constitutional Hypothesis' [2006] *Public Law* 562, 579.

Chapter 4 will examine the judicial crises that had occurred in each of the three jurisdictions in which monumental constitutional confrontations between the legislature/executive and the judiciary went on to shape and impact the current constitutional relations between the co-ordinate branches of government.

This above investigation into the interplay of law and politics in Asia will set the stage for my analysis in Chapter 5 of how these Asian courts, notwithstanding the absence of the structural mechanisms found in the UKHRA or NZBORA, can still engage in a collaborative conversation with their respective legislatures on rights-protection. The focus of this chapter is on the development of judicial techniques and canons of interpretation that allow courts to preserve the right of the legislature to disagree with the courts' decisions using the ordinary political processes, such that an override via a constitutional amendment can be avoided and any adverse backlash from the political branches reduced. This dialogic form of judicial review is politically more efficacious in common law Asia as each of the three territories has been governed by the same ruling party/coalition since decolonization, and will continue to be so governed for the foreseeable future.[13] In essence, where the judiciary operates within a constitutional system dominated by a semi-permanent party/coalition in government, the pursuit of a dialogic form of judicial review is also the politically expedient way for the courts to engage in a valuable but less confrontational colloquy with the political institutions about the requisites of a constitutional democracy. Techniques to be discussed in Chapter 5 include the judicial observance or recognition of one or more of the following sub-constitutional norms/practices: (1) provisional or advisory determinations in constitutional matters; (2) administrative review; (3) common law liberties or statutory rights that are reversible by the ordinary political process; (4) procedural constitutional rules; (5) rational basis review of legislative actions; and (6) delayed declarations of invalidity.

Chapters 6 to 9 will be a comparative study on how these judicial techniques and canons of interpretation can be applied in four core constitutional areas: (1) freedom of expression; (2) freedom of religion; (3) right to equality; and (4) criminal due process rights. Each chapter (from Chapters 6 to 9) will be a comparative focus on one of the above topics. These chapters

[13] Since the establishment of the Hong Kong Special Administrative Region, an informal coalition of political parties and independent legislators that usually supports the agenda of the Hong Kong executive government (the pro-establishment camp) has been able to command an overall majority of the seats in the Legislative Council. Malaysia has been ruled by the same political coalition since its independence, that is the Alliance Party which was renamed Barisan Nasional (National Front) in 1974. The People's Action Party has been the ruling party in Singapore since its independence and the party has controlled over 90% of the elected seats in Parliament since 1968.

will examine and critique the case law and examine how these cases can be reconsidered or re-decided in view of the dialogic form of judicial review that I propose.

This book will essentially demonstrate how dialogic judicial review can take place in common law Asia. This mode of judicial review promotes a form of deliberative democracy, a model which eschews the rule of judges as philosopher kings, but also one that holds the promise of transformative change beyond the confines of the ballot box.

2

Defending Dialogue

Domestic courts are commonly perceived today as being engaged in a collaborative and dialectical conversation with their respective national legislatures on rights-protection, and the term 'dialogue' has become a ubiquitous and fashionable term to describe this particular form of constitutional discourse.

Dialogic constitutional theorists have however focussed generally on those Commonwealth legal systems where the national legislatures have adopted bills of rights under which lawmakers are empowered to ignore or reverse judicial decisions they disagree with, without the need to seek change via constitutional amendments.[1]

For Canada, the use of the Section 33 of the constitution 'notwithstanding' constitutional clause allows the federal Parliament or a provincial legislature to declare expressly that an impugned statutory provision shall continue to operate notwithstanding an adverse constitutional ruling from the courts. In the United Kingdom, a declaration of incompatibility issued under Section 4 of the Human Rights Act 1998 (UKHRA) does not affect the validity, continued operation, or enforcement of the impugned legislative provision in question. With regard to New Zealand, Section 4 of the New Zealand Bill of Rights Act (NZBORA) expressly bars the courts from invalidating or rendering ineffective any statutory provision for being inconsistent with the NZBORA.

Notwithstanding the plethora of academic literature on dialogic review, its supporters generally focus on *how* their respective national courts can structure this interactive and dialectical conversation with their political branches of government, and they often fail to explain *why*, as a constitutional theory, dialogic review is normatively superior to the alternatives of legislative

[1] Peter W Hogg & Allison A Bushell, 'The Charter Dialogue Between the Courts and Legislatures (Or Perhaps the Charter of Rights Isn't Such a Bad Thing After All)' (1997) 35 *Osgoode Hall Law Journal* 75; Tom Hickman, *Public Law after the Human Rights Act* (Oxford, Hart Publishing 2010); Alison Young, *Parliamentary Sovereignty and the Human Rights Act* (Oxford, Hart Publishing 2009); Petra Butler, 'Human Rights and Parliamentary Sovereignty in New Zealand' (2004) 35 *Victoria University Law Review* 341.

or judicial supremacy.[2] The need to defend the normative value of dialogic review is crucial, especially in view of the trenchant attacks by its deriders. On one side, we have judicial sceptics who champion legislative supremacy as the preferred response to the 'counter-majoritarian difficulty'[3] associated with judicial review.[4] At the other end of this constitutional spectrum, we may find legislative sceptics who argue in favour of judicial supremacy as they doubt the relative capacity of the political branches of government to be sufficiently stable or impartial to serve as the ultimate arbiter of fundamental rights.[5] This chapter will thus seek to fill this gap in the literature by explicating and defending the normative merits of dialogic judicial review against its critics on both ends of this continuum.

Section I of this chapter begins with an examination of the case for legislative supremacy as advanced by eminent jurists, such as Jeremy Waldron[6] and Adrian Vermeule.[7] Section II will proceed by exploring the arguments in favour of judicial supremacy as commonly advanced by luminary scholars, like Larry Alexander,[8] Frederick Schauer,[9] Trevor Allan,[10] and Jeffrey Jowell.[11] Finally, in Section III, I shall seek to defend dialogic review as the constitutional ideal that mediates the extremities and excesses of judicial and legislative supremacy.

I. Legislative Supremacy and its Critics

Professor Jeremy Waldron has been a strident and prominent advocate for legislative supremacy, and the target of his attack is any system with 'strong judicial review';[12] but for him, this would include any constitutional practice whereby 'courts have the authority to decline to apply a statute in a particular case... or to modify the effect of a statute to make its application conform

[2] Hickman (n 1); Butler (n 1); Young (n 1) 128, however has briefly advanced two justifications for dialogic review that apply to the United Kingdom HRA regime: (1) dialogue is 'a method through which the right answer can be reached as to the scope and application of a human right' and (2) dialogue is a 'more legitimate process by which to resolve disputes about rights'.

[3] Alexander Bickel, *The Least Dangerous Branch: The Supreme Court at the Bar of Politics* (2nd edn, New Haven, Yale University Press 1986) 16–19.

[4] Jeremy Waldron, *Law and Disagreement* (Oxford, Clarendon Press 1999); Adrian Vermeule, *Law and the Limits of Reason* (Oxford, Oxford University Press 2008).

[5] Larry Alexander & Fredrick Schauer, 'On Extrajudicial Constitutional Interpretation' (1997) 110 *Harvard Law Review* 1359; TRS Allan, *Constitutional Justice: A Liberal Theory of the Rule of Law* (Oxford, Oxford University Press 2001); Jeffrey Jowell, 'Parliamentary Sovereignty under the New Constitutional Hypothesis' [2006] *Public Law* 562, 579.

[6] Waldron, *Law and Disagreement* (n 4). [7] Vermeule (n 4).

[8] Alexander & Schauer (n 5). [9] Ibid. [10] Allan (n 5). [11] Jowell (n 5).

[12] Jeremy Waldron, 'The Core of the Case Against Judicial Review' (2006) 115 *Yale Law Journal* 1346, 1354.

with individual rights (in ways that the statute itself does not envisage)'.[13] It is thus evident that Waldron takes issue not only with the United States–style of strong-form review but also with the weaker forms of review as provided in the Canadian Charter of Rights and Freedoms.

For Waldron, such stronger forms of judicial review are politically illegitimate, so far as democratic values are concerned. As he argues:

> By privileging majority voting among a small number of unelected and unaccountable judges, it disenfranchises ordinary citizens and brushes aside cherished principles of representation and political equality in the final resolution of issues about rights.[14]

Therefore, so far as the unelected judiciary is empowered to override or set aside the consensus of the elected representatives of the people, the citizenry's right to participate in the political processes would be violated. For Waldron, this disenfranchisement of the populace is a loss to democracy even if the judicial decision is substantively correct.[15] This judicial disempowerment of ordinary citizens and the concomitant loss to democracy become more acute when the electorate is faced with a reasonable disagreement about the moral principles that should guide one's political system and the courts foreclose the debate. More importantly and controversially, for Waldron, this right to political participation is paramount, and it cannot be limited or traded off against other instrumentalist goals or in furtherance of other principles of political morality.

Waldron's discomfort with strong judicial review is premised on the assumption that most members of society have a persisting, substantial, and good faith disagreement about the content and application of the constitutional rights in question. Where such reasonable disagreements exist, the necessity for settlement arises, but the resolution should not be a judicial one. After all, since there is a fundamental bona fide disagreement about what is the correct result in such cases, the only alternative is to eschew a result-oriented approach and for the political system in question to resort to a dispute resolution mechanism that is procedurally fair. According to Waldron, the procedurally fairest method of resolving such contested claims is to observe the 'principle of majority decision (MD)'.[16] As he argues:

> Better than any other rule, MD is neutral as between the contested outcomes, treats participants equally, and gives each expressed opinion the greatest weight possible

[13] Ibid. [14] Ibid. 1353.

[15] Jeremy Waldron, 'A Right-Based Critique of Constitutional Rights' (1993) 13 *Oxford Journal of Legal Studies* 18.

[16] Waldron, 'The Core of the Case Against Judicial Review' (n 12) 1388. See also *Law and Disagreement* (n 4) 239–43.

compatible with giving equal weight to all opinions. When we disagree about the desired outcome, when we do not want to bias the matter up-front one way or another, and when each of the relevant moral participants has a moral claim to be treated as an equal in the process, then MD—or something like it—is the principle to use.[17]

More importantly, vis-à-vis the judiciary, the use of MD to elect the legislators and the use of MD for decision-making amongst the elected representatives would provide a better 'approximation of the use of MD as a decision-procedure among the citizenry as a whole (and so a reasonable approximation of the application of the values underlying MD to the citizenry as a whole)'.[18]

Before I lay out my disagreements with some of Waldron's arguments, I shall first assess some of the critiques and rebuttals advanced by other eminent jurists.

Professor Richard Fallon has advanced an insightful critique of Waldron's arguments, to which I will now turn.[19] In essence, Fallon concedes that courts are no better than legislatures at defining rights correctly, but his justification for 'strong' judicial review rests on the assumption that 'it is presumptively worse for legislation to be enacted than not enacted, largely because of the threat that legislation might violate individual rights';[20] and hence, for instrumentalist reasons, a society might reasonably want to 'create multiple veto points so that governmental action could not occur if either a court or the legislature thought that the action would violate individual rights'.[21] However, as observed by Professor Mark Tushnet, Fallon's argument rests on a libertarian and questionable assumption that private violations of fundamental rights are less serious or pervasive than legislative violations of fundamental rights, especially since private actions that result in the denials of fundamental rights occur not in a vacuum but as a consequence of the way the background rights of contract, property, and torts are defined and distributed.[22]

[17] Ibid. [18] Waldron, 'The Core of the Case Against Judicial Review' (n 12) 1388.

[19] Richard Fallon, 'The Core of an Uneasy Case for Judicial Review' (2008) 121 *Harvard Law Review* 1693.

[20] Ibid. 1707.

[21] Ibid. 1705. Fallon however concedes that his argument does not apply in zero-sum controversies in which fundamental rights are pitted against one another and the over-enforcement of one entails the under-enforcement of the other, and in situations where the national constitutions expressly protect social and economic rights which are typically better promoted by legislative rather than judicial action.

[22] Mark Tushnet, 'How Different Are Waldron's and Fallon's Core Cases For and Against Judicial Review?' (2010) 30 *Oxford Journal of Legal Studies* 49, 63.

Moreover, Fallon's arguments are also premised on another questionable assumption that constitutional review merely acts as a brake or veto on legislative action and may not mandate legislation. He analogizes constitutional review to the United States Presidential veto against Congressional legislation or bicameral lawmaking, but this analogy is misleading. This analogy suggests that both branches of government can legally veto each other's actions and in the absence of mutual agreement, no action is taken. However, this is not wholly accurate. In any constitutional system with strong-form judicial review, judges may not only invalidate pre-existing legislation, they may also require the legislature to enact certain statutes to fulfil certain constitutional mandates. Such court mandates may include judicial directions to the legislature to enact certain social welfare legislation (even if the constitution does not expressly protect such rights) or matrimonial statutes for same-sex couples. Seen in this light, constitutional review can thus act not only as a shield but also as a sword. If so, it is not evidently clear why judicially directed legislative action is superior to or epistemically more correct than legislative self-directed action when a society is seeking to resolve contestable rights.

Aileen Kavanagh has advanced an elegant critique of Waldron's views, and I would focus here on two crucial arguments. First, she argues that the intrinsic value of political participation does not compromise the central importance of designing political institutions such that they are likely to 'make political decisions in accordance with right reason'.[23] As she argues, popular preference does not transform a morally wrong act, like rape, into one that is morally right, even if some people might believe otherwise.[24] The design that is most likely to yield the most morally right decisions is thus most justified. Second, Kavanagh argues that if disagreement over the best means of protecting rights is the ground on which we should reject the institution of judicial review, it is difficult then to see why participatory majoritarianism is not impugned on the very same grounds. After all, since reasonable people may disagree over whether majority voting is the desirable way of making political decisions, Waldron's case for prioritizing the right to participate on equal terms would therefore not be immune from the sort of disagreement which he argues is fatal to all other modes of political decision making.[25]

[23] Aileen Kavanagh, 'Participation and Judicial Review: A Reply to Jeremy Waldron' (2003) 22(5) *Law and Philosophy* 451, 460.

[24] Ibid. 460–1.

[25] Kavanagh, 'Participation and Judicial Review' (n 23) 468; Joseph Raz, 'Disagreement in Politics' (1998) 43 *American Journal of Jurisprudence* 25, 47.

Certainly, Kavanagh has successfully argued that 'the instrumentalist condition of good government'[26] is the fundamental criterion for judging the success of any constitutional arrangement, and she has equally undermined Waldron's process-based arguments in favour of majority voting on the basis that participatory majoritarianism, as a method of dispute resolution, would equally be subject to the same sort of rights-disagreement that Waldron argues delegitimizes other forms of political decision-making. However, Kavanagh's arguments cannot be used to establish why, when there is a reasonable rights-disagreement in society, it would be *instrumentally* better for the constitutional system to confer the *final* resolution of such rights on the courts.[27] So far as Kavanagh has argued that, on instrumentalist grounds, constitutional review is a valuable channel of political participation, her arguments are unassailable. However, all the instrumentalist arguments she harnesses in favour of constitutional review only establish, at best, the case for allowing the judicial invalidation of legislation in circumstances where Parliament retains the right to disagree with the courts; they do not establish the case for allowing the courts to have the final say on any rights-controversy on the ground that judges are epistemically more reliable than legislators in getting such decisions right. Even if Kavanagh may indeed agree with me, I would like to make this point clear. In essence, Kavanagh's arguments cannot be read to support a proposition for foreclosing the ability of the political branches of government, after deliberation, to overrule the judicial understanding of rights via the ordinary political processes.

Dimitrios Kyritsis has also argued that Waldron's objection to judicial review overlooks the fact that legislators' conception of rights may not be reflective of the people they represent. In his view, a legislator is like a trustee rather than a proxy of the people; he or she exercises independent judgment in the choices he or she makes and he or she is 'under no institutional duty to keep equal distances from every reasonable view actually held by his constituents'.[28] Therefore, so far as Waldron argues that the legislature offers the best approximation of popular will, he overlooks the fact that legislators, in exercising their best independent judgments, may indeed go against the view of some or most of their constituents. *A fortiori*, Kyritsis argues, the only way to ensure that the legislature does not misuse its liberty to

[26] Joseph Raz, *Ethics in the Public Domain: Essays in the Morality of Law and Politics* (Oxford, Clarendon Press 1994) 117.

[27] Kavanagh may not have any intentions of advancing such a view. See Aileen Kavanagh, *Constitutional Review under the UK Human Rights Act* (Cambridge, Cambridge University Press 2009) 406–21.

[28] Dimitrios Kyritsis, 'Representation and Waldron's Objection to Judicial Review' (2006) 26 *Oxford Journal of Legal Studies* 733, 745.

exercise independent judgment is to conceive of a safeguard; to be effective, this safeguard must also be sufficiently independent of the organ it seeks to superintend.[29] Therein is the justification for the judicial review of legislation.

Kyritsis is certainly right that a legislator's job is not to strive as far as possible to accurately reflect the convictions of the people he or she represents; but so far as a legislator has to account, on a regular basis, for his or her views at the ballot box, a legislator who seeks re-election would have every incentive to ensure that the law he or she supports does not deviate too far from those convictions held by a majority of his or her constituents. The same cannot be said of judges who do not need to seek popular endorsement of their job performances for the continuance of their tenure in office. There may indeed be many good reasons, as I will explore later, why the judicial insulation from electoral pressures is instrumentally desirable, but as Professor James Allan astutely observes, '[p]ointing to the flaws in a particular legislature's democratic credentials does not improve those same credentials of the judiciary'.[30] Furthermore, Kyritsis has argued convincingly that an independent judiciary should be the branch of government conferred with the right to supervise the legislature as we need a separate, independent branch of government to check another branch's exercise of powers, and courts are better placed vis-à-vis other branches to resist any political pressure. But in view of Kyritsis' concession that judges do not necessarily have sharper moral insights than legislators,[31] his arguments cannot be read to support the proposition that, vis-à-vis the legislature, courts should possess the final say on the resolution of any rights-controversy. In other words, instrumentalist arguments in support of the judiciary's right to review the propriety of any rights-infringing legislation do not further demonstrate why the legislature, via the use of ordinary democratic processes, should be barred from overruling the court's interpretation of rights.

In the foregoing discussions, we have examined how Waldron's process-based arguments are incomplete so far as he eschews instrumentalist justifications for or against constitutional review. It is plausible that in the context of the protection of rights, the loss of some self-governance rights in a specific legal system might be more than compensated by the judicial protection of other rights that have been disregarded by the legislature.[32] However, notwithstanding the instrumentalist justifications for judicial review advanced

[29] Ibid. 746–7.

[30] James Allan, 'Bill of Rights and Judicial Power—a Liberal's Quandary' (1996) 16 *Oxford Journal of Legal Studies* 337, 349.

[31] Kyritsis (n 28) 747.

[32] Wojciech Sadurski, 'Judicial Review and the Protection of Constitutional Rights' (2002) 22 *Oxford Journal of Legal Studies* 275, 280.

by Kavanagh and Kyritsis, as discussed above, we have also observed how Waldron's critics do not demonstrate why, even after legislative deliberation, the judiciary should be the branch of government entrusted to provide the final determination on the optimum balance of rights and limitations in any democratic constitutional system.

However, Waldron has equally not established his case against the weaker forms of judicial review that allow for the legislature to harness the ordinary political processes to override the court's reading or invalidation of legislation. Waldron opposes what he terms 'strong judicial review' in Canada, but he says he is not against the 'weak judicial review' that operates under the UKHRA. Yet, by Waldron's definition of 'strong judicial review', the operation of the UKHRA should be classified as strong-form review too. Waldron disavows any constitutional practices whereby the courts are empowered to modify the effect of a statute to make its application conform to individual rights in ways that the statute itself does not envisage.[33] But this is indeed the practice of the United Kingdom courts under Section 3 of the UKHRA when they rectify statutory terms in order to render them compatible with the European Convention on Human Rights.[34]

As discussed earlier, Waldron's main objection to 'strong judicial review', as defined, is that it disenfranchises the electorate of the right to equal participation in the determination of public policy. But the people's right to equal participation is in no way affected if the legislature retains the right to use the ordinary political processes to reverse any judicial invalidation/reading of legislation that it disagrees with, unless Waldron also considers any judicial attempts to slow down the legislative processes or be involved in lawmaking as undemocratic. But this claim proves too much; it would also bring into question the legitimacy of the court's exercise of its administrative law functions or engagement in common law adjudication.[35] In fact, Waldron has conceded that such '"slowing-down" devices may also be supported in the political community by values associated with "the rule of law"'[36] and this would not be an affront to democracy.

While Waldron has championed legislative supremacy on philosophical and jurisprudential grounds, Professor Adrian Vermeule has attacked judicial review with pragmatic tools drawn from social science. He argues that if we focus on consequentialist inquiries about institutional choices, there

[33] Waldron, 'The Core of the Case Against Judicial Review' (n 12) 1354.

[34] *R v A (No 2)* [2002] 1 AC 45 (HL), 68. See also Aileen Kavanagh, *Constitutional Review under the UK Human Rights Act* (Cambridge, Cambridge University Press 2009) 19–47.

[35] Leighton McDonald, 'Rights, "Dialogue" and Democratic Objections to Judicial Review' (2004) 32 *Federal Law Review* 1, 23.

[36] Waldron, *Law and Disagreement* (n 4) 305–6.

are no epistemic reasons to believe that judicial review is superior to the legislative determination of rights. The claim of superior judicial competence over rights-adjudication primarily rests on the ground that courts are comparatively freer from politically induced bias, but Vermeule argues that such arguments favouring judicial review over legislative supremacy are often based on a form of 'nirvana fallacy':

> This sort of view generates an idealised picture or best-case scenario for judicial law-making and compares it to the worst-case scenario for legislative law-making. In an even handed comparison, the epistemic superiority of legislative law-making emerges under a broad range of conditions.[37]

Legislators are connected to constituents, and have greater fact-finding capabilities of identifying the factual components and causal consequences of constitutional decisions; but, in turn, the need to secure re-election can distort their assessments. Judges are insulated from the political winds and are arguably more impartial; but comparatively, they are limited in their access to the requisite empirical evidence to make a fully informed constitutional judgment and they lack the necessary training to weigh accurately the social or economic consequences of such constitutional decisions. The main trade-off in institutional design is thus between freedom from bias and information.[38]

Vermeule then invokes the Condorcet Jury Theorem to defend the overall epistemic superiority of legislatures. The Condorcet Jury Theorem is a model of information aggregation which states that where there is a binary choice for which a right answer exists, the probability of a correct answer, reached by a majority of the group, increases toward 100 per cent as the group gets bigger.[39] The central point of this Jury Theorem is that groups will perform better than individuals and larger groups will outdo smaller ones, so long as two conditions are satisfied: (1) majority rule is used; and (2) each person in the group is more likely than not to be correct.[40] According to Vermeule, the legislatures have an overwhelming Condorcetian advantage: legislators have greater institutional tools to acquire information, and though they may use them in a more biased fashion at an *individual* level, legislative diversity at a large *group* level will help wash out the biases.[41] As Vermeule argues:

> What matter for the Jury Theorem purposes is not bias in the abstract but whether biases are correlated across the group. Because legislators as a group are more diverse

[37] Vermeule (n 7) 4. [38] Vermeule (n 7) 86. [39] Ibid. 19.

[40] See Sunstein, *A Constitution of Many Minds: Why the Founding Document Doesn't Mean what it Meant Before* (Princeton, Princeton University Press 2009) 9.

[41] Vermeule (n 7) 87.

than the judges, along professional and other margins, biases are less tightly correlated and will tend to cancel out.[42]

Therefore, although the electoral connection diminishes the competence of individual legislators, Vermeule argues that it is a fallacy of composition to assume that this diminishes the competence of the legislature. Turning to the judiciary, Vermeule argues that the aggregation of the dozens of judicial minds ameliorates the informational problem they face, but this does not 'plausibly offset the large advantages of numbers, professional diversity, intra-institutional specialization, and sheer information that legislators enjoy in the Condorcetian framework'.[43]

Convincing as Professor Vermeule's arguments on the epistemic superiority of legislatures may be, he has only made a case against the final judicial resolution of constitutional rights. He has not made a case against dialogic forms of review which allow for a layer of judicial scrutiny that can, on Condorcetian grounds, improve the overall epistemic capabilities of the system while preserving the right of the legislature to use the ordinary political processes to disagree with the court's reading of the constitutional mandates. Vermeule argues that '"cumulative epistemic competence" cannot co-exist because if judges prefer their own views, and invalidate the statute, they are not adding epistemic competence to the system, but subtracting the legislators' epistemic competence from the rule-making process'.[44] This argument is however premised on an assumption that the judicial reading of the constitution is final, in the absence of a constitutional amendment. However, if the court's constitutional interpretations are merely provisional or if they can be overruled by legislative overrides as provided in some human rights charters or if the court's constitutional mandates are only enforced by common law norms which in turn can be overturned by ordinary legislation, Vermeule's arguments against judicial review will fall away. After all, under the Condorcetian framework, dialogic judicial review will only enhance the epistemic reliability of the decisions reached when the views of the comparatively more independent, legally trained minds are included in the constitutional deliberation and when the legislature retains the right to resolve the constitutional dispute in question by an ordinary majority.

II. Judicial Supremacy and its Critics

On the other end of the constitutional spectrum, we may find judicial supremacists who argue that the judiciary should be the final arbiter of

42 Ibid. 43 Vermeule (n 7) 87. 44 Ibid. 95.

constitutional rights. Professors Larry Alexander and Fredrick Schauer, in a joint article, have embraced 'judicial primacy without qualification'[45] on the basis that the benefits yielded by the authoritative settlement of the law—stability, reliability, and coordination—are pre-eminent and paramount constitutional values and that these substantive values are best secured by the courts.

Alexander and Schauer are absolutely right so far as they underscore the settlement function of the law as a cornerstone of constitutionalism. An authoritative constitution resolves disputes by providing uniform decisions on issues for which people have divergent views; it helps coordinate the decisions of atomistic, self-interested actors in the advancement of common interests, and provides a stable environment for the citizenry to conduct their affairs.[46] However, while these scholars have demonstrated why legal stability is a critical constitutional value, they have not explained why legal settlement should be determinative or should trump other constitutional values. As Professor Mark Tushnet has pointed out, all they have established is that 'the rule of law requires that a legal system have a set of institutional arrangements sufficient to ensure that degree of stability necessary to guarantee that the law's settlement function will be performed acceptably'.[47] After all, a constitution is not simply a mechanism for addressing coordination problems; it is also a focal point for public discourse on constitutional meanings that can only thrive with open debate and ceaseless deliberation.[48] Thus, while there may be instrumental reasons for resolving some constitutional controversies,[49] even in the face of underlying disagreement, so that society can properly function, it is not self-evident why we need to settle all constitutional ambiguities such that future generations are foreclosed from debating and deciding those issues for themselves. A charter of rights imposes both constitutional rules and constitutional standards, and where vague, open-textured language like 'equal protection of the law' and 'freedom of expression' are used, premature settlement and fixation of the exact contours of its meanings will impoverish and thwart a civic debate on its relevance and its new modes of application in a changing world. Settlement of the law is vital, but equally important is the need for the law to remain relevant to its times and change

[45] Alexander & Schauer (n 5) 1362. [46] Ibid. 1371–6.

[47] Mark Tushnet, *Taking the Constitution Away from the Courts* (Princeton, Princeton University Press 1999) 27.

[48] Ibid. 185–94.

[49] Examples that Alexander and Schauer gave include decisions on whether the legislature should be elected on a proportional or 'first past the post' basis or the length of an office holder's term of office. See Larry Alexander & Frederick Schauer, 'Defending Judicial Supremacy: A Reply' (2000) 17 *Constitutional Commentary* 455, 469.

when circumstances require so. The constitution is an enduring instrument with constitutional silences and spaces in place for future generations to fill according to their evolving circumstances. All that is required and desirable is sufficient stability for the settlement function of the law to be performed optimally.

Even if we accept Alexander and Schauer's arguments that the settlement function of the law is the pre-eminent constitutional value, it is unclear why the judiciary is the institution best suited to settling the law. Alexander and Schauer are of the view that the courts should wield this settlement authority as they are relatively insulated from the political winds and their adherence to precedent allows them to 'settle constitutional issues more permanently than can the political branches'.[50] At the outset, one must note that the question of whether judicial decisions are more stable than legislative acts is an empirical one, and Alexander and Schauer have conceded that they have not undertaken the necessary empirical analysis to reach a definitive judgment.[51] Other scholars have contested this assumption and argued that legislatures are regulated by norms that also encourage the maintenance of the status quo.[52] However, even if we assume that empirically Alexander and Schauer are right and that judicial decisions are generally more permanent than legislative acts, their arguments still suffer from a logical fallacy. Just because judicial decisions are more permanent than legislative acts does not mean that courts are better settlers of the law than the legislature. In other words, just because court decisions tend to be more stable, this does not demonstrate how judges are better or more likely to be correct when they first seek to settle an area of constitutional law. *Ex post* stability as a result of internal institutional constraints against change does not confer *ex ante* accuracy on the correctness of the decisions reached.

Across the Atlantic Ocean, there are legal scholars who argue that the judiciary, rather than the legislature, should be the final arbiter of constitutional rights, and it is to them we now turn. Unlike their American counterparts however, the British scholars do not defend judicial supremacy on the basis that judicial decisions are more permanent or stable than legislative ones. Instead, the common thread that joins their arguments lies in their unwavering faith in the judiciary's duty and ability to uphold the moral force of the rule of law.

[50] Alexander & Schauer, 'Defending Judicial Supremacy: A Reply' (n 49) 455, 477; See also 'On Extrajudicial Constitutional Interpretation' (1997) 110 *Harvard Law Review* 1359, 1373–6.

[51] Alexander & Schauer, 'Defending Judicial Supremacy: A Reply' (n 49).

[52] Tushnet (n 47) 28.

These judicial supremacists thus argue that the moral demands of the rule of law require the recognition of certain basic individual rights that are 'beyond serious legislative encroachment'.[53] In the context of the United Kingdom, which does not have a written constitution, Sir John Laws has observed that the 'doctrine of Parliamentary sovereignty cannot be vouched by Parliamentary legislation; a higher-order law confers it, and must of necessity limit it'.[54] According to the judicial supremacists in the United Kingdom, the rule of law encapsulates a substantive ideal and serves as the anvil on which the morality of legislation is tested. For Sir John Laws, the rule of law ideal may be unpacked 'by reference to three ideas: freedom, certainty, and fairness'.[55] According to Professor Trevor Allan, respect for the 'equal dignity of citizens, and its implications for fair treatment and respect for individual autonomy'[56] vindicates the ultimate meaning of the rule of law. Professor (Sir) Jeffrey Jowell has also expressed hope for a constitutional reality in the United Kingdom where 'the rule of law enforced by the courts is the ultimate controlling factor'[57] on which the United Kingdom's unwritten constitution is based. *A fortiori*, this would mean that if a legal system has a written constitution, no constitutional amendments may be passed in ways that are inconsistent with the rule of law and the fundamental liberties it embodies.

The trouble with this elusive, divine rule of law ideal is not that people will disagree with its normative force in the abstract but that this higher-order law, if enforceable, must be given substance, be interpreted, and be applied.[58] The appeal to a divine ideal may be irresistible but the devil is in the details. Judges do not uphold the rule of law in the abstract but have to apply these sacrosanct rights of free expression and equality to specific and particularized facts that come before them. It is noteworthy that the judicial supremacists do not clarify in concrete terms the scope and specifications of these rights. Does the right to free speech exclude any legislative attempts to ban hate speech that incites violence against racial or sexual minorities? Does the right to free speech trump legislation passed to cap the campaign expenditure of politicians? Does the right to equality exclude all forms and varieties

[53] TRS Allan, 'Parliamentary Sovereignty: Law, Politics, and Revolution' (1997) 113 *Law Quarterly Review* 443, 449.

[54] John Laws, 'Law and Democracy' [1995] *Public Law* 72, 87.

[55] John Laws, 'The Constitution: Morals and Rights' [1996] *Public Law* 622, 630.

[56] TRS Allan, *Constitutional Justice: A Liberal Theory of the Rule of Law* (Oxford, Oxford University Press 2001) 2.

[57] Jeffrey Jowell, 'Parliamentary Sovereignty under the New Constitutional Hypothesis' [2006] *Public Law* 562, 579.

[58] JAG Griffith, 'The Brave New World of Sir John Laws' (2000) 63 *Modern Law Review* 159, 165.

of race-based affirmative action programmes that the legislature may pursue? Does the right to equality require the state to pass legislation to allow same-sex couples to marry according to the same statutory procedure as heterosexual couples? The rule of law is a vague, contestable ideal and is consistent with a variety of understandings and institutional arrangements.[59] If the judicial supremacists are right that the courts should stand at the apex of any constitution, they must demonstrate how judges, vis-à-vis the legislature, are better at resolving such constitutional disputes.

Laws and Allan have sought to provide an instrumental justification for judicial supremacy: judges stand above the rancour of politics as they do not need to face re-election and are duty-bound to reach reasoned judgments such that they are well placed to reach morally correct results. This might be true but as we have discussed earlier, there is a trade-off between information and the freedom from bias. The insulation from the masses and independence from the political branches allow judges to be comparatively freer from bias during constitutional adjudication, but it is this insulation that hampers the judges' fact-finding capabilities. Due to their professional homogeneity, judges also lack the necessary non-legal training and expertise to assess accurately the social and economic consequences of their constitutional decisions. Therefore, judicial supremacists tend to view the courts through rose-tinted glasses; they only see the institutional advantages that the judiciary enjoys in rights adjudication and fail to account for the institutional disadvantages inherent in the office.

Furthermore, Jowell and Laws have denied that the demise of legislative supremacy would transfer unfettered powers to the unelected judiciary as, in reality, the courts exercise final authority over different and distinct spheres. According to Laws, judges exercise judicial power while legislatures exercise elective power; the latter 'consists in the authority to make decisions of policy within the remit given by the electorate... with which neither the judges nor anyone else have any business to interfere'[60] while the former rests in the guarantee that the constitutional framework of fundamental principles will be vindicated. Jowell has been more explicit about the distinct spheres of influence that the two branches of government occupy:

(L)egislative authority inevitably contains a wide area of discretion to make social and economic policy, over which the courts have no dominium. It is not for the

[59] Jeffrey Goldsworthy, 'Homogenising Constitutions' (2003) 23 *Oxford Journal of Legal Studies* 483, 505.

[60] Laws, 'Law and Democracy' (n 54) 92.

judges to second-guess the legislature on utilitarian considerations of the social good. Their role is strictly confined to the limited issue of whether the various inherent elements of democracy have been infringed by other branches of government and therefore cannot be sustained.[61]

In essence, the learned scholars are arguing that judicial supremacy is not undemocratic as judges are only supreme within their limited sphere of stewardship as constitutional guardians of democratic principles/rights while legislatures are supreme in their exercise of policy, in particular over social and economic policy. With respect, this distinction between 'rights' and 'policy' is untenable. Every alleged rights-infringing legislative measure stems from a social or economic policy that lawmakers seek to pursue. When legislatures carve away due process protections for criminal defendants, they are (rightly or wrongly) pursuing a certain social policy on crime control. If lawmakers decide to exclude certain racial groups from receiving welfare benefits, the right to equality is most trenchantly violated by this economic policy, even if the legislature may be merely making utilitarian calculations of the social good. There is thus no self-evident way how one can delineate the domain of 'rights' from 'policy' such that courts can be stewards only of the former and not the latter. In many constitutional disputes, there may be clashes of rights for which the legislature's 'policy' may indeed just be parliamentary attempts to advance the rights of one group over the other. Even for those legislative measures, for example social welfare statutes, which Jowell may describe as mere policies, others may describe them as rights-implementing or rights-limiting statutes. Ultimately, this rights/policy dichotomy is unconvincing as rights legislation or adjudication inevitably involves the making of a myriad of policy choices in a political environment that is pervaded by moral disagreement.[62]

In the final analysis, an appeal to judicial supremacy often rests on questionable assumptions that judges are the best settlers of the law or that courts are merely enforcing determinate and non-controversial rights. But in a complex world where judges have to give content to the rule of law and balance controversial and competing rights, and especially in light of the informational gap that is an inherent institutional disadvantage of the courts, we cannot rely on judges' good faith application of reason alone to ensure that the correct moral decision is reached. Therefore, so far as judicial supremacists argue that judges should be the final and exclusive arbiters of constitutional rights, their claim must be rejected.

[61] Jowell, 'Parliamentary Sovereignty under the New Constitutional Hypothesis' (n 57) 578–9.

[62] Richard Ekins, 'Judicial Supremacy and the Rule of Law' (2003) 119 *Law Quarterly Review* 127, 140.

III. Dialogic Judicial Review and its Critics

Dialogic judicial review is premised on an understanding that courts should and can engage in a 'continuing colloquy with the political institutions and with society at large'[63] on the requisites and demands of a constitutional democracy. So far as judges are more immune from electoral pressures and insofar as adjudication provides an effective forum for opposing views to be argued, deliberated, and reasoned, judicial review offers a unique contribution to our constitutional discourse. Such institutional advantages that the courts enjoy are especially apparent when one seeks to protect unpopular or systemically under-valued minorities, for example criminal defendants, racial, or sexual minorities, that may not be seriously represented by popular initiatives or legislative majorities, and it should be no surprise that it is for these discrete and insular groups that judicial review has made the most difference.[64] Yet, where a constitutional system provides for structural mechanisms that enable the legislature to reverse, modify, or avoid a judicial decision it disagrees with, or where courts apply judicial techniques and canons of interpretation that permit responses and disagreements from the political branches of government on an interpretation of constitutional values, any concern that the judicial discourse will serve as a veto on politics is thus misplaced. As Professor Mark Tushnet has observed:

> Dialogic review capitalizes on the institutional advantage courts have in constitutional attentiveness by allowing courts to bring constitutional values, in connection with specific problems, into focus in the legislative forum. This advances the constitutional value of limitations on democratic self-governance. With issues brought to the legislature's attention, we can then advance the democratic self-governance by leaving the final decision to the legislature.[65]

Dialogic review thus embodies a constitutional framework that harnesses the advantages of judicial review; but, at the same time, it allows for legislatures to make reasoned judgments about alternative interpretations of fundamental liberties, without resorting to the onerous process of a constitutional amendment.

Professor Luc B Tremblay has however argued that the theory of institutional dialogue lacks normative content as it is premised only on a 'negative'

[63] Bickel (n 3) 240.

[64] Erwin Chemerinsky, 'In Defence of Judicial Review: A Reply to Professor Kramer' (2004) 92 *California Law Review* 1013.

[65] Mark Tushnet, 'Dialogic Judicial Review' (2008) 61 *Arkansas Law Review* 205, 212.

claim: judicial review is legitimate not because it possesses some positive legitimate justification but because it does not prevent the democratic institutions from accomplishing their prior objectives.[66] Professor Keith Ewing has equally made the same point: '[I]f judicial review is to be justified, it must be for reasons of principle which are intrinsic to the process itself, and not because the process is not as intrusive or as expansive in practice as might otherwise be claimed by the opponents of judicial review of legislation.'[67] Dialogic theorists thus have to provide an affirmative justification for allowing the courts to serve alongside the legislature as fellow interlocutors of the requisite demands of a constitutional democracy. However, since dialogic theorists do not argue that judges should be the final and exclusive arbiters of constitutional freedoms, we do not have the burden of proving that judges are epistemically more reliable than legislators are in reaching the correct constitutional determination, assuming a single right answer can be determined in the first place.

The central justification for dialogic judicial review is that rights-violations often occur as a result of legislative neglect and that the judiciary can play a positive role in placing such issues on the legislative agenda for the lawmakers' deliberation and response. The bureaucratic inertia that must be overcome before the ruling government can be provoked to act on human rights is often very prohibitive. In instances where the rights of the politically marginalized conflict with the wishes of a sizable segment of the society, the vested interest of any administration committed to preserving its incumbency would be to preserve the status quo until the pressure for initiating reforms is greater than the convenience of leaving things unchanged. If judges are empowered to invalidate legislation on the basis that the statute violates human rights or read an existing statute in a rights-compatible way, the benefit of legislative inertia is then bestowed upon the aggrieved political minority as they are now provided with a tangible remedy. At the same time, if Parliament, after deliberation, is empowered to respond, reverse, or avoid the court's decision, by harnessing the ordinary political processes when it wants to correct a perceived judicial error, any concern about an overzealous judiciary thwarting democratic prerogatives would equally be addressed.

FL Morton has however questioned whether Parliament can always reinstate the old law as it was after the judicial (mis)reading or invalidation. According to him, certain issues like gay rights and abortion cut across

[66] Luc B Tremblay, 'The Legitimacy of Judicial Review: The Limits of Dialogue Between Courts and Legislatures' (2005) 3 *International Journal of Constitutional Law* 617, 645.

[67] Keith Ewing, 'Human Rights' in Peter Cane & Mark Tushnet (eds), *The Oxford Handbook of Legal Studies* (Oxford, Oxford University Press 2003).

normal lines of partisan cleavage and are so divisive that any change in the law would create a new 'judicially-created policy status quo'.[68] Elaborating on this point, Morton argues that these issues often involve a tussle between two minority camps and an apathetic majority; in such instances, the legislature's preferred choice is to do nothing, as legislative activity on behalf of either camp would trigger the wrath of the other. In the same vein, Professor Mark Tushnet has argued that judicial review can lead to 'policy distortion' when legislators take the judicially articulated constitutional norms as dispositive and refrain from adopting a statute that would reinstate or reaffirm their original views.[69]

While I agree with Morton that judges often do change the status quo when they intervene in disputes over gay rights or abortion and I agree with Tushnet that policy distortion occurs when lawmakers, as a result of judicial review, pursue a policy different from their original one, I would however consider this power transfer a virtue rather than a vice. Under a dialogic model of judicial review, courts serve as an interlocutor of rights in a constitutional democracy by allowing legislators to have their way if they so choose, but the lawmakers must openly deliberate and take political responsibility for their courses of action. If Parliament is unwilling or unable to garner a simple majority vote to overturn a judicial decision, this only demonstrates that the court's decision is not so egregious (if at all) for such legislative consensus to be reached. So far as the judiciary has imposed a new 'policy status quo' on the legislature or caused a 'policy distortion', the result is just an inevitable trade-off for a system of human rights enforcement by an independent institution of government. Dialogic judicial review provokes legislatures to confront issues of principle that they would rather ignore, by placing important but uncomfortable issues on the legislative agenda, but so far as the electoral majoritarian preferences can still be vindicated by the ordinary political processes in statutes that revise or reverse the judicial decisions, the political process would have been enriched by the fuller deliberation in Parliament and the court's contribution to this discourse on rights and freedoms.[70]

Furthermore, as Professor Rosalind Dixon has observed, dialogic judicial review draws the attention of lawmakers to 'legislative blind spots'[71] and provides them with an opportunity to address inadvertent infringements of rights

[68] FL Morton, 'Dialogue or Monologue? A Reply to Hogg and Thornton' [April 1999] *Policy Options* 23, 23–4.

[69] Mark Tushnet, 'Policy Distortion and Democratic Debilitation: Comparative Illumination of the Countermajoritarian Difficulty' (1995) 94 *Michigan Law Review* 245, 265.

[70] Kent Roach, 'Dialogic Judicial Review and its Critics' (2004) 23 *Supreme Court Law Review* 49, 54.

[71] Rosalind Dixon, 'The Supreme Court of Canada, Charter Dialogue and Deference' (2009) 47 *Osgoode Hall Law Journal* 235.

and freedoms. Such legislative blind spots can take three forms: (1) blind spots of application arise when legislators, faced with hundreds of bills in any given session, fail to study how individual pieces of legislation may limit rights in ways they did not appreciate; (2) blind spots of perspective occur when legislators lack the appropriate incentives to reach out to minority voices that are very different from the median voter's and inadvertently fail to consider certain perspectives in lawmaking; and (3) blind spots of accommodation arise when legislators, as a result of time and expertise constraints, focus only on achieving the relevant legislative objective and overlook opportunities for the accommodation of rights, even if such accommodation represents only a minimal cost to the legislature's policy aims.[72] Dialogic judicial review is thus well suited to ameliorate rights-infringement that results from legislative inadvertence as the adjudicatory forum allows judges to examine the application of general laws to specific circumstances and specified groups that legislators may have failed to consider.

Professor Mark Tushnet has however expressed concern that political 'veto points' in the legislature can allow a minority in the legislative house to stall legislative proposals from moving forward and estop lawmakers from overturning a judicial decision with an ordinary majority; in this sense, weak-form review can escalate into strong-form review.[73] Nonetheless, this concern over veto points is not one exclusive to judicial review. Veto points are present when a legislature seeks to pass any legislation, not just one that seeks to override or avoid a judicial decision. Building coalitions and consensus among legislators is part and parcel of the ordinary legislative process; any concerns that such slowing measures are democratically debilitating would have to be accepted as necessary trade-offs for a constitutional system where the legislature can be forced to take political responsibility for its actions.

Alon Harel and Adam Shinar have also argued that dialogic review or 'constrained judicial review' should be justified on the basis that it offers the aggrieved the right to a hearing.[74] The aggrieved is given an opportunity to raise his or her grievance; this right invariably triggers a concrete examination of the reasons underlying the decision taken against the aggrieved, and the State is given an opportunity to reconsider its initial decision against the aggrieved.[75] In the same vein, Ronald Den Otter[76]

[72] Ibid. 258–9.

[73] Mark Tushnet, 'New Forms of Judicial Review and the Persistence of Rights and Democracy-Based Worries' (2003) 38 *Wake Forest Law Review* 813, 831.

[74] Alon Harel & Adam Shinar, 'Between Judicial and Legislative Supremacy: A Cautious Defence of Constrained Judicial Review' (2012) 10 *International Journal of Constitutional Law* 950.

[75] Ibid. 967.

[76] Ronald Den Otter, *Judicial Review in an Age of Moral Pluralism* (Cambridge, Cambridge University Press, 2009).

and Tamas Gyorfi[77] have equally defended judicial review on the basis that governmental policies should be subjected to reasoned, public justification. So far as courts facilitate the airing of the public's grievances and induce the political institutions to attend to them, courts provide a forum for rights-violations to be formally addressed, but they do not foreclose the legislature from making a final determination on the outcome.

This dialogic institutional division of labour rests on the assumption that major sources of rights-violations occur as a result of legislative inadvertence or deliberate neglect, faults that can be 'cured by thoroughly airing the issues of principle in a judicial forum'.[78] At the same time, precisely because the legislature can use the ordinary political processes to overturn any judicial decisions, lawmakers retain the right to correct any perceived judicial errors without having to seek an extraordinary consensus usually required for a constitutional amendment. What dialogic judicial review does is that it can compel governments to confront issues of principle that they may be inclined to ignore, but the judiciary cannot force a committed legislature to accept the court's resolution of such matters.[79] These sentiments were indeed what Lord Hoffmann was echoing when he observed as follows in *Regina v Secretary of State for the Home Department Ex parte Simms*:[80]

> But the principle of legality means that Parliament must squarely confront what it is doing and accept the political cost. Fundamental rights cannot be overridden by general or ambiguous words. This is because there is too great a risk that the full implications of their unqualified meaning may have passed unnoticed in the democratic process.

Professor Luc Tremblay has however argued that so far as the courts recognize a second-order rule of constitutional interpretation that provides for judges to accept formally all legislative reversals and avoidances of former judicial nullification, the application of this rule would 'entail a radical form of judicial deference or submission to the judgments of the legislatures'.[81] With respect, this objection is misconceived. Judicial deference *ex post* must be distinguished from judicial deference *ex ante*. Judicial deference *ex ante* takes place when the courts prematurely yield to the legislative understanding of a rights-limitation when the impugned legislation is first challenged. *Ex ante* deference deprives the judiciary of an opportunity to offer to the legislature its own institutional best understandings of rights. On the other hand, if the judiciary has already

[77] Tamas Gyorfi, 'Between Common Law Constitutionalism and Procedural Democracy' (2013) 33 *Oxford Journal of Legal Studies* 317.

[78] Paul Weiler, 'Rights and Judges in a Democracy: A New Canadian Version' (1984) 18 *Journal of Law Reform* 51, 84.

[79] Roach (n 70) 75.

[80] [2000] 2 AC 115 (HL), 131.

[81] Tremblay (n 66) 637.

advanced its own view in a prior constitutional challenge and the legislature has responded in disagreement, judicial deference *ex post* to this legislative sequel is merely an acknowledgement that the legislature, after deliberation in Parliament, is entitled to disagree with a judicial conception of indeterminate rights. *Ex ante* judicial deference deprives the political process of the insights that the judiciary can provide to the polity's shared understandings of rights, while *ex post* deference accords respect to the political process that has already been enriched by the fuller deliberation in Parliament and the court's contribution to this constitutional discourse.

In this way, as Professor Kent Roach has observed, there are important continuities between the common law and dialogic constitutionalism.[82] Courts, in developing the common law, are commonly responding to legislative inertia, which can be viewed as an implied delegation of authority.[83] Nonetheless, this delegation of authority is revocable as the legislature can always reclaim the field by enacting ordinary legislation to supersede the judicial decision that is perceived to have gone awry. In this way, the benefits or costs of dialogic constitutionalism are no more ambitious or no less modest than the common law interpretive functions that such courts have exercised for centuries. Dialogic constitutional review is merely the extension of the situs for dialogue between the courts and the legislature that has already been taking place for centuries under the common law. The aim of dialogic review is to merely introduce 'new ideas, perspectives, or even equilibriums into the political process, all with the view to encouraging the legislature and the broader constitutional culture to reconsider its allegiance to the previous status quo'.[84]

IV. Conclusion

The dialogic model of judicial review allows for the legislature and the courts to be fellow collaborators in upholding the rule of law. Neither the legislature nor the judiciary is a perfect institution. The former is vulnerable to the whims of populist needs, while the latter is composed of unelected officials who are unaccountable to the public and lack the information-gathering capacities of the legislature.

[82] Kent Roach, *The Supreme Court on Trial: Judicial Activism or Democratic Dialogue* (Toronto, Irwin Law 2001).

[83] Kent Roach, 'A Dialogue about Principle and a Principled Dialogue: Justice Iacobucci's Substantive Approach to Dialogue' (2007) 57 *University of Toronto Law Journal* 499, 456.

[84] Rosalind Dixon, 'Creating Dialogue about Socioeconomic Rights: Strong-form versus Weak-form Judicial Review Revisited' (2007) 5 *International Journal of Constitutional Law* 391, 407.

As astutely observed by Professor Stephen Gardbaum:

> The relative weaknesses of legislatures are the potential rights-relevant pathologies to which they may be subject. The relative advantage of courts here is independence from these potential electorally induced pathologies... but the weaknesses are the parallel tendencies towards pathologies of their own and the general problem of relying exclusively on ex post regulation.[85]

Judicial supremacists may argue that the courts have a democratic mandate either conferred by their constitution or their human rights instrument to interpret rights; but this argument, while true, in no way refutes the critique that judges are less accountable to the public than lawmakers and that they are equally capable of making egregious blunders of moral judgment.[86] Dialogic theory therefore represents a concession that Ronald Dworkin's Hercules—a legendary judge that can always be trusted to reach reliably right answers—is no more than a myth.[87] On the other hand, legislative supremacists pay scant attention to the fact that legislators have every incentive to preserve their own incumbency and are open to neglecting the needs of the politically vulnerable. Given that both institutions are equally fallible, an ideal vision of constitutional democracy must provide a space for both the judiciary and the legislature to provide independent insights to the optimal specification of a human rights norm. While neither institution can be relied upon exclusively to further the demands of a rights-based democracy, the risks of constitutional blunders (as perceived by current or future generations) are significantly reduced when both institutions are allowed to act in tandem to defend the rights of all.

Legislative supremacists may argue that judicial review disenfranchises voters of the right to equal participation in the determination of public policy,[88] but the people's right to equal participation is in no way affected if the legislature retains the right to use the ordinary political processes to reverse any judicial invalidation/reading of legislation that it disagrees with. Certainly, such judicial interventions may create a new 'judicially-created policy status quo'[89] or lead to 'policy distortion'[90] such that it may be politically unfeasible for lawmakers to reinstate or reaffirm their original views. In this regard, commentators have observed, in particular, that the Canadian Section 33 override bears such opprobrium that it has fallen into desuetude,

[85] Stephen Gardbaum, *The New Commonwealth Model of Constitutionalism: Theory and Practice* (Cambridge, Cambridge University Press 2013) 63.

[86] See eg *Korematsu v United States* 323 US 214 (1944) (United States Supreme Court); *Dred Scott v Sandford* 60 US 393 (1856) (United States Supreme Court).

[87] Roach (n 70) 67.

[88] Waldron (n 4) 254. [89] Morton (n 68). [90] Tushnet (n 69) 265.

such that the legislatures are usually forced to take the judicially articulated constitutional norms as dispositive.[91] However, where the Canadian or any legislature is politically unwilling or unable to garner even a simple majority vote to overturn the court's decision, for fear of any adverse public reaction, this only demonstrates that the judicial decision is not so egregious (if at all) for such legislative consensus to be reached. It is the democratic process that has determined what is or is not politically feasible, and it does not follow that the judiciary has therefore trumped the democratic process.[92]

On the other hand, judicial supremacists may argue that this dialogic model of judicial review, where Parliament can prevail by avoiding or reinstating its original views with a simple majority, may cure human rights violations that occur as a result of legislative inadvertence or neglect, but it will not prevent a hostile legislature from intentionally violating fundamental liberties, especially against the interests of political minorities, with the majority's blessings. This may well be true, but it assumes that the judiciary is staffed by a 'bevy of Platonic Guardians'[93] who will always reach morally correct results and is right to have thwarted the wishes of the majority whenever it so intervenes. But the American experience with *de facto* judicial supremacy abounds with examples where judges have committed egregious moral blunders.[94] To allow the courts to have the exclusive and final say on our constitutional fundamentals, we are ultimately only making a choice to live with judicial errors over legislative ones. Finally, even if the judiciary is allowed to be the ultimate arbiter of the constitution, where its views go against the common opinion of both the legislature and the electorate, it is highly unlikely that the court's judgment would be dutifully enforced anyway. The sad reality is that while the courts can perhaps save the people from the legislature, with neither purse nor sword, there is no way the judiciary can save the people from themselves. If Parliament, with the overwhelming support of the people, decides to dismantle every vestige of democracy in a modern state, it would be futile for the judiciary to stand as a bulwark against an electorate gone mad. As the American Judge Learned Hand so eloquently expressed:

> a society so riven that the spirit of moderation is gone, no court can save; that a society where that spirit flourishes, no court need save; that in a society which evades

[91] See Tushnet (nn 69, 73); Morton (n 68).

[92] Jeffrey Goldsworthy, 'Judicial Review, Legislative Override, and Democracy' in Tom Campbell, Jeffrey Goldsworthy & Adrienne Stone (eds), *Protecting Human Rights Instruments and Institutions* (Oxford, Oxford University Press 2003) 268.

[93] Learned Hand, *The Bill of Rights* (Cambridge, Harvard University Press 1958) 74.

[94] n 86.

its responsibility by thrusting upon the courts the nurture of that spirit, that spirit in the end will perish.[95]

The resources and expertise of the judiciary would thus be more profitably utilized if they were harnessed instead to structure a constitutional dialogue with the legislature. The virtue of such review lies in the heightened scrutiny that is brought to bear on the validity of governmental action and not in the promise for a judicial resolution of societal conflicts concerning rights.

Dialogic judicial review essentially celebrates a model of 'judicial penultimacy'[96] whereby courts are engaging in a continuing constitutional colloquy with the political institutions, and the society at large,[97] and participating in a dynamic process in which constitutional meanings have evolved conversationally and are not perfected unilaterally.

[95] Learned Hand, *The Spirit of Liberty* (New York, Alfred A Knopf 1953) 164.

[96] Michael Perry, 'Protecting Human Rights in a Democracy: What Role for the Courts?' (2003) 38 *Wake Forest Law Review* 635, 673.

[97] Bickel (n 3) 244.

3

Overview of the Constitutional Systems

In the previous chapter, I have explored the normative justifications for dialogic review and have demonstrated *why* as a constitutional theory it is normatively superior to the alternatives of legislative or judicial supremacy.

In this chapter, I shall provide an overview of the three Asian constitutional systems under discussion. Section I will examine Hong Kong's constitutional model. Section II will continue with Malaysia's constitutional model and Section III will conclude with Singapore's developments. In each section, I shall provide a brief sketch of the respective jurisdiction's constitutional history, the constitutional powers assigned to the three branches of government, that is the legislature, the executive, and the judiciary, the constitutional rights regime provided, and its constitutional amendment procedures. The highlighted constitutional features would also be particularly salient to my later discussions on how dialogic review can take place in the jurisdictions discussed.

I. Hong Kong

A. Constitutional History of Hong Kong

The acquisition of Hong Kong by the British government was achieved via the conclusion of three treaties with China over the span of approximately 60 years.[1] Following the confiscation and destruction of opium stocks belonging to the British in 1839, war broke out between the British government and the imperial Chinese government, and this culminated in the Treaty of Nanking in 1842 that formally ceded in perpetuity Hong Kong Island

[1] For more information, see Yash Ghai, *Hong Kong's New Constitutional Order* (2nd edn, Hong Kong, Hong Kong University Press 1999) 1–80; Johannes Chan & CL Lim, *The Law of the Hong Kong Constitution* (Hong Kong, Sweet & Maxwell 2011) 5–33; Albert Chen, 'From Colony to Special Administrative Region: Hong Kong's Constitutional Journey' in Raymond Wacks (ed), *The Future of the Law in Hong Kong* (Hong Kong, Oxford University Press 1989).

to Britain. Following another altercation between the two governments in 1856, the British government went on to occupy Beijing in 1860 and compelled China to conclude a second treaty, the Convention of Peking, which ceded the Kowloon peninsula in perpetuity to Britain. Subsequently, as Britain observed how Japan, Russia, France, and Germany had successfully obtained leases over different ports in China, it decided to follow suit, and this culminated in the third treaty, the Convention of Peking of 1898, which provided for a 99-year lease of the immediate hinterland of Kowloon, including land still known today as the New Territories. The lease would expire on 30 June 1997, an event too remote and far into the future for the British government then to consider the consequences following its expiration.

As a Crown Colony, Hong Kong was governed pursuant to the Letters Patent of 1843, which, as amended through the years, formed the Constitution of Hong Kong until 30 June 1997. The People's Republic of China was established in 1949, but it was not till the 1970s that the two governments met to discuss the future of Hong Kong. By 1976, the devastating Cultural Revolution had come to an end. With the demise of Mao Zedong and the ascendance of Deng Xiaoping in Chinese politics, China embarked on its new policy of economic reforms and liberalization. At the same time, the demands of commerce were prompting the British government to resolve the future of the territory as the Hong Kong administration was unable to grant leases beyond 1997, and businesses equally faced immense uncertainties when they sought to raise loans from financial institutions. Nevertheless, negotiations between 1978 and 1982 reached an impasse as the British wanted to continue with the administration of Hong Kong after 1997, while the Chinese government was adamant about resuming its sovereignty over land that it claimed was wrongfully annexed via unequal treaties. It was only in 1983, after the British government conceded to relinquishing any authority over Hong Kong after 1997, that some headway was finally made in the negotiations. By then, the British government had decided to focus on safeguarding Hong Kong's autonomy from the Chinese government, and on preserving its pre-existing economic, legal, and social infrastructures. Further negotiations also led to the conclusion of the Sino-British Joint Declaration in 1984, a legally binding treaty, signed by both governments.

The Sino-British Joint Declaration essentially provided that China would resume the exercise of sovereignty over Hong Kong with effect from 1 July 1997 and that Hong Kong would henceforth be administered as a Special Administrative Region. The Hong Kong Special Administrative Region (HKSAR) would enjoy a high degree of autonomy, except in foreign and defence affairs which are the responsibilities of the Central People's

Government. The HKSAR would be vested with executive, legislative, and independent judicial power, including that of final adjudication, and the laws currently in force in Hong Kong would remain basically unchanged. The basic policies of the People's Republic of China regarding Hong Kong would be further stipulated in a Basic Law of the HKSAR and these would remain unchanged for 50 years. A Sino-British Joint Liaison Group, an advisory body, was also established to ensure a smooth transfer of government in 1997.

The primary responsibility for the drafting of the Basic Law was shouldered by the Basic Law Drafting Committee (BLDC). It was composed of 59 members; 36 of them were from China and 23 from Hong Kong, all of whom were nominated by the Chinese government. The Hong Kong members, in particular, were dominated by the business elites. The BLDC was assisted by a Basic Law Consultative Committee (BLCC), an advisory body that actively solicited the views of the Hong Kong people on various drafts of the Basic Law. In comparison, the BLCC was a more diverse body as some of its 180 members were nominated or elected by professional bodies. The first Basic Law draft was published in April 1988 and after the first consultation, 100 revisions were made. The second draft was published in February 1989 and 24 further revisions were made after the second round of consultation. The Basic Law was eventually finalized and promulgated by the National People's Congress, China's highest law-making body, on 4 April 1990, and was slated to come into effect on 1 July 1997.

B. Relationship between the Chinese Authorities and the HKSAR

The Basic Law provides that the HKSAR shall be a local administrative region of the People's Republic of China, which shall enjoy a high degree of autonomy and come directly under the Central People's Government.[2] National laws shall not be applied in the HKSAR except for those listed in Annex III to the Basic Law, which are confined to matters relating to defence, foreign affairs, and other matters outside the limits of the autonomy of the Region.[3] The socialist system and policies shall not be practised in the HKSAR, and the previous capitalist system and way of life shall remain unchanged for 50 years.[4] Article 21 also authorizes Chinese citizens among the residents of

[2] Hong Kong Basic Law, Article 12.

[3] Ibid. Article 18. Some of these National Laws include the Resolution on the Capital, Calendar, National Anthem, and National Flag of the People's Republic of China; the Resolution on the National Day of the People's Republic of China; and the Declaration of the Government of the People's Republic of China on the Territorial Sea.

[4] Ibid. Article 5.

the HKSAR to locally elect deputies of the Region to the National People's Congress and to participate in the work of the highest organ of state power.

C. Hong Kong Legislature

Under the Basic Law, the Legislative Council constitutes the legislature of the HKSAR. It is a unicameral body, although it is composed of members who are elected via two different electoral methods. Currently, 35 seats in the Legislative Council are constituted via universal suffrage in Geographical Constituencies (GC) elections. Another 35 seats, however, are constituted via Functional Constituencies (FC) elections, a system in which the right to vote depends upon a person's membership or registration in a recognized social, economic, industrial, commercial, political advisory, or professional body represented in the legislature.[5] Legislative Council elections are now held every four years. Currently, there are 28 FCs in the Legislative Council, which include the Legal, Financial Services, and Insurance FCs etc. Each FC is allowed to return one FC legislator, except the Labour FC which is permitted to return three members and the District Council FC which is permitted to return six members. The FC system was first introduced by the British government in 1985, as part of an overall plan to develop representative government in Hong Kong. The aims of such FC elections were to allow the economic and professional sectors to be well-represented in the legislature and to maintain Hong Kong's stability and prosperity after the hand-over.

However, this FC electoral system is not without its controversies. First, in many of the FCs, for example Insurance, Transport, Tourism, Finance, Labour etc., it is not individuals working in these professions that are eligible to vote; instead, in such FCs, it is only the recognized corporate bodies operating in these professions that are eligible to vote, and they would select their authorized representatives to vote as their proxies. Secondly, the inclusion of corporate voting raises the problem of 'packing'; conglomerates with several subsidiaries and associate companies could easily 'pack' a single or even a few FCs with multiple corporate electors that are subject to the singular control of the parent company.[6] The full extent in which 'packing' takes place in the FCs is practically impossible to verify as the recording or copying of any information from the public register of FC electors for research purposes is

[5] For a critique on the FC system, see Simon Young & Anthony Law, 'Privileged to Vote: Inequalities and Anomalies of the FC System' in Christine Loh (ed), *Functional Constituencies: A Unique Feature of the Hong Kong Legislative Council* (Hong Kong, Hong Kong University Press 2006) 59.

[6] See Ibid. 98–9.

prohibited by law. Thirdly, the size of the constituency base in each FC differs such that the relative voting power of an elector in a small FC would be far greater than that of another in a large FC. The FC with the smallest electorate base is Heung Yee Kuk, a statutory body that represents the indigenous inhabitants of the New Territories in advising the government on socio-economic matters pertaining to their welfare, and it had an electoral base of 147 registered individual electors in 2012. On the other hand, the Education FC had an electoral base of 92,957 registered individual electors in 2012. The variation in constituency size thus invariably affects the relative weight that each vote carries in determining the voter's preferred candidate in the relevant FC.

Christopher Patten, the last governor of colonial Hong Kong, had attempted to expand the electoral base for the FCs in the mid-1990s by replacing corporate voting with voting by individuals or employees in all the FCs; and he further created nine new FCs that included all of the working population. The Legislative Council elections of 1995 took place on this basis. China had objected to these political reforms and perceived them to be inconsistent with the Basic Law. These reforms were of particular concern to China as both governments had reached a tacit understanding, when the Basic Law was enacted, that the last legislature of colonial Hong Kong would form the first legislature of the HKSAR. When the Patten reforms were passed, China decided to establish a Provisional Legislative Council (PLC) in 1997. The PLC was a temporary legislature, with a term-limit of one year, tasked by China to take charge of Hong Kong's legislative affairs before the first Legislative Council could be elected. One of the PLC's first tasks was to repeal the Patten electoral reforms. The first Legislative Council elections took place in 1998, pursuant to the pre-Patten electoral laws reinstated by the PLC; and since then, elections have taken place in 2000, 2004, 2008, and 2012.

Nevertheless, in view of the public pressure for electoral reform, the Basic Law was amended in 2010 to allow for five GC seats (constituted by universal suffrage elections) and five District Council FC seats to be added to the Legislative Council for the 2012 elections. (Previously, there was only one District Council FC seat in the Legislative Council.) District Councils (DCs) are local municipalities that advise the government on the well-being of the people and the provision of public services in the respective 18 localities across Hong Kong. With regard to the five new DC seats added in the 2012 Legislative Council FC elections, all registered voters who previously did not have the right to vote in any pre-existing FC could now vote for candidates contesting for these five FC seats, but eligible DC candidates had to be first nominated by the elected District Councillors. With these constitutional reforms, each registered Hong Kong voter now has two votes, one to be cast for his or her preferred GC candidate and the other for his or her chosen FC candidate. However, with the massive increase in the electoral base for the new District Council FCs, the disparity in the relative weight that each vote carries in different FCs is now further exacerbated. In the 2012 elections, the added District Council FCs had about 3,220,000 registered electors. Notwithstanding this, Article 68 of the Basic Law provides that the 'ultimate aim' in Hong Kong's political transition is for all the members of the Legislative Council to be elected by universal suffrage, but this must be done in light of the 'actual situation in the Hong Kong Special Administrative Region and in accordance with the principle of gradual and orderly progress'.

Pursuant to Article 74 of the Basic Law, all private members' bills relating to government policies may only be proposed with the Chief Executive of the HKSAR's consent; private members' bills relating to 'public expenditure or political structure or the operation of the government' may not be introduced at all. Furthermore, Annex II of the Basic Law provides that bills introduced by the government shall require only a simple majority vote of the members of the Legislative Council present, while bills introduced by individual members of the Legislative Council shall require a simple majority vote of each of the two groups of the Legislative Council members present, that is a majority of the FC legislators and a majority of the GC legislators must vote for the bill. In other words, Hong Kong effectively has a bicameral legislature when members of the opposition seek to pass bills in the Legislative Council.

This constitutional feature is particularly noteworthy in light of Hong Kong's political realities. Since the 1980s, there have been two main political camps in Hong Kong—the pro-China/pro-establishment camp and the pro-democracy camp (or more commonly known today as the 'pan-democrats' camp). The pro-establishment camp is composed of an informal coalition of political parties and independent legislators that usually supports the agenda of the Hong Kong executive government. This informal coalition includes the Democratic Alliance for the Better of Hong Kong (DAB), the pro-Beijing political party that currently has the most number of seats in the Legislative Council, and the Liberal Party, a pro-business party whose vested interests often align with the government's. It is significant that since the establishment of the HKSAR, while the pan-democrats camp has consistently won over 60 per cent of the popular vote in the GC elections and has a slight lead in the GCs, the pro-establishment camp has unsurprisingly dominated the FC elections, such that the pro-establishment camp is able to command an overall majority of the seats in the Legislative Council.[7] In the 2012

[7] Ma Ngok, 'Political Parties and Elections' in Lam, Lui, Wong, & Holliday (eds), *Contemporary Hong Kong Politics: Governance in the Post-1997 Era* (Hong Kong, Hong Kong University Press

Legislative Council elections, the pro-establishment camp won 17 of the 35 GC seats and 26 of the FC seats.[8] Therefore, since the Hong Kong executive government is heavily reliant on the support of the pro-establishment camp in the legislature for the passage of its bills, unrestricted elections by universal suffrage for all the seats in the Legislative Council would unlikely be allowed till the pro-establishment camp is able to form a clear majority in the Legislative Council, without the use of the FC system as a political crutch.

D. Hong Kong Executive Government

The Chief Executive is the head of the HKSAR and head of the government. He or she serves for a term of five years and for no more than two terms.[9] Under the Basic Law, he or she is tasked to lead the government of the Region, to decide on government policies, and to be responsible for the implementation of its laws.[10]

The current Chief Executive, Leung Chun-ying, was elected in 2012 by members of an Election Committee composed of 1,200 members, with 300 members fielded from each of the following four sectors: (1) the industrial, commercial, and financial sectors; (2) the professions; (3) labour, social services, religious, and other sectors; and (4) members of the Legislative Council, representatives of district-based organizations, Hong Kong deputies to the National People's Congress, and representatives of Hong Kong members of the National Committee of the Chinese People's Political Consultative Conference.[11] Nevertheless, Article 45 of the Basic Law provides that the ultimate aim in Hong Kong's political transition is for the Chief Executive to be elected by universal suffrage upon nomination by a broadly representative nominating committee in accordance with democratic procedures. Before an elected Chief Executive can assume office, he or she must also be appointed by the Central People's Government in Beijing. The Chinese Government has emphasized that this power of appointment enshrined under Article 15 of the Basic Law is substantive in nature, and therefore it has the discretion to refuse the appointment of a candidate successfully elected.

The Chief Executive is assisted by a ministerial team that he or she appoints. They are composed of Principal Officials who are in charge of

2007) 117, 131–2. See also Sonny Lo, *Competing Chinese Political Visions* (Santa Barbara, Praeger 2010) 130–1.

[8] See 'Poll Creates Stumbling Block for Leung' *South China Morning Post* (Hong Kong, 11 September 2012) 1.

[9] Hong Kong Basic Law, Article 46. [10] Ibid. Article 48. [11] Ibid. Annex I.

various portfolios, which include Finance, Justice, and Home Affairs. Article 54 also provides for an Executive Council to advise the Chief Executive on policy making. All Principal Officials are now members of the Executive Council, but the Chief Executive also appoints legislators and other leading public figures onto the Council.[12] The appointment or removal of any member of the Executive Council is decided by the Chief Executive.[13]

E. Hong Kong Judiciary

The judiciary in Hong Kong is composed of the Court of Final Appeal (CFA), the High Court (which includes the Court of Appeal and the Court of First Instance), the District Court, magistrates' courts, and other special courts established by law. The CFA is empowered to invite judges from other common law jurisdictions[14] to participate in the appeals it decides, and judicial recourse to the common law and the rules of equity are maintained.[15] The judges on all levels of the courts are appointed by the Chief Executive on the recommendation of an independent commission composed of local judges and persons from the legal profession.[16]

While Article 82 vests the power of final adjudication in the CFA, Article 158 vests the power of interpretation of the Basic Law in the Standing Committee of the National People's Congress (SCNPC). Nonetheless, the SCNPC shall authorize the courts of the HKSAR to interpret on their own, in adjudicating cases, the provisions of the Basic Law which are within the limits of the autonomy of the HKSAR. However, on affairs which are the responsibility of the Central People's Government or concerning the relationship between the Central Authorities and the HKSAR and if such judicial interpretation will affect the judgments on the cases, the courts of the HKSAR shall, before making their final judgments which are not appealable, seek an interpretation of the relevant provisions from the SCNPC. When the Standing Committee makes an interpretation of the provisions concerned, the courts of the Region, in applying those provisions, shall follow the interpretation of the Standing Committee.

F. Fundamental Rights in Hong Kong

Fundamental rights in Hong Kong are protected in Chapter III of the Basic Law. Notably, Article 39 expressly provides that any rights-restrictions shall

[12] See Hong Kong Basic Law, Article 55. [13] Ibid. [14] Ibid. Article 82.
[15] Ibid. Article 8. [16] Ibid. Article 88.

not contravene the provisions of the International Covenant on Civil and Political Rights (ICCPR) and the International Covenant on Economic, Social, and Cultural Rights (ICESCR), as applied to Hong Kong, which shall remain in force and be implemented through the laws of the HKSAR.

Before the Basic Law came into force in 1997, the Bill of Rights Ordinance (BORO) was passed in 1991 by the colonial government to 'bring home' the rights the British government acceded to in 1976 when it ratified the ICCPR and extended its application to Hong Kong.[17] The passage of the BORO was, in particular, triggered by the violent suppression of the student demonstrators in Tiananmen Square over the summer of 1989. In its original form, Section 3 of the BORO provided that all pre-existing legislation that did not admit of a construction consistent with this Ordinance was, to the extent of the inconsistency, repealed; but this provision was excised by the Provisional Legislative Council in 1998. Although the BORO was and still is a mere statute such that its provisions could be repealed by a legislative majority, the Hong Kong Letters Patent was amended to provide that no law of Hong Kong shall be made after these changes to restrict the rights and freedoms enjoyed in Hong Kong in a manner which was inconsistent with the ICCPR as applied to Hong Kong. With the repeal of the Letters Patent after China's resumption of sovereignty over Hong Kong, Article 39 of the Basic Law arguably retains the BORO's semi-constitutional status, such that the BORO provisions may be used to invalidate any rights-infringing legislation, though the content of these rights-provisions may be changed by a mere legislative majority.

Nevertheless, Chapter III of the Basic Law enshrines most of the BORO rights, thereby expressly conferring constitutional status on these rights. Some of these rights include the right to free expression, the right to assembly, the right to equality, the freedom of religious belief, and the right against arbitrary arrest and imprisonment. Nevertheless, there are a number of BORO rights that are not protected in the Basic Law. The BORO expressly protects a person's right against slavery and forced labour, but this right is absent from the Basic Law. Some BORO rights are more circumscribed in the Basic Law. The BORO protects a person's right against torture and cruel, inhuman, or degrading treatment[18] but the Basic Law only prohibits torture;[19] there is a general right to privacy under the BORO[20] but the Basic Law only protects

[17] See Richard Swede, 'One Territory—Three Systems? The Hong Kong Bill of Rights' (1995) 44 *International and Comparative Law Quarterly* 358–78.

[18] Bill of Rights Ordinance (Cap 383), Article 3.

[19] Hong Kong Basic Law, Article 28.

[20] Bill of Rights Ordinance (Cap 383), Article 14.

the privacy of one's communication.[21] Notably, the Basic Law also protects certain rights exclusively; these rights include the right of abode and the right to social welfare.

G. Constitutional Amendment Procedures in Hong Kong

According to Article 159 of the Basic Law, the power of amendment is vested in the National People's Congress in China. The power to propose bills for any amendments is vested in the Standing Committee of the National People's Congress, the State Council of the People's Republic of China, and the HKSAR. Amendment bills from the HKSAR can only be submitted to the National People's Congress by the delegation of the HKSAR to the National People's Congress after obtaining the consent of two-thirds of the deputies of the HKSAR to the National People's Congress, two-thirds of all the members of the Legislative Council, and the Chief Executive of the HKSAR. Therefore, the amendment process for a HKSAR-sponsored change is incredibly onerous.

Since its inception, the Basic Law has only been amended once, in 2010, where the composition of the Legislative Council was increased by five GC seats and five FC seats, and the composition of the Election Committee for the selection of the Chief Executive expanded from 800 to 1,200 members.

Article 159 also provides that no amendment to the Basic Law shall contravene the established basic policies of the People's Republic of China regarding Hong Kong, though the Basic Law is silent on what these basic policies are.

II. Malaysia

A. Constitutional History of Malaysia

Between 1786 and 1824, the British East India Company established trade outposts in Penang, Singapore, and Malacca; and these outposts later formed the Straits Settlements, which came under the administration of the British Colonial Office in 1867.[22] Between 1874 and 1889, Britain also concluded

[21] Hong Kong Basic Law, Article 30.

[22] For more information, see Tan Sri Mohammed Suffian, *An Introduction to the Constitution of Malaysia* (Kuala Lumpur, Di-chetak di-Jabatan Chetak 1972); Sheridan & Groves, *The Constitution of Malaysia* (4th edn, Singapore, Malayan Law Journal 1987); Rais Yatim, 'The Road to Merdeka' in Andrew Harding & HP Lee (eds), *Constitutional Landmarks in Malaysia: The First Fifty Years 1957–2007* (Kuala Lumpur, LexisNexis 2007). See also Andrew Harding, *The Constitution of Malaysia: A Contextual Approach* (Oxford, Hart Publishing 2012).

treaties with the state Rulers of Perak, Selangor, Negeri Sembilan, and Pahang whereby each Ruler agreed to accept a British Resident whose advice had to be acted upon on all matters, other than those concerning the Islamic faith, in his state in exchange for British protection. In 1895, the four states of Perak, Selangor, Pahang, and Negeri Sembilan formed a federation known as the Federated Malay States (FMS), which was administered under the advice of the British Government. The Unfederated Malay States of Kedah, Perlis, Kelantan, Terengganu, and Johor also came under British protection following the signing of separate treaties between 1909 and 1923. In East Malaysia, North Borneo and Sarawak also became protected British States in 1888, though they were administered by the British North Borneo Company and the Brooke family respectively.

Following the end of the Second World War, the Straits Settlement disbanded and Singapore became a separate Crown Colony. The new Crown Colony of North Borneo was formed with the merger of the former North Borneo and Labuan, which became a British colony in 1846 after being ceded from Brunei. Similarly, Sarawak also became a Crown Colony. Penang, Malacca and the rest of the Malay States were amalgamated to form the Malayan Union in 1946. This Union was however short-lived as there was an outcry by the Malays against the loss of the rights and privileges of the state Rulers and the common citizenship conferred on all races. The Malayan Union was thus replaced by the Federation of Malaya in 1948. The Federation of Malaya was headed by a British High Commissioner with executive powers but the Federal Legislative Council would consist of 52 unofficial seats to be filled by elections. Citizenship rules were tightened, and the powers and the privileges of the Rulers enhanced. The Alliance Party, a coalition that consists of United Malays National Organisation (UMNO), the Malaysian Chinese Association (MCA), and the Malaysian Indian Congress (MIC), won 51 out of 52 seats in the 1955 Legislative Council elections; and Tunku Abdul Rahman, the Alliance's leader, went on to assume the office of Chief Minister.

Subsequently, Tunku Abdul Rahman spearheaded a mission to London and negotiated for Malaya's independence. After rounds of negotiation in London between representatives of the Rulers, representatives of the Alliance government and representatives of the British government, an Independent Constitutional Commission was appointed in 1956 to draft a Constitution that provided full independence for the Federation of Malaya. This Constitutional Commission was chaired by Lord Reid and is now commonly termed the Reid Commission. The Commission duly submitted its report in 1957 and a Working Committee was appointed to examine its recommendations. The final draft of the Constitution of the Federation of Malaya was soon agreed upon, and the Federation of Malaya became an independent sovereign state on 31 August 1957.

Following a referendum in Singapore and elections in North Borneo (renamed Sabah in 1963) and Sarawak, plans were laid for the above-mentioned three territories to join an enlarged federation in 1963. The federation would be renamed Malaysia and the new member states would have significant autonomy under the new federal Constitution of Malaysia. Days before Malaysia came into being, the state of Kelantan brought a court challenge against the merger on the basis that the proposed decision to admit new states would require the prior consent of each constituent state in the original federation, but this challenge unsurprisingly failed as the Constitution of the Federation of Malaya 1957 did not impose such a requirement.[23] Malaysia was formally established on 16 September 1963; but, two years later, on 9 August 1965, Singapore separated to form an independent republic on its own, thus leaving 13 states in the federation today. Furthermore, the Federal Territory of Kuala Lumpur was created in 1973; the Federal Territory of Labuan (ceded from Sabah) was established in 1984; and finally, the Federal Territory of Putrajaya was constituted in 2001.

B. Malaysia's Federal Legislature

Malaysia has a bicameral federal Parliament, consisting of the House of Representatives (Dewan Rakyat) and the Senate (Dewan Negara). The Constitution also divides legislative power between the federal Parliament and the individual state Assemblies.[24]

With regard to the House of Representatives, there are currently 222 members representing their respective single-member electoral constituencies in the states and Territories, and they are elected on a first past the post basis. Such elections have to be held at least every five years.[25]

The Senate is currently composed of 26 elected members, with each state electing two members.[26] The King, the Yang di-Pertuan Agong, on the advice of the government, also appoints two members from the Federal Territory of Kuala Lumpur, and one each from the Federal Territories of Labuan and Putrajaya. Forty additional senators can be appointed by the King, on the advice of the government. Therefore, the Constitution provides

[23] *The Government of the State of Kelantan v The Government of the Federation of Malaya* (1963) 29 MLJ 355 (Federal Court of Malaysia).

[24] See Part VI of the Malaysia Constitution read with the Ninth Schedule.

[25] Malaysia Constitution, Article 55(3).

[26] Ibid. Article 45(1)(a).

for 44 appointed senators in all. The term of office in the Senate is fixed at three years and each senator may not serve more than two terms in office.[27]

The Constitution provides that a money bill may only originate from the House of Representatives, and the Senate may only delay its passage by a month.[28] For a non-money bill, the Senate may delay its passage by one year.[29] For bills seeking to amend the Constitution, the concurrence of at least two-thirds of the members in both the House of Representatives and the Senate is generally required.[30] Therefore, the legislative powers of the Senate are nominal, except where it is faced with bills seeking to amend the Constitution.

It is noteworthy that Malaysia has been ruled by the same political coalition since its independence, that is the Alliance Party which was renamed Barisan Nasional (National Front) in 1974. It is significant, however, that National Front, for the first time, lost more than a third of the seats in the House of Representatives following the 2008 general election. In the latest general elections held in May 2013, the National Front coalition won 133 out of 222 federal Parliamentary seats and was thus returned to power again.

C. Malaysia's Federal Executive Government

The Prime Minister is the head of the administration in Malaysia, and he or she is usually the leader of the political party dominating the coalition that controls the most number of seats in the House of Representatives. The Prime Minister is assisted by his or her cabinet of Ministers and all Ministers in Malaysia are concurrently members of either house of Parliament.

The King of Malaysia, also known as the Yang di-Pertuan Agong, exercises the executive authority of the federation, but he is primarily a ceremonial head and usually acts on the advice of the Cabinet. The term of office of the King is five years and he is elected or removed by the Conference of Rulers. The Conference of Rulers is comprised of the hereditary Rulers of the nine Malay States and the four Governors of Malacca, Penang, Sabah, and Sarawak. A hereditary Ruler in each Malay State reigns for life while a Governor is appointed for renewable terms of four years. Although a Governor is a member of the Conference of Rulers, he does not participate in any proceedings relating to the election or removal of the King or matters concerning the honours and dignities of royalties, or religious observances and ceremonies. The consent[31] of the Conference of Rulers is required before any law that

[27] Ibid. Articles 45(3), 45(3A). [28] Ibid. Article 68(1). [29] Ibid. Article 68(2).

[30] Ibid. Article 159(3).

[31] Where the Conference of Rulers cannot reach a unanimous decision, the decision taken by a majority of the members voting shall prevail, though the King may only be removed from office with at least five votes. See also Third and Fifth Schedules of the Malaysia Constitution.

affects the privileges, position, or dignities of the rulers, or any legislation seeking to change the boundaries of the states can be passed.[32] Furthermore, their consent is needed before certain types of constitutional amendments can be passed, as would be discussed in a later section.[33]

Prior to 1993, no proceedings could be brought in any court against the King or any Ruler of a state in his personal capacity. However, following the Ruler of Johor's alleged assault on a school hockey coach in 1992,[34] a constitutional amendment was passed to strip the King and Rulers of their immunity from suit and to provide for a Special Court presided by the Lord President of the Supreme Court (now known as the Chief Justice of the Federal Court of Malaysia) to try the King and Rulers for any offences or civil wrongs committed. Unsurprisingly, the Conference of Rulers refused to give consent to this constitutional amendment. Subsequently, the government retaliated by withdrawing all ancillary perks which the Rulers enjoyed that were not expressly provided by law. A media war, under the influence of the government, was also waged against the Rulers whereby their extravagant lifestyles were disclosed to the public. The Conference of Rulers eventually caved in and agreed to an amendment that was similar to the original one, but modified so far as any proceeding against the King or a Ruler may only be instituted with the consent of the Attorney General.[35]

D. Malaysia Judiciary

Prior to 1988, Article 121 of the Malaysian Constitution expressly declared that 'the judicial power' of the federation shall be vested in the courts but the term 'judicial power' has since been excised.[36] The Federal Court of Malaysia is the court of final resort in Malaysia. It hears appeals from the Court of Appeal, which in turn hears appeals from two coordinate High Courts, one in Malaya and the other in Sabah and Sarawak. Inferior courts may also be created by federal law. The Federal Court, however, has original jurisdiction over disputes between states or between the federation and the states, or on federalism matters.[37] There is thus no separate state court system in Malaysia that applies only state laws. The Malaysia federal judiciary also does not have any 'jurisdiction in respect of any matter within the jurisdiction of

[32] Malaysia Constitution, Article 38(6)(c).

[33] Ibid. Article 159(5).

[34] For a fuller discussion, see HP Lee, *Constitutional Conflicts in Contemporary Malaysia* (Kuala Lumpur, Oxford University Press 1995).

[35] Malaysia Constitution, Article 183.

[36] These developments will be discussed more comprehensively in Chapter 4.

[37] Malaysia Constitution, Article 128(1).

the syariah courts',[38] which adjudicate over matters concerning the practice of the Islamic faith in Malaysia. Malaysia abolished appeals, on criminal and constitutional matters, to the Privy Council in 1978, and all ties were severed in 1985 when appeals on civil matters were also abolished. The Federal Court was renamed the Supreme Court in 1985, but it reverted back to its original title in 1994. Pursuant to Article 130 of the Constitution, the King may also refer to the Federal Court for its advisory opinion on any question as to the effect of any provision of the Constitution which has arisen or appears to him likely to arise.

The Federal Court is presided by the Chief Justice and it usually hears cases in panels composed of three or five members. The Chief Justice, the Judges of the Federal Court, the Judges on the Court of Appeal, and the Judges of the High Court are appointed by the King, on the advice of the Prime Minister, after consulting the Conference of Rulers.[39] A Judicial Appointments Commission, chaired by the Chief Justice of the Federal Court, was established in 2009 to recommend to the Prime Minister suitably qualified persons for judicial appointments on the superior courts. The Prime Minister may now only select candidates that are short-listed by the Judicial Appointments Commission. Judicial independence is secured under the Constitution to the extent that all of the abovementioned categories of judges, once appointed, have tenure until they reach the age of 66[40] and the judges' remuneration may not be altered adversely after their appointment.[41] These judges may also not be removed from office unless they have been found to have breached a prescribed code of ethics by a tribunal consisting of no less than five persons who hold or have held offices as judges on the Federal Court, Court of Appeal, a High Court, or equivalent offices in any court in the British Commonwealth.[42] It is noteworthy that in 1988, the Lord President (now re-titled as Chief Justice) Tun Salleh and two other judges on the Supreme Court (now re-titled as the Federal Court) were impeached for acts of 'misbehaviour', the term used in Article 125(3) of the Constitution then, and were removed from office. It is generally believed that these judicial dismissals were politically motivated, as will be discussed in the next chapter.

The subordinate court judges in Malaysia do not have tenure, and they are under the supervision of the Judicial and Legal Service Commission headed by the Chairman of the Public Services Commission.[43] The Constitution also allows for the appointment of temporary judges on the two High Courts,

[38] Ibid. Article 121(1A).
[39] Ibid. Article 122(B)(1).
[40] Ibid. Articles 125(1), 125(9).
[41] Malaysia Constitution, Articles 125(7), 125(9).
[42] Ibid. Articles 125(3), 125(9).
[43] Ibid. Article 138.

known as Judicial Commissioners, to facilitate the disposal of business in the High Courts, and they exercise the same powers as High Court judges.[44]

E. Fundamental Liberties in Malaysia

Fundamental liberties in Malaysia are protected in Part II of the Malaysia Constitution. These rights include the freedom from slavery or forced labour, the right not to be criminally sanctioned by retrospective criminal laws, the right to equality, the right to property, the freedom of speech and assembly. While most constitutional rights are guaranteed to all persons, the freedom of expression and assembly is only guaranteed to Malaysian citizens.

Islam is the official religion of Malaysia, though any other religions may be practised in peace and harmony with it in any part of Malaysia.[45] Article 11(1) protects a person's right to profess and practise his or her religion, though this is subject to Article 11(4) that expressly allows for legislation to be passed that 'control[s] or restrict[s] the propagation of any religious doctrine' among Muslims. One must note that the Malaysian federal judiciary also does not have any 'jurisdiction in respect of any matter within the jurisdiction of the syariah courts'.[46]

The constitutional right to equality must also be read against Article 153 which allows the federal and state governments to safeguard the special position of the Malays and the natives of Sabah and Sarawak by reserving lands, positions in public service, places in educational institutions, scholarships, permits and licences for businesses, for these preferred ethnic groups.

In the wake of the racial riots in May 1969 that were sparked by the inflammatory speeches made by various politicians, and also compounded by the perceived disparity in wealth between the poorer Malay majority and the wealthier Chinese minority, the Malaysian government implemented the New Economic Policy that provided greater affirmative action for the social and economic advancement of ethnic Malays. A constitutional amendment was also passed in 1971, now found in Article 10(4) of the Constitution, to authorize Parliament to pass any law prohibiting the questioning of any matter relating to the constitutional provisions concerning citizenship, the national language, the special privileges accorded to the Malays and the natives of Sabah and Sarawak, and the sovereignty of the Rulers, though one may question the implementation of these provisions.[47]

It is also significant that Article 149 authorizes any statutory measures passed to counter organized violence, public disorder, or racial disharmony,

[44] Ibid. Article 122AB.
[45] Malaysia Constitution, Article 3(1).
[46] Ibid. Article 121(1A).
[47] Ibid. Article 10(4).

notwithstanding any derogation from certain constitutional rights of due process, right to free expression and assembly, right to movement, and right to property, if Parliament observes the requisite drafting formula provided within Article 149 when passing such legislation. The Internal Security Act (ISA) was passed pursuant to Article 149; it allowed for the government to detain persons for up to two years without trial, and the detention period was renewable ad infinitum. The ISA was however repealed in 2012, and it is replaced with the Security Offences (Special Measures) 2012 Act (SOSMA), which allows the police to detain suspects for up to 28 days and subjects the detention to judicial oversight.

Article 150 also authorizes the King, on the advice of the Government, to issue a Proclamation of Emergency when he is satisfied that a grave emergency exists in any part of the federation. Any Ordinances promulgated in these circumstances may derogate from all constitutional rights except those relating to religion, citizenship, or language. Since 1957, there have been four such Proclamations and the last one was invoked in 1977.[48] A constitutional amendment was also introduced in 1981 to oust the court's jurisdiction to determine any question concerning any Proclamation or any Ordinance promulgated pursuant to it.[49] It is noteworthy that these Emergency Proclamations were only officially lifted in 2011.

F. Constitutional Amendment Procedures in Malaysia

Four methods of amending the Constitution are provided in Article 159. First, any amendments to the constitutional provisions concerning the Conference of Rulers,[50] citizenship,[51] the Malay National Language,[52] the special privileges of the Malays, and the natives of Sabah and Sarawak,[53] and some provisions pertaining to the Rulers and the King[54] require the support of at least two-thirds of the total number of members in each House of Parliament and the consent of the Conference of Rulers.[55] Notably, any amendments to Article 10(4) that authorize Parliament to pass any law prohibiting the questioning of any matter relating to the constitutional provisions concerning citizenship, the Malay National Language, the special privileges of the Malays, and the natives of Sabah and Sarawak, and the Rulers' sovereignty are also subject to this amendment procedure.

[48] For more information on the history of the four Proclamations, see Andrew Harding, *Law, Government and the Constitution of Malaysia* (The Hague, Kluwer Law International 1996) 160–3.
[49] Malaysia Constitution, Article 150(8). [50] Ibid. Article 38.
[51] Ibid. Part III. [52] Ibid. Article 152. [53] Malaysia Constitution, Article 153.
[54] Ibid. Articles 70, 70 (1). [55] Ibid. Article 159(5).

Secondly, any amendments to the constitutional provisions that provide certain safeguards for the states of Sabah and Sarawak may not be passed unless they receive the support of at least two-thirds of the total number of members in each House of Parliament and the concurrence of the Governor of the state concerned.[56] Such safeguards include their right to Malaysian citizenship, the special treatment of their natives, matters which their state legislatures may legislate on, and the financial arrangements between the federation and these states.

Thirdly, the most common procedure applicable for an amendment is provided in Article 159(3) of the Malaysia Constitution and such amendments require the support of at least two-thirds of the total number of members in each House of Parliament. The fundamental liberties enshrined in Part II of the Constitution are generally subject to this amendment procedure. Interestingly, any amendments to laws passed under Article 10(4), as discussed above, are also subject to this onerous amendment procedure.

Finally, a few constitutional amendments may however be passed by ordinary law in Parliament.[57] These include amendments to supplementary provisions on citizenship,[58] forms provided on oaths and affirmations,[59] the election procedure for Senators,[60] and the admission of new states to the federation.[61]

III. Singapore

A. Constitutional History of Singapore

The modern history of Singapore can be traced to 1819 when Sir Stamford Raffles claimed this small island for the British East India Company.[62] From 1826, Singapore, alongside Malacca and Penang in present-day Malaysia, were administered jointly as the Straits Settlements. With the abolishment of the East India Company in 1858, the British colonial government assumed

[56] Ibid. Article 161E(2).

[57] Malaysia Constitution, Article 159(1) read with Article 159(4)(a).

[58] Ibid. Part III of 2nd Schedule.

[59] Ibid. 6th Schedule.

[60] Ibid. 7th Schedule.

[61] Ibid. Article 159(4)(bb). This clause is subject to Article 161E which enshrines the constitutional safeguards for Sabah and Sarawak.

[62] For a more extensive study of Singapore's constitutional history, see Kevin Tan, 'A Short Legal and Constitutional History of Singapore' in Kevin Tan (ed), *The Singapore Legal System* (Singapore, National University of Singapore Press 1999) 26–66. See also Victor Ramraj & Po Jen Yap, 'Singapore' in Gerhard Robbers (ed), *Encyclopedia of World Constitutions* (New York, Facts on File 2007) 817.

immediate supervision of the Straits Settlement and this state of affairs lasted till 1942 when the British surrendered to the Japanese armed forces during World War II.

After the British resumed control of Singapore in 1945, they decided that the Straits Settlement should be dissolved and Singapore administered as a separate Crown Colony. This policy took effect in 1948 when Singapore's own Constitution, the Singapore Colony Order-in-Council, came into force. In 1953, the British government established the Rendel Commission to recommend constitutional changes in Singapore; this culminated in the implementation of a new Constitution, known popularly as the Rendel Constitution, in 1955, which allowed for 25 elected members in a 32-member legislative council, of which six elected members could serve on the Council of Ministers. Subsequently, after protracted negotiations, the British Parliament passed the State of Singapore Act in 1958, thereby transforming the colony formally into a self-governing state. A new legislative assembly was established, composed of 51 elected members and headed by a prime minister. The British government, however, retained control over defence and external affairs.

The People's Action Party (PAP) won 43 of the 51 seats in the first general legislative elections, and its leader, Lee Kuan Yew, became Singapore's first Prime Minister in 1959. Soon after its electoral success, the PAP began to campaign for a merger between Singapore and its northern neighbour, the Federation of Malaya. This move was prompted by the government's desire to achieve political independence from the British and to anchor Singapore's economic survival to a rich hinterland. The proposal for an enlarged Malaysian federation was accepted by the British on condition that the military bases in Singapore remain under British control and that the people living in the various territories were in favour of such a union. In Singapore, 71 per cent of the electorate voted in favour of a merger. The Federation of Malaysia would compose of the states of Singapore, North Borneo, Sarawak, and the existing states of the Federation of Malaya. Singapore formally joined the federation in September 1963. Under the agreement reached, the federal government in Malaysia would manage Singapore's internal security, defence, and foreign affairs, but Singapore's daily administration would be left to the state government.

The merger proved to be short-lived as relations between the Malaysian federal government and the Singapore state government soon soured over the perceived interference of the PAP in federal politics and Singapore's apparent non-compliance with federal mandates. These internal politics within the federation were played out against the backdrop of communist threats and communalistic strife, which eventually convinced the

Malaysian Prime Minister to expel Singapore from the federation in August 1965.

Singapore's independence was effected by a series of constitutional changes. The Republic of Singapore Independence Act (RSIA) vested the legislative and executive powers, relinquished by Malaysia, in Singapore's legislature and executive. It also extended the application of certain provisions of the Malaysian Federal Constitution, for example fundamental liberties, to Singapore. The Constitution of Singapore (Amendment) Act was also passed to bring the Singapore State Constitution in line with its new found independent status and to allow for a simple majority in the legislature to make any constitutional changes. Therefore in 1965, Singapore's Constitution was to be found in three separate documents: the RSIA, the State Constitution of Singapore (and its amendments), and the applicable provisions of the Malaysian Federal Constitution. This untidy state of affairs was to persist till 1979 when a constitutional amendment was passed to authorize the Attorney General to make such necessary or expedient modifications, and publish a consolidated reprint of the Singapore Constitution. The amendment process for the Constitution was also changed, such that a two-thirds majority in Parliament would be required for future constitutional amendments.

B. Singapore Legislature

Singapore has a unicameral legislature. Currently, its Parliament is composed of 87 elected members returned, on a first past the post basis, at general elections that have to be held at least every five years.[63]

Singapore's electoral system is unique so far as it provides for both single-member constituencies and multi-member group constituencies in the Parliamentary elections. Such multi-member group constituencies are known as Group Representative Constituencies (GRC) and each GRC is formed by merging several single wards into one mega-constituency; all the electoral candidates in a GRC currently contest in teams composing of four to six persons and each elector would cast one vote for the team he or she supports. The GRC model was first introduced, following a constitutional amendment in 1988, ostensibly to ensure racial diversity in Parliament as at least one team member must be an ethnic minority. Initially, each GRC would be composed of only three members. But, in 1991, this was increased to four; and later in 1996, the ceiling was raised to six. While the entrenchment of minority representation in Parliament is a laudable political end, the

[63] Singapore Constitution, Article 65(4).

integrity of this justification is undercut by the expansion of the GRC size. In fact, the GRC system is widely perceived to be merely an electoral mechanism for the ruling party, the People's Action Party, to ensure the election of new promising but unknown candidates with Ministerial calibre by fielding them in GRC teams alongside party stalwarts with mass electoral appeal. Currently, there are 12 Single Member Constituencies (SMCs) and 15 GRCs in Singapore. In the last general election held in 2011, the PAP won 81 of the 87 elected seats, but it is noteworthy that it lost a GRC for the first time to an opposition party. In a by-election held in 2013, the PAP lost another seat to the Workers' Party, the main opposition party in Singapore. Nevertheless, the PAP has been the ruling party in Singapore since its independence; and since 1968, the PAP has controlled over 90 per cent of the elected seats in Parliament. Anti-hopping provisions are entrenched in the Constitution that provides for the vacation of a seat in Parliament when the elected member ceases to be a member of the political party for which he or she stood in the elections.[64]

Besides the elected members of Parliament, the Constitution also provides for up to nine opposition party members to be appointed as Non-Constituency Members of Parliament (NCMP).[65] These NCMPs must be composed of defeated opposition party candidates who garnered the highest percentage of the popular vote in the prior general elections, but not less than 15 per cent of the total number of votes in the constituency. Furthermore, up to nine Nominated Members of Parliament (NMP) who are nonpartisan citizens that have distinguished themselves in the fields of arts and letters, culture, the sciences, business, industry, the professions, social or community service, or the labour movement, can be appointed by the President on the recommendation of a Parliamentary Special Select Committee to foster greater Parliamentary debate and ensure a wide representation of community views in Parliament.[66] It is noteworthy that both groups of non-elected Members of Parliament may not vote on the budget or appropriation bills, bills to amend the constitution, or motions of no confidence in the government.[67]

C. Singapore Executive Government

The Prime Minister is the head of the administration in Singapore, and he or she is usually the leader of the political party that wins the most elected seats at the general election. The Prime Minister is assisted by his or her cabinet of

[64] Singapore Constitution, Article 46(2)(b).
[65] Ibid. Article 39(1)(b).
[66] See Singapore Constitution, Article 39(1)(c) read with 4th Schedule.
[67] Singapore Constitution, Article 39(2).

Ministers and all Ministers in Singapore are concurrently elected members of Parliament.

In 1991, the Constitution was amended to introduce an Elected Presidency.[68] Prior to this, the President was a ceremonial head of state chosen by Parliament; now, the President is elected by the people directly and he or she serves for a term of six years. The Elected President is vested with a degree of independent, executive powers to withhold assent to certain money bills that draw on the nation's financial reserves[69] and to veto key public officer appointments, such as Supreme Court judges, the Attorney General, the Chief of the Defence Force, members on the Presidential Council of Minority Rights etc.[70] made by the government of the day. The Elected President exercises only reactive powers and was conceived as an institutional check on any errant future governments that may raid the nation's coffers to buy popularity or pack the public service with its cronies. One must however note that the Presidential veto herein is only absolute if it is exercised in tandem with the recommendations of the Council of Presidential Advisors.[71] Otherwise, the veto may be overridden by a two-thirds Parliamentary majority.[72] The President also has the power to veto restraining orders and detention orders issued by the government under the Maintenance of Religious Harmony Act and the Internal Security Act respectively, but his or her veto is only effective if it concurs with the recommendations of the administrative tribunal that oversees the operation of the legislation in question.[73]

The qualifications that a presidential candidate must meet are extremely stringent. Under Article 19(2) of the Constitution, a presidential candidate must have held key public or private office appointments such as cabinet minister, chief justice, chairman, or chief executive officer of a company with a paid-up capital of at least 100 million Singapore dollars. The Presidential Elections Committee (PEC)[74] may in its discretion make

[68] See also Kevin Tan, 'The Presidency in Singapore: Constitutional Developments' in Tan & Lam, *Managing Political Change in Singapore: The Elected Presidency* (New York, Routledge 1997) and Li-ann Thio, 'Singapore: (S)electing the President—Diluting Democracy?' (2007) 5 *International Journal of Constitutional Law* 526.

[69] Singapore Constitution, Article 21(2).

[70] Singapore Constitution, Article 22.

[71] The Council of Presidential Advisers is composed of six members: two are appointed by the President acting in his own discretion, two are appointed by the President on the advice of the Prime Minister, one is appointed by the President on the advice of the Chief Justice, and one is appointed by the President on the advice of the Chairman of the Public Service Commission. See Singapore Constitution, Article 37(B).

[72] Singapore Constitution, Article 22(2).

[73] Ibid. Article 22I; ibid. Article 151(4).

[74] Ibid. Article 18(2) provides that the PEC shall consist of the Chairman of the Public Service Commission, the Chairman of the Accounting and Corporate Regulatory Authority and a member of the Presidential Council for Minority Rights nominated by the Chairman of that Council.

exceptions if it believes that the presidential candidate has occupied comparable positions of seniority and responsibility in other organizations of equivalent complexity.

D. Singapore Judiciary

Article 93 of the Constitution vests the judicial power of Singapore in the Supreme Court and the subordinate courts created by law. The Supreme Court consists of the Court of Appeal and the High Court. Prior to 1993, the Privy Council sitting in London was the highest appellate court in Singapore, but such ties have since been cut, and the Singapore Court of Appeal is now the nation's court of final resort. The Court of Appeal is presided by the Chief Justice and it usually hears appeals in panels comprising of three members. The courts in Singapore are empowered under Article 4 of the Constitution to invalidate any legislative provision that is inconsistent with the nation's supreme law.

As discussed earlier, the Chief Justice, the Judges of Appeal, and the Judges of the High Court are appointed by the President if he or she, acting in his or her discretion, concurs with the advice of the Prime Minister.[75] Judicial independence is secured under the Constitution to the extent that a Supreme Court judge, once appointed, has tenure until he or she reaches the age of 65[76] and the judge's remuneration may not be altered adversely after his or her appointment.[77] It is also noteworthy that the term of office of a Supreme Court judge may be extended contractually when he or she reaches 65; the subordinate court judges in Singapore do not have tenure and they may be transferred between appointments in the executive or judicial branches as decided by the Judicial Service Commission headed by the Chief Justice. The Constitution also allows for the appointment of temporary judges on the Supreme Court, known as Judicial Commissioners, to facilitate the disposal of business in the Supreme Court, and they exercise the same powers as Supreme Court judges.[78]

Pursuant to Article 100 of the Constitution, the President may also refer to a tribunal consisting of not less than three Judges of the Supreme Court for its advisory opinion on any question as to the effect of any provision of the Constitution that has arisen or appears to him or her likely to arise.

[75] Singapore Constitution, Article 95(1). [76] Ibid. Article 98(1).
[77] Ibid. Article 98(8). [78] Ibid. Article 94(4).

E. Fundamental Liberties in Singapore

Fundamental liberties in Singapore are enshrined in Part IV of the Singapore Constitution. These rights include the freedom from slavery or forced labour, the right not to be criminally sanctioned by retrospective criminal laws, the right to equality, the freedom of speech and assembly, and the freedom of religion. While most constitutional rights are guaranteed to all persons, the freedom of expression and assembly is only guaranteed to Singapore citizens.

Article 149 authorizes any statutory measures passed to counter organized violence, racial disharmony, or security threats, notwithstanding any derogation from the constitutional rights of due process, right to free expression and assembly, right to movement, and right to equality, if Parliament observes the requisite drafting formula provided within Article 149 when passing the legislation. This 'notwithstanding' clause was only added, by a 1989 constitutional amendment, in response to the Singapore Court of Appeal's decision[79] that it was constitutionally required for the judges to objectively review the Ministerial exercise of discretion to detain personnel under the Internal Security Act, a piece of legislation passed pursuant to Article 149 of the Constitution.

Article 152 also provides that it shall be the responsibility of the Government constantly to care for the interests of the racial and religious minorities in Singapore. Specifically, the Government has to recognize the special position of the Malays who are the indigenous people of Singapore; and accordingly, it shall be the responsibility of the Government to protect, safeguard, support, and promote their political, educational, religious, economic, social and cultural interests, and the Malay language. To these ends, the Constitution provides for the establishment of a Presidential Council of Minority Rights (PCMR) whose function is to report on any legislative bill or subsidiary legislation which it perceives to be a differentiating measure that affects persons of any racial or religious community in Singapore.[80] Notwithstanding an adverse report from the PCMR, a differentiating bill may still be presented to the President for his or her assent if two-thirds of the total membership of Parliament so concur.[81] The PCMR also has no powers to review any money bills, any bill certified by the Prime Minister as being one that affects the defence or the security of Singapore or that relates

[79] *Chng Suan Tze v Minister of Home Affairs* (1988) 2 SLR 132 (Singapore Court of Appeal). Chapter 4 will elaborate on the origins and development of this saga.

[80] Singapore Constitution, Articles 76, 77. The Constitution provides that the PCMR shall consist of a Chairman appointed for a period of three years, up to ten members appointed for life, and up to ten members appointed for a period of three years. There are currently 16 members on the PCMR and it is chaired by the Chief Justice.

[81] Ibid. Article 78(6)(c).

to public safety, peace, or good order in Singapore, or a bill certified by the Prime Minister to be so urgent that it is not in the public interest to delay its enactment.[82] These broad exemptions essentially afford the Prime Minister much latitude to bypass the PCMR if he or she so chooses. In any case, to date, the PCMR has never issued an adverse report on any legislative bill or subsidiary legislation in Singapore.

F. Constitutional Amendment Procedures in Singapore

Most provisions in the Singapore Constitution can be amended with the concurrence of at least two-thirds of the total number of elected legislators in Parliament.[83]

In 1972, a constitutional amendment was passed to prohibit any surrender, either wholly or in part, of the sovereignty of Singapore as an independent nation, whether by way of merger or incorporation with any other sovereign state or federation, unless such surrender or relinquishment has been supported by not less than two-thirds of the total number of votes cast in a national referendum.[84]

Interestingly, two novel constitutional amendment procedures were introduced in 1991 and 1996. The first, Article 5(2A) provides that, unless the President concurs, any bill that seeks to amend provisions in Part IV (clauses protecting fundamental liberties), Part V, Chapter 1 (clauses on the Presidency), Articles 65 and 66 (clauses on the general elections and the dissolution of Parliament) must be passed by Parliament and also be supported by not less than two-thirds of the total number of votes cast in a national referendum. The second, Article 5A, provides that the President may veto any constitutional amendments, apart from those implicating Article 5(2A), which circumvent or curtail, directly or indirectly, the discretionary powers he or she possesses under the Constitution. However, if the advisory tribunal established under Article 100 is of the view that the amendments do not curtail the Presidential discretionary powers, he or she would be deemed to have assented to the amendments. If the tribunal upholds the President's views, these amendments may only be passed with the support of at least two-thirds of the total number of votes cast in a national referendum. However, despite the introduction of both amendment procedures, they remain inoperative in Singapore as the government considers this amendment scheme a work-in-progress, and it has no immediate plans to bring these two provisions into force.

[82] Ibid. Article 78(7). [83] Ibid. Article 5(2).

[84] This amendment is now found in Singapore Constitution, Article 6.

4

Judicial Crises

In the previous chapter, I have provided an overview of the three Asian constitutional systems under discussion. In this chapter, I shall examine the judicial crises that erupted in each of the three jurisdictions, where monumental standoffs between the legislature/executive and judiciary went on to shape and impact the current constitutional relationship between the judiciary and its respective political branches of government.

This investigation into the interplay of law and politics in Asia will also underscore why, in these Asian courts, the dialogic form of judicial review is not only normatively defensible, as demonstrated in Chapter 2, its use would also be politically more efficacious. As discussed in Chapter 3, within Hong Kong, Malaysia, and Singapore, there has been a dominant party/coalition in control of the government since decolonization and this state of affairs will persist for the foreseeable future. In each of these jurisdictions, a constitutional decision may only be reversed internally if there is a super-majoritarian consensus amongst the legislators. As it currently stands, save Singapore, the dominant ruling party/coalition would be required to secure the support of the opposition parties to initiate such a constitutional amendment, and this would rarely be feasible in practice. Therefore, if the judiciary consciously preserves the right of the legislature to disagree with the court's decision via the use of the ordinary political processes, such that an override via a constitutional amendment can be avoided, any strain on the inter-branch relations and any potential backlash from the dominant ruling government could equally be minimized.

Section I of this chapter examines the seminal decision in *Ng Ka Ling v Director of Immigration*,[1] where the Hong Kong Court of Final Appeal (CFA) proclaimed that the Hong Kong judiciary had the requisite duty and power to declare any legislative acts of the National People's Congress (NPC) (or its Standing Committee, SCNPC) to be inconsistent with the Basic Law.[2] This

[1] [1999] 1 HKLRD 315 (Hong Kong Court of Final Appeal).

[2] *Ng Ka Ling* (n 1) 337.

bold assertion naturally triggered the wrath of the Mainland and HKSAR government, and was the catalyst to an unfortunate constitutional stand-off between the CFA and Beijing, which culminated in the First Interpretation by the Standing Committee of the NPC (SCNPC) that overturned the CFA's decision. Section II explores the events leading up to and following from the Malaysian judicial crisis of 1988, where Lord President (now known as Chief Justice) Tun Salleh and two other judges on the Supreme Court of Malaysia (now Federal Court of Malaysia) were impeached for judicial misconduct and removed from office. Finally, in Section III, I analyse the landmark Singaporean decision of *Chng Suan Tze v Minister of Home Affairs*[3] where the Court of Appeal, after surveying a litany of Commonwealth precedents, quashed a preventive detention order issued under the Internal Security Act (ISA) against various alleged Marxist conspirators and also concluded that the Ministerial discretion to detain personnel under the ISA would be subject to an 'objective' test of review by the courts. This decision proved to be sufficiently disquieting to the Executive; the government quickly overturned this decision via a series of constitutional and statutory amendments within a month of the judgment, and henceforth restricted judicial review in ISA cases to only procedural grounds.[4]

I. Judicial Crisis in Hong Kong

Few would have expected a constitutional crisis to erupt within two years of the HKSAR's establishment, let alone in response to the first decision handed down by its Court of Final Appeal (CFA).

In *Ng Ka Ling v Director of Immigration*,[5] a few children born in the Mainland to Hong Kong permanent residents argued that their constitutional right of abode in Hong Kong, as provided under Article 24(2)(3) of the Basic Law,[6] was violated by two Immigration Ordinances that were passed by the

[3] [1988] 1 MLJ 133 (Singapore Court of Appeal).

[4] Article 149(3) was added to the Singapore Constitution and it provides that nothing in Article 93 of the Singapore Constitution, i.e. the constitutional clause that vests the judicial powers in the courts, shall invalidate any anti-subversion law passed by Parliament, regardless whether the proceedings were instituted before or after the commencement of this clause. Section 8B(2) was added to the Internal Security Act and it provides that 'there shall be no judicial review in any court of any act done or decision made by the President or the Minister under the provisions of this Act save in regard to any question relating to compliance with any procedural requirement of this Act governing such act or decision'.

[5] *Ng Ka Ling* (n 1).

[6] Article 24(2)(3) of the Basic Law provides that the permanent residents of the Hong Kong Special Administrative Region shall be persons of Chinese nationality born outside Hong Kong of (1) Chinese citizens born in Hong Kong before or after the establishment of the

Hong Kong Provisional Legislative Council days *after* China's resumption of sovereignty over Hong Kong. The impugned statutory provisions required any Mainland Chinese seeking to exercise their Hong Kong right of abode, arising by descent, first to obtain the mainland authorities' permission to leave for Hong Kong. (At that time, China only issued about 150 of such travel documents, known as one-way permits, a day.) Furthermore, criminal sanctions were imposed retrospectively on parties who entered Hong Kong, without such permits, after the entry of the Basic Law but before the enactment of the relevant immigration provisions. Moreover, a child born out of wedlock would not have the right of abode, unless the child was subsequently legitimated by the parents' marriage.

The claimants were unsuccessful in the lower courts but they eventually found favour with the CFA. On 29 January 1999, the court unanimously agreed that the impugned statutory provisions violated the applicants' right of abode; and in so ruling, the CFA also made several pronouncements that were of momentous constitutional significance in Hong Kong.

First, Chief Justice Andrew Li, on behalf of a unanimous bench, held that:

> In exercising their judicial power conferred by the Basic Law, the courts of the Region have a duty to enforce and interpret that Law. They undoubtedly have the jurisdiction to examine whether legislation enacted by the legislature of the Region or acts of the executive authorities of the Region are consistent with the Basic Law and, if found to be inconsistent, to hold them to be invalid.[7]

Although Hong Kong courts have been empowered since 1991 to invalidate any legislation that is inconsistent with the International Covenant on Civil and Political Rights (ICCPR) as applied to Hong Kong, this pronouncement was significant as the CFA was asserting in its first decision that the judiciary would continue to serve as a constitutional check on any perceived excesses of the Hong Kong government after the handover.

More controversial, however, was the CFA's second pronouncement that sparked off the inevitable standoff with Beijing. The judiciary held that the Hong Kong courts have the jurisdiction and duty to declare any legislative acts of the NPC or its Standing Committee invalid if found to be inconsistent with the Basic Law.[8] According to the CFA, Article 159(4) of the Basic Law enshrined China's commitment, pursuant to the Sino-British

Hong Kong Special Administrative Region or (2) Chinese citizens who have ordinarily resided in Hong Kong for a continuous period of not less than seven years before or after the establishment of the Hong Kong Special Administrative Region.

[7] *Ng Ka Ling* (n 1) 25.

[8] Ibid. 26; for a critique of *Ng Ka Ling*, see Po Jen Yap, '10 Years of the Basic Law: The Rise, Retreat and Resurgence of Judicial Power' (2007) 36 *Common Law World Review* 166.

Joint Declaration, to maintain the status quo in Hong Kong for 50 years; the courts' jurisdiction to enforce and interpret the Basic Law necessarily entailed the jurisdiction over acts of the NPC and its Standing Committee to ensure their consistency with the Basic Law.[9] In other words, if the Hong Kong courts do not have the power to invalidate NPC or SCNPC legislative acts that are inconsistent with the Basic Law, the regional courts would be impotent in the face of any attempt by China to breach its treaty obligations under the Joint Declaration or its constitutional obligation under Article 159(4) to preserve the established basic policies regarding Hong Kong.

This arguably is the best justification that one can advance in favour of such an assertion of judicial power. However, read against Article 158 of the Basic Law, the tenability of this reading collapses. Article 158(1) unambiguously vests the power of interpretation in the SCNPC. Article 158(2) continues by adding that the SCNPC shall 'authorize' the courts of Hong Kong to interpret, on their own, provisions of the Basic Law which are within the limits of the HKSAR's autonomy. Since, pursuant to Article 158(2), the power of Interpretation granted to the Hong Kong courts is a delegated power from the SCNPC, it would be legally untenable for the grantee/delegatee to possess any powers to override the acts of the grantor/delegator. Article 158(3) of the Basic Law confirms my reading:

> If the courts of the Region, in adjudicating cases, need to interpret the provisions of this Law concerning affairs which are the responsibility of the Central People's Government, or concerning the relationship between the Central Authorities and the Region, the Courts of the Region shall, before making their final judgments which are non appealable, seek an interpretation of the relevant provisions from the Standing Committee of the National People's Congress through the Court of Final Appeal of the Region. When the Standing Committee makes an interpretation of the provisions concerned, the courts of the Region, in applying those provisions, shall follow the interpretation of the Standing Committee.

Certainly, the question of whether the Hong Kong judiciary has the authority to invalidate NPC legislative acts concerns 'the relationship between the Central Authorities and the Region'; so far as the courts have a constitutional obligation to refer this matter to the SCNPC for its consideration, the judiciary is therefore deprived of any a priori power to invalidate them for being inconsistent with the Basic Law.

One must also note that this CFA dictum was not only provocative, it was also gratuitous. On the facts here, the CFA was not confronted with a NPC or SCNPC legislative act; the immigration procedures and the

[9] Ibid. 27.

'one-way permit' scheme for Mainland Chinese citizens seeking to relocate to Hong Kong were provided in a Chinese administrative law regulation passed by the State Council of the PRC.[10] Even if the CFA felt compelled to invalidate the offending administrative regulation in question, there was no need for the court to also assert the right to invalidate any NPC or SCNPC legislative acts when none was at issue.

Furthermore, the CFA's refusal to refer the interpretation of Articles 22(4) and 24(3) to the SCNPC for consideration also engendered significant controversy. Essentially, in *Ng Ka Ling*, the CFA was confronted with two conflicting Basic Law provisions. Article 22(4) states that for entry into Hong Kong, people from other parts of China must apply for approval from the competent authorities of the Central Government. Notwithstanding Article 22(4), Article 24(2)(3) states that persons of Chinese nationality born outside Hong Kong of HKSAR permanent residents shall have the right of abode. It was thus unclear whether persons who derived their right of abode, under Article 24(2)(3), were exempted from or subjected to the immigration requirements imposed by Article 22(4). It is also significant that Article 22(4) is an excluded provision, that is a provision concerning affairs which are the responsibility of the Central People's Government. Nevertheless, the CFA held that a duty to make a SCNPC reference would only arise under Article 158 if two conditions were satisfied: (1) the Basic Law provisions under examination concerned affairs which were the responsibility of the Central People's Government or the relationship between the Central Authorities and Hong Kong (henceforth termed 'the classification condition'); and (2) the CFA needed to interpret such provisions as the interpretation would affect the judgment on the case (henceforth termed the 'necessity condition'). Interestingly, the court held that, on the facts, the classification condition was not satisfied as the predominant provision that required interpretation was Article 24(2)(3) (a provision that fell within the limits of Hong Kong's autonomy) and not Article 22(4) (an excluded Basic Law provision). According to the CFA, if the predominant provision was not an excluded provision, 'no reference needs to be made, although an excluded provision is arguably relevant to the construction of the non-excluded provision even to the extent of qualifying it'.[11]

Unfortunately, the CFA did not offer any reasons why Article 24(2)(3), and not Article 22, was the predominate provision; it merely explained

[10] See Interim Measures for the Control of Chinese Citizens Travelling on Private Business to and from Regions of Hong Kong and Macao, approved by the State Council of the PRC on 3 December 1986 and promulgated on 25 December 1986.

[11] *Ng Ka Ling* (n 1) 33.

cursorily that Article 24 was the 'very source of the right which is sought to be enforced by the applicants in these appeals'.[12] Certainly, the claimants were relying on Article 24 to establish their right of abode; but the mere identification of the constitutional provision that the applicants' claim rested upon did not further demonstrate how the Article in question was the predominant provision that trumped the conflicting Article 22.

The central interpretive ambiguity concerning Article 24(2)(3) was whether the right of abode conferred on Mainland-born Chinese citizens claiming their residency status by descent was either independent of or qualified by the Article 22 immigration scheme. Where there is a clash of two Basic Law provisions, one which falls within the limits of Hong Kong's autonomy and another which concerns the affairs of the Central People's Government, it is impossible to interpret one provision independently of the other; it is certainly plausible that any interpretive attempts to reconcile the conflicting provisions herein should be resolved by the SCNPC. In any case, as argued above, the CFA had not explained how the predominant provision might be identified and had merely declared Article 24 to be the predominant one.

Consequently, the CFA held that the Immigration Ordinance was unconstitutional to the extent that it required permanent residents of the HKSAR residing in the Mainland to obtain a one-way permit before they could enjoy the constitutional right of abode. To the extent that the Ordinance applied retrospective criminal sanctions, the court also expunged the offending provision. The statutory exclusion that prevented illegitimate Mainland children, born to men who were Hong Kong Permanent Residents, from enjoying the right of abode by descent was also readily excised. Moreover, in *Chan Kam Nga v Director of Immigration*,[13] a judgment issued on the same day as *Ng Ka Ling*, the CFA also invalidated a statutory bar that excluded children, who were born before their parents acquired the right of permanent residency, from claiming their right of abode by descent in Hong Kong.

Naturally, the Central Government in Beijing was infuriated as it perceived the CFA's provocative grab for power as a direct challenge to its sovereignty and interpretive mandate. About a week after *Ng Ka Ling* was handed down, on 7 February 1999, four leading Chinese law professors, who were also former members of the Basic Law Drafting Committee, vehemently criticized the CFA's decisions, especially its claim over the right to review legislative acts of the NPC and the SCNPC. The Hong Kong government then requested the CFA to 'clarify' its decision in *Ng Ka Ling*. The court acceded to this request, in view of the controversy this decision had engendered, and

[12] Ibid. [13] [1999] 1 HKLRD 304 (Hong Kong Court of Final Appeal).

issued a clarification. In a very terse judgment, handed down on 26 June 1999, the court accepted that the SCNPC had the authority to issue a constitutional Interpretation under Article 158, and this Interpretation would have to be followed by the courts of the region.[14] But more interestingly, the court followed this concession with a veiled re-assertion of judicial power:

> The Court accepts that it cannot question the authority of the National People's Congress or the Standing Committee to do any act which is in accordance with the provisions of the Basic Law and the procedure therein.[15]

This statement seemed to suggest that the court was amenable to questioning or invalidating any legislative acts of the NPC or the SCNPC which the judges deemed not to be in accordance with the Basic Law. Oddly, the subversive nuances in *Ng Ka Ling (No 2)* were lost on the Central Government and Beijing was sufficiently appeased by this clarification.[16]

The Hong Kong government was however not placated. It was more concerned about the practical ramifications that would result from the massive influx of Mainland Chinese immigrants into Hong Kong and the strain this would put on the city's healthcare, housing, and social welfare system. Consequently, the government waged a media war by raising the ominous spectre of 1.67 million Mainlanders trooping into Hong Kong over the next seven years if the decisions were implemented and the tide of public opinion inevitably turned against the court. The HKSAR government also returned to Beijing and sought an Interpretation from the SCNPC to reverse *Ng Ka Ling* and *Chan Kam Nga* definitively.[17]

Soon after the request was made, the SCNPC issued its First Interpretation under the Basic Law on 26 June 1999, stating unequivocally that Mainland children born to Hong Kong Permanent Residents had to first obtain the requisite one-way permits before they could acquire the right of abode in Hong

[14] *Ng Ka Ling v Director of Immigration (No 2)* [1999] 1 HKLRD 577 (Hong Kong Court of Final Appeal).

[15] Ibid. 141.

[16] See Albert Chen & Anne Cheung, 'Debating the Rule of Law in Hong Kong' in Randall Peerenboom (ed), *Asian Discourses of Rule of Law* (London, Routledge 2004) 257.

[17] According to the Hong Kong government, Article 43 of the Basic Law provided that the Chief Executive was accountable to the Central People's Government and he was also tasked under Article 48(2) to implement the Basic Law; therefore, Article 43 read with Article 48(2) conferred upon the Chief Executive an implied right to seek such an Interpretation from the SCNPC. Professor Christopher Forsyth and Dr Mark Elliott, in a joint article, have expressed their disagreement with this view as according to the authors, such a reading of the Basic Law would render the constitutional safeguards provided in Articles 158(3) and 159 otiose. See Mark Elliott and Christopher Forsyth, 'The Rule of Law in Hong Kong: Immigrant Children, the Court of Final Appeal and the Standing Committee of the National People's Congress' (2000) 8 *Asia Pacific Law Review* 53, 67.

Kong. Furthermore, for this right to arise under Article 24(2)(3), either parent of the child had to be a Hong Kong Permanent Resident at the time of the child's birth. Interestingly, the Interpretation did not disturb the CFA's extension of the right of abode to illegitimate children born to Hong Kong Permanent Residents nor did it restore the retrospective criminal sanctions originally imposed by the Immigration Ordinance. The original parties in the *Ng Ka Ling* and *Chan Kam Nga* litigations were also held not to be affected by this Interpretation, but the rights of all others would be determined by reference to the Interpretation.

But this was not the end to the 'right of abode' saga. After the CFA handed down its decisions in *Ng Ka Ling/Chan Kam Nga,* but prior to the issue of the SCNPC Interpretation, the Director of Immigration had sought to remove 17 Mainland-born Chinese, each of whom had at least one parent who was a Hong Kong Permanent Resident, who had overstayed in Hong Kong without the requisite one-way permits. These Mainland-born Chinese subsequently went to court to have their removal orders quashed. Their challenge failed in the High Court but they succeeded in the Court of Appeal. Nevertheless, before the Court of Final Appeal, the court in *Director of Immigration v Lau Kong Yung,*[18] by a majority of 4–1,[19] affirmed the Director's right to issue the removal orders.

While the CFA might have been divided on whether the Director had the legal authority to issue the removal orders in question, the CFA was unanimous in recognizing the complete and plenary powers of the SCNPC to interpret every provision of the Basic Law:

> The power of interpretation of the Basic Law conferred by Article 158(1) is in general and unqualified terms.[20]

This was an important concession. After all, counsel for the abode-seekers had sought to argue that the SCNPC could only issue an Interpretation when there had been a judicial reference from the CFA over a dispute on an excluded provision. This appeared also to be the view advanced by Professor Christopher Forsyth and Dr Mark Elliott.[21] With respect, this view was

[18] [1999] 3 HKLRD 778 (Hong Kong Court of Final Appeal).

[19] Although the Director of Immigration had issued the removal orders before the issue of the SCNPC Interpretation, the majority did not consider that his decisions were not vitiated by any relevant error of law, since the legal position pursuant to the Interpretation would have been even less favourable to the applicants and the Director had no legal duty in the first place to take into account humanitarian considerations when making his decisions. Bokhary PJ, in his lone dissent, argued that the removal orders should be quashed as the removal orders were decided upon under a different legal regime and the applicants should be allowed to ask the Director, on humanitarian grounds, not to remove them.

[20] *Lau Kong Yung* (n 18) 323.

[21] See Elliott & Forsyth (n 17) 65–7.

rightly rejected by the CFA. The authority of interpretation that the CFA possesses, under Article 158(2) and (3), is a delegated one from the general power of Interpretation that the Basic Law vests in the SCNPC under Article 158(1). While the Basic Law framers, in drafting Article 158, drew inspiration from the judicial reference mechanism provided in Article 177 of the European Economic Treaty (EEC),[22] one must note a fundamental distinction. Under the EEC Treaty, the national courts' power of interpretation was not a delegated one from the European Court of Justice; this is unlike Article 158 where the SCNPC grants the Hong Kong courts the right to exercise the power of interpretation over some matters on its behalf. The SCNPC does not divest itself of the power to interpret the Basic Law; it merely authorizes the Hong Kong judiciary to do so on its behalf on some issues. Therefore, it would be rather odd for one to argue that the SCNPC, the original delegator of the interpretive power, is denied the power to interpret those Basic Law provisions that it has merely authorized the Hong Kong courts to perform on its behalf, except when the delegatee of the interpretive power first consents to it.

Interestingly, the CFA went on to express support for the view that the power of the SCNPC to interpret the Basic Law is 'plenary in that it covers all the provisions of the Basic Law; this power may be exercised in the absence of litigation'.[23] Therefore, the CFA admitted that the SCNPC not only could interpret the excluded provisions, it could also interpret those provisions that concerned only affairs relating to Hong Kong's autonomy. While this observation may be legally accurate, such a concession was unnecessary. After all, the CFA was not confronted with a Basic Law provision that was of a purely local nature and it did not have to pre-emptively rule herein on the SCNPC's right to interpret such provisions too.

Notwithstanding the CFA's recognition of the SCNPC's interpretive supremacy, the court announced that the retrospective criminal sanctions imposed by the Immigration Ordinance were still unconstitutional. Although the Interpretation resurrected the legality of the Immigration Ordinance so far as it re-subjected Mainland children born of Hong Kong Permanent Residents to the regulatory exit permit scheme, and required either parent to be a Permanent Resident at the time of the child's birth before he or she could enjoy the right of abode by descent, the court held that the Interpretation was silent on the court's invalidation of the retrospective

[22] See Albert Chen, 'Ng Ka Ling and Article 158(3) of the Basic Law' (2002) 5 *Journal of Chinese and Comparative Law* 221.

[23] *Lau Kong Yung* (n 18) 324, citing Professor Yash Ghai, *Hong Kong's New Constitutional Order* (2nd edn, Hong Kong, Hong Kong University Press 1999) 198.

criminal sanctions. Since this ground was not affected by the Interpretation, the court held that the retrospective provisions remained invalid.[24] Although this judicial manoeuvre had minimal practical impact, that is it only protected immigrants who arrived in Hong Kong between 1 July and 9 July from criminal sanctions, this holding, nonetheless, was of great constitutional significance. Henceforth, while the Hong Kong judiciary would abide by the free-standing interpretive mandate of the SCNPC, it would read any such Interpretation narrowly and strictly. If the SCNPC seeks to overturn a CFA decision, the Interpretation must openly and expressly convey such intentions.

After being chastised by the SCNPC for judicial over-reach in *Ng Ka Ling*, the fundamental jurisprudential conundrum the CFA faces is how it can preserve the judiciary as a separate and independent branch of government while assuaging any anxieties from the Mainland that Hong Kong courts, if left unleashed, would turn the Island into another 'renegade province' in the South. If the Hong Kong courts are perceived to be too aggressive in rights-adjudication, they might be censured again by the SCNPC and have their judicial powers further fettered. On the other hand, if the judiciary is too indulgent on the HKSAR government, the Basic Law would be reduced to a mere hollow shell that only protects constitutional rights on paper but not in practice.

After serving for over a decade as HKSAR's first Chief Justice, Andrew Li retired in 2010 and he was succeeded by Geoffrey Ma, who was the Chief Judge of the High Court of Hong Kong prior to his elevation. A Permanent Judge of the Court of Final Appeal, Kemal Bokhary retired in 2012 after he reached the retirement age of 65. Some speculate that his term of office was not contractually extended by the government as it was displeased with his 'liberal' record on the bench.[25] He remains in the CFA, however, as a Non-Permanent Judge and hears cases occasionally.

II. Judicial Crisis in Malaysia

The judicial crisis of 1988 was sparked off by a letter Tun Salleh, the Lord President of the Supreme Court of Malaysia (now retitled Chief Justice of the Federal Court of Malaysia), wrote to the King on 26 March 1988 about the judiciary's concern over its deteriorating relationship with the Executive.

[24] Ibid. 327.

[25] Former judge Bokhary, 'I was ousted for being too liberal' *South China Morning Post* (Hong Kong, 5 November 2012).

Back in 1987, there were already simmering tensions between the Malaysian government and the judiciary. The Prime Minister, Mahathir Mohamad, had expressed his displeasure, on several occasions, within and outside Parliament, over various recent decisions of the Malaysian courts.[26] In *Berthelsen v Director General of Information*,[27] the Supreme Court of Malaysia had quashed the cancellation of an employment pass, originally granted to an Asian Wall Street Journal staff correspondent, on the ground that he was not afforded the right to make representations before his employment pass was terminated. Subsequently, in *Public Prosecutor v Dato' Yap Peng*,[28] the Supreme Court, by a 3–2 majority, invalidated Section 418A of the Criminal Procedure Code,[29] which allowed the Public Prosecutor to transfer a criminal case pending before a subordinate court to the High Court, on the basis that this statutory provision encroached upon the judicial powers conferred on the courts by Article 121(1) of the Constitution. (The government responded to this decision by excising the term 'judicial power' from Article 121(1) of the Constitution in a constitutional amendment effected on 10 June 1988.)

The pivotal case that hardened Prime Minister Mahathir's stance against the judiciary was probably *Mohd Noor Bin Othman v Mohd Yusof Jaafar*,[30] or more commonly known as the UMNO-11 case. In this dispute, 11 dissatisfied members of UMNO, the dominant party in the ruling National Front coalition, challenged the results of the internal party elections held in 1987 on the ground that a number of the UMNO branches were not registered under the Societies Act[31] and therefore decisions taken by the delegates from these branches were null and void. The plaintiffs also sought a declaration that the election of the office-bearers in the UMNO general assembly of 1987 was null and void, and for fresh elections to be called. (These internal UMNO elections were of particular importance to Mahathir, as traditionally the person who was elected President of UMNO would also become the Prime Minister.) In particular, Section 12(3) of the Societies Act provided that where a registered society established a branch without the prior approval of the Registrar of Societies, the registered society and the branch so established would be deemed unlawful societies. On 4 February 1988, the High Court handed down its judgment where it stated that, by virtue of Section 12(3), UMNO and those unregistered branches were unlawful societies, but

[26] See Andrew Harding, 'The 1988 Constitutional Crisis in Malaysia' (1990) 39 *International and Comparative Law Quarterly* 57, 74–7.

[27] (1987) 1 MLJ 134 (Supreme Court of Malaysia).

[28] (1987) 2 MLJ 311 (Supreme Court of Malaysia).

[29] Criminal Procedure Code (Laws of Malaysia Act 153).

[30] (1988) 2 MLJ 129 (High Court of Malaysia).

[31] Societies Act (Laws of Malaysia Act 335).

the plaintiffs were not entitled to any relief as they 'cannot acquire any right which is founded on that which is unlawful'.[32] For the ruling coalition to be declared unlawful naturally unnerved the government and it proceeded to register a new party 'UMNO Baru' (New UMNO) in mid February 1988.

It was in this tense political climate that the Lord President was prompted, on 25 March 1988, to summon a meeting of all the Supreme Court and High Court judges, resident in Kuala Lumpur, to discuss the escalating tensions between the judiciary and the executive. Twenty judges attended the meeting and it was collectively decided that the Lord President would send a letter to the King, expressing the judiciary's concerns and anxieties. A draft of this letter was circulated to all the judges before it was delivered on 26 March 1988 to the King and copied to all the Malay Rulers.

The letter was signed by the Lord President but was written on behalf of all the judges in Malaysia. It stated that the judges were all 'disappointed with the various comments and accusations' made by Prime Minister Mahathir against the judiciary that have 'brought shame' to them and left them 'mentally disturbed' and they were thus conveying these sentiments to the King, 'with the hope that all of those unfounded accusations will be stopped'.[33]

Unfortunately, the King took offence at the letter as he perceived that the Rulers would be brought into a conflict with the government if he had intervened on behalf of the judiciary. On 1 May 1988, in an audience with the Prime Minister, the King conveyed his displeasure about the letter and asked for appropriate action to be taken against the Lord President. On 5 May 1988, the Prime Minister wrote to the King where he explained that the only legal recourse available was the removal process provided under Article 125 of the Constitution, and he would revert on a later date on whether there was any evidence that justified the Lord President's dismissal from the bench. Soon after, on 25 May 1988, the Prime Minister informed the King that there was evidence of misbehaviour that justified the removal of Tun Salleh, and the King was advised to appoint a Tribunal to adjudicate over the removal process; in the interim, the Lord President was suspended from his duties till the Tribunal's report was made available.

All this while, the Lord President remained in the dark over the palace intrigue that was taking place. On 26 May 1988, the Supreme Court scheduled the appeal over the UMNO-11 case, for 13 June 1988, before a bench

[32] *Mohd Noor Bin Othman* (n 30) 134.

[33] The English translation of the letter is reproduced in the Report of the Tribunal Established under Article 125(3) and (4) of the Federal Constitution: Re: YAA Tun Dato' Hj Mohammed Salleh Abas. See also HP Lee, *Constitutional Conflicts in Contemporary Malaysia* (Kuala Lumpur, Oxford University Press 1995) 44.

of nine judges. The very next day, on 27 May 1988, the Lord President was summoned to the Prime Minister's office, where he was invited to resign or a Tribunal would be constituted under Article 125 with a view to removing him. On the same day that he was suspended from office, the UMNO-11 case was removed from the court's schedule. Tun Salleh had originally wanted to resign but decided against this on 29 May 1988. Instead, he held a press conference and also gave a British Broadcasting Corporation interview the next day.

The Tribunal was convened very quickly, and the hearing was scheduled for 27 June 1988. There were six members and they included the Chief Justice of Malaya, the Chief Justice of Borneo, a retired Federal Court judge, a retired High Court judge, the Chief Justice of Sri Lanka, and a Supreme Court judge from Singapore. Tun Salleh's lawyers objected to the composition of the Tribunal as it was chaired by the Chief Justice of Malaya who was appointed the Acting Lord President, and was thus next in line to succeed Tun Salleh if he was successfully removed; and only one member of the Tribunal, the Chief Justice of Sri Lanka, could be regarded to have held an appointment equal to that of the Lord President's. His lawyers also wanted a public hearing, instead of a closed-door session.

These objections were rejected by the Tribunal but it was willing to adjourn the hearing to 29 June 1988; the proceedings commenced that fateful day without the presence of Tun Salleh as he had decided not to further participate in the inquiry. On 28 June 1988, Tun Salleh filed an application in the High Court, where he sought a judicial order to restrain the Tribunal from submitting its report to the King. On 2 July 1988, the High Court judge hearing this application adjourned the hearing till 4 July 1988, so that the Attorney General could submit more evidence, and refused to grant Tun Salleh an interim stay order against the Tribunal. That afternoon, on 2 July, counsel for Tun Salleh appeared before a special sitting of the Supreme Court, and five judges unanimously granted an interim stay order that prohibited the Tribunal from submitting its report to the King. This order was then served on the Tribunal.

This special sitting of the Supreme Court was convened by Supreme Court judge Tan Sri Wan Suleiman who had been apprised in advance that this urgent application would take place should the High Court refuse to grant a temporary stay order. Wan Suleiman and George Seah (another Supreme Court judge) were scheduled for a court session at Kota Bahru that weekend, but they deliberately remained in Kuala Lumpur for this special sitting.

On 5 July 1988, Abdul Hamid Omar, Chairman of the Tribunal, in his capacity as Acting Lord President, made a representation to the King that the five Supreme Court judges, in issuing the temporary restraining order against the Tribunal, should also be removed from office for misbehaviour. The Prime Minister also supported Abdul Hamid Omar's representation. The King agreed and ordered for a Second Tribunal to be convened to investigate the conduct of the five Supreme Court judges; these judges were also suspended from office, pending the Second Tribunal's report, with effect from 6 July 1988.

On 7 July 1988, the First Tribunal completed its report and recommended the removal of Tun Salleh. Interestingly, on the next day, the High Court dismissed Tun Salleh's initial application for a restraining order. On 22 July 1988, a different panel of the Supreme Court set aside the temporary restraining order issued by the five judges in the earlier sitting. The First Tribunal's report was submitted to the King on 31 July. On 6 August, the Prime Minister's Department issued a press release, announcing that the King agreed with the First Tribunal's recommendation for the removal of Tun Salleh, and the dismissal would take effect from 8 August 1988.

On 8 August 1988, the UMNO-11 case was also heard in the Supreme Court and the appeal was dismissed. On 12 August, the Second Tribunal, constituted by a different panel of judges from the first one, was tasked to inquire into the conduct of the five judges. The Second Tribunal submitted its report on 26 September; in early October, the King dismissed Wan Suleiman and George Seah, and reinstated the other three judges, as recommended by the Second Tribunal. Unsurprisingly, the Acting Lord President, Abdul Hamid Omar, was officially appointed the Lord President on 10 November 1988.

The first Tribunal found Tun Salleh guilty on all five charges laid against him.[34] The first two charges related to the public speeches he gave in 1987 and 1988, where he allegedly undermined the public's confidence in the government. The third charge alleged that he acted with improper motives when an appeal concerning a minor's choice of religion was adjourned *sine die*. The fourth charge was directed at the allegedly false statements he made in the letter he sent the King. Finally, the fifth charge concerned the allegedly untrue statements he made to the media after his suspension. Under Article 125(3) of the Constitution existing then, a Supreme Court judge may be removed for acts of 'misbehaviour', but this vague term was unfortunately left undefined. The First Tribunal held that misbehaviour would include any 'unlawful conduct or immoral conduct such as bribery, corruption, acts done with improper motives relating to the office of a judge and which would affect the due administration of justice or which would shake

[34] For fuller details on the allegations, see FA Trindade, 'The Removal of the Malaysian Judges' (1990) 106 *Law Quarterly Review* 51, 59–66.

the confidence of the public in a judge'.[35] Subsequently, the First Tribunal unanimously decided that the above-mentioned five charges were proved on a balance of probabilities, and hence recommended his removal from office.[36]

With regard to the other five Malaysian Supreme Court judges, they were all charged in relation to their intentional participation in the special sitting of the Supreme Court on 2 July 1988, without the prior permission of the Acting President. George Seah was additionally charged for abandoning his scheduled sitting at Kota Bahru without reasonable cause. Wan Suleiman, in turn, was further charged for staying away from his assigned Kota Bahru hearing without due cause and directing George Seah to do the same.[37] Interestingly, the Second Tribunal, unlike the first one, decided that all the charges against the judges had to be proven beyond reasonable doubt. Judicial misbehaviour was also construed to include any improper exercise of, or wilful and unjustifiable absence from duty or refusal to perform one's official duties, but any such errors of judgment must be attributed to improper motives, that is dishonest, oppressive, or corrupt motives, or partiality, or malice.[38] On the facts, the Tribunal found that the judges had not misbehaved by merely participating in the special sitting on 2 July as they had acted in the honest belief that Wan Suleiman (as the most senior judge after the Acting President) was entitled to convene the special sitting since the Acting Lord President, as the Chairman of the Tun Salleh Tribunal, would experience a conflict of interest in such a proceeding. The Second Tribunal also held that there was also no evidence that the five judges had conspired in advance to grant an interim stay order against the Tun Salleh Tribunal. Nevertheless, by a majority of three to two, the Second Tribunal agreed that George Seah's absence from his scheduled Kota Bahru hearing constituted judicial misbehaviour that was sufficiently serious to justify removal from the bench. Similarly, by a majority of four to one, the Second Tribunal found that Wan Suleiman's deliberate absence from his Kota Bahru hearing, and his direction to George Seah to do the same, was actuated by an improper motive to help his friend, Tun Salleh, and this constituted judicial misbehaviour that was sufficiently serious to justify removal from the bench.[39] All three judges were eventually cleared of any wrongdoing nearly two decades

[35] Tun Salleh Tribunal Report (7 July 1988), 49.

[36] For a critique on the findings, see FA Trindade (n 34) 59–66 and HP Lee (n 33) 60–6.

[37] Wan Suleiman also directed Supreme Court judge Harun Hashim to attend the Special Sitting of the Federal Court on 2 July, even though the latter was already assigned to Kota Bahru hearing, but Harun Hashim had declined to do so.

[38] Second Tribunal Report (23 September 1988), 38.

[39] For a critique on the findings, see FA Trindade (n 34) 82–5 and HP Lee (n 33) 67–73.

later in 2008 by an independent Panel of Eminent Persons, though no formal apology was offered by the Malaysian government.

Naturally, public confidence in the independence of the judiciary was eroded after the removal of the three Supreme Court judges. Unfortunately, matters did not improve as the members of the Malaysian judiciary, soon after, were embroiled in scandals of corruption and perceived acts of impropriety. During the tenure of Tun Eusoff Chin as Chief Justice of Malaysia (1994–2000), many allegations surfaced that lawyers could 'shop' for the presiding judges over their disputes. In the most controversial of such cases, *Ayer Molek Rubber v Insas Bhd*,[40] the plaintiffs, in a commercial dispute over share transfers, obtained an *ex parte* mandatory injunction against the defendants in the Appellate and Special Powers Division of the High Court, instead of the Commercial Division as procedures required. On appeal, the Court of Appeal admonished the High Court judge for granting an *ex parte* injunction in a non-urgent matter and for requiring such an injunction to be complied with within two working days, especially since the writ was filed in the wrong Division in the first place. The Court of Appeal expressed concern that there might be public perception that litigants could choose the judge before which they wished to appear and that 'something is rotten'[41] in the courts. On further appeal,[42] Chief Justice Eusoff Chin expressed outrage at the Court of Appeal's allegations of judicial impropriety; rather extraordinarily, he ordered for portions of the Court of Appeal's judgment to be expunged from the record. Interestingly, one member of this Federal Court panel was only a High Court judge and its composition was thus inconsistent with Article 122(2) of the Malaysia Constitution, which permitted the Chief Justice to co-opt only Court of Appeal judges to hear Federal Court cases.[43] In 2000, it further surfaced that Chief Justice Chin had taken a holiday in 1994 with VK Lingam,[44] a prominent lawyer, and Lingam's family in New Zealand. No action was taken against the judge but he retired that year.

Furthermore, in September 2007, there was public outrage when a 2002 video recording surfaced where VK Lingam, the same above-mentioned lawyer, was unknowingly filmed having a phone conversation with an undisclosed party about how he could influence Prime Minister Mahathir to appoint specific individuals to senior judicial posts. The party on the other

[40] [1995] 2 MLJ 734 (High Court of Malaysia). [41] Ibid. [23].

[42] [1995] 2 MLJ 833 (Federal Court of Malaysia).

[43] A decade later, in *Dato' v Kanagalingam v David Samuels* [2006] 6 MLJ 521 (High Court of Malaysia), the High Court expressly declared that this Federal Court decision was null and void, as it was composed in violation of the Malaysia Constitution.

[44] Interestingly, VK Lingam was also counsel for the party that sought the *ex parte* mandatory injunction in *Ayer Molek Rubber v Insas Bhd.*

end of the phone line was widely believed to be Ahmad Fairuz, who was the Chief Justice of Malaysia from 2003 to 2007. (At the time that the phone conversation occurred, Ahmad Fairuz was the Chief Judge of Malaya.) Chief Justice Ahmad Fairuz retired in November 2007 when his tenure in office came to an end. A Royal Commission of Inquiry was later established by Prime Minister Abdullah Badawi and its findings were published in May 2008. The Commission affirmed the authenticity of the video tape, recommended that further investigations and appropriate action be taken against VK Lingam, Ahmad Fairuz, and Mahathir, and proposed the establishment of a Judicial Appointments Commission (JAC). Only the last recommendation was taken up by the government and a JAC was established in 2009.

In the aftermath of the 1988 judicial crisis and the corruption scandals that plagued the judiciary in the years following, the central struggle for the Malaysian courts has been to restore public confidence in the integrity of the nation's legal system. There are promising signs that the Malaysian judiciary, encouraged by a re-energized electorate and civil society, is reasserting its independence vis-à-vis the government,[45] and senior judges are now also more conscious about being fair and transparent in the discharge of their public functions.[46] While the jury is out on whether these aspirations for change and reform will be realized, it is undeniable that the Malaysian courts have embarked on the long and winding road to constitutional redemption.

III. Judicial Crisis in Singapore

The judicial crisis in Singapore also followed from a controversial decision handed down by the Singapore Court of Appeal. In 1987, four individuals were arrested and detained without trial under the Internal Security Act[47] (ISA) for their alleged involvement in a Marxist conspiracy to subvert the existing political system in Singapore and destabilize the country. They were, in fact, primarily only Catholic social workers who were seeking to raise awareness and organize activities to assist the poor and underprivileged in

[45] See also *Sivarasa Rasiah v Badan Peguam Malaysia* [2010] 2 MLJ 333 (Federal Court of Malaysia).

[46] See Speech by Chief Justice Arifin Zakaria, Opening Address of the Legal Year 2012, 'As Judges We Are Accountable to No One But the Law Which Must be Administered Without Fear or Favour, Affection or Ill Will' (14 January 2012) <http://www.kehakiman.gov.my/sites/default/files/document3/Penerbitan%20Kehakiman/KetuaHakim.pdf> accessed 15 March 2012.

[47] Internal Security Act, (Cap 143).

Singapore. Thereafter, the detainees filed for *habeas corpus* and their consolidated appeals eventually came before the Court of Appeal.

The judgment of the Court of Appeal in *Chng Suan Tze v Minister for Home Affairs*[48] has since fascinated legal scholars, practitioners, and students alike, and it remains the single most important constitutional decision that the Singapore judiciary has ever handed down. The appeal primarily turned on the court's interpretation of Section 8(1) of the ISA, which authorized the Minister of Home Affairs to issue a detention order if the President of Singapore was satisfied that this was necessary to prevent that person from acting in any manner prejudicial to the security of Singapore. On the facts, the detention orders were signed only by the Permanent Secretary of Home Affairs and the affidavit he signed merely testified to the fact that the government was satisfied that the detention orders were necessary. The court held unanimously that this recital was insufficient. Instead, the court opined that, in the absence of direct evidence from the President, the Cabinet or the authorized Minister must provide evidence that the Cabinet (or the authorized Minister) was satisfied and that the President, after receiving the government's advice, was satisfied that these measures were necessary.[49] Therefore, the Court of Appeal seized on this technical irregularity, invalidated the detention orders, and ordered the release of the detainees.

What proved to be most interesting was the court's subsequent extended discussion on its right to review the propriety of detentions without trial. After surveying a litany of Commonwealth precedents, the court overruled a prior Singapore High Court precedent of *Lee Mau Seng v Minister of Home Affairs*[50] and declared that henceforth, the courts would objectively review the exercise of the President's discretion to issue a detention order. In a widely celebrated[51] passage of the judgment, Chief Justice Wee Chong Jin, on behalf of a unanimous Court of Appeal, boldly observed:

> In our view, the notion of a subjective or unfettered discretion is contrary to the rule of law. All power has legal limits and the rule of law demands that the courts should be able to examine the exercise of discretionary power.[52]

Nevertheless, the court acknowledged that 'those responsible for national security are sole judges of what action is necessary in the interests of national security',[53] and hence the scope of review over the exercise of such discretions would be limited to 'the normal judicial review principles of "illegality,

[48] [1988] 2 SLR 132 (Singapore Court of Appeal). [49] Ibid. [39].
[50] [1971–73] SLR(R) 135 (High Court of Singapore).
[51] See Li-ann Thio, 'Lex Rex or Rex Lex? Competing Conceptions of the Rule of Law in Singapore' (2002) 20 *UCLA Pacific Basin Law Journal* 1.
[52] *Chng Suan Tze* (n 48) [86]. [53] Ibid. [89].

irrationality or procedural impropriety" ...'[54] Yet, strangely, despite all the lengthy observations on how the judiciary would review the President's exercise of his discretion under the ISA, the Court of Appeal held that it was unnecessary to decide whether the detention orders were invalid on these substantive grounds.[55] Scholars have speculated whether the court was perhaps offering the government a face-saving way out of the crisis by giving the government the chance to 'voluntarily' abandon the detentions rather than be judicially chided for illegally or irrationally detaining political dissidents under the ISA.[56]

But the Singapore government was not to be cowed or deterred by its judiciary. The detainees were released, in compliance with the judicial decision, but they were re-arrested, within minutes of their release, and served with new detention orders that were signed this time by the rightful authorities. Furthermore, within a month of the judicial decision, Parliament passed a series of constitutional[57] and statutory amendments, ousting all judicial review over executive decisions made under the ISA save in regard to any question relating to the compliance with any procedural requirement of the said statute governing that decision.[58] Interestingly, the then newly introduced Section 8B(1) of the ISA also provides that the law governing judicial review of any decision 'shall be the same as was applicable and declared in Singapore on the 13th day of July 1971', that is the day that the Singapore High Court handed down its decision in *Lee Mau Seng*. The Minister of Home Affairs justified this series of changes on the basis that the government could not allow for Singapore's law on national security matters to be governed by overseas cases decided in countries where conditions were totally different from those of Singapore.[59] The Minister also emphasized that judges lacked national security expertise and security assessments by the executive should thus not be subject to an objective evaluation by the courts.[60]

Naturally, the re-arrested applicants filed for *habeas corpus* again and their applications once again came before the Court of Appeal. It is noteworthy that in *Teo Soh Lung v Minister of Home Affairs*,[61] the dispute came before the

[54] Ibid. [119]. [55] Ibid. [127].

[56] Michael Hor, 'Law and Terror: Singapore Stories and Malaysian Dilemmas' in Michael Hor, Victor Ramraj & Kent Roach (eds), *Global Anti-Terrorism: Law and Policy* (Cambridge, Cambridge University Press 2005) 284.

[57] Article 149(3) was added to the Singapore Constitution and it provides that nothing in Article 93 of the Singapore Constitution, i.e. the constitutional clause that vests the judicial powers in the courts, shall invalidate any anti-subversion law passed by Parliament, regardless whether the proceedings were instituted before or after the commencement of this clause.

[58] See Section 8B(2) of the Internal Security Act (Cap 143).

[59] 52 Singapore Parliamentary Debates, cols 468–73. [60] Ibid. col 527.

[61] [1990] 1 SLR(R) 347 (Singapore Court of Appeal).

same panel of three judges that decided *Chng Suan Tze*. Nevertheless, this time, in view of the constitutional and statutory overrides, the judges were significantly more subdued. But one must note that the Court of Appeal did not just capitulate to all of the government's demands. Parliament had, via statutory amendments to the ISA, sought to restrict the court's role in such disputes to procedural review and reinstate *Lee Mau Seng* as the law of the land. But the court demurred. While the court would no longer objectively review the President's exercise of his discretion, the court was resistant to applying *Lee Mau Seng* strictly.

The High Court in *Lee Mau Seng* had held that even if the President was *mala fides* insofar as he exercised his discretion on 'vague, irrelevant or incorrect grounds and facts',[62] such that he subjectively knew that the detention was imposed not with a view to prevent the detainee from acting in any manner prejudicial to the security of Singapore, *mala fides* was not a justiciable issue in the context of the ISA.[63] This was indeed the position taken by the High Court in *Teo Soh Lung*.[64] But the Court of Appeal was unwilling to grant to the executive such unbridled powers. Instead, the court held that the judiciary would still intervene if a person was detained for reasons which had nothing to do with national security, but the onus was on the applicants to prove that the 'Government did not take into account national security considerations as a factor in re-detaining'[65] them. On the facts, the applicants could not discharge this burden of proof and their appeal failed on this ground.

Teo Soh Lung was also striking so far as the Court of Appeal refused to decide whether the constitutional amendments passed to override *Chng Suan Tze* were invalid for violating the implied basic structure of the Singapore Constitution.[66] This reticence on the part of the Court of Appeal contrasted sharply with the lower court's express finding that there were no implied basic features to the Singapore Constitution, and that 'Parliament has the power to amend any provision of the Constitution so long as the special procedure required for amendment is followed'.[67]

Shortly after *Teo Soh Lung* was decided, Chief Justice Wee Chong Jin retired from the bench in 1990, after serving over 25 years as Singapore's first Chief Justice. Wee was replaced by Yong Pung How and the judiciary lurched to the far-right under his leadership as the courts entered a period

[62] *Lee Mau Seng* (n 50) [58]. [63] Ibid. [59].

[64] *Teo Soh Lung v Minister for Home Affairs* (1989) 1 SLR 461 (High Court of Singapore).

[65] *Teo Soh Lung* (Singapore Court of Appeal) (n 61) [28]. [66] Ibid. [44].

[67] *Teo Soh Lung* (High Court of Singapore) (n 64) [59].

of extreme rights-conservatism.[68] Nevertheless, with Yong's retirement from the bench, Chan Sek Keong, one of the three judges on the Court of Appeal panels in *Chng Suan Tze* and *Teo Soh Lung*, assumed the position of Chief Justice in 2006. Alongside the new appointments to the Court of Appeal,[69] Chief Justice Chan was perceived to have embarked on a path to mitigate the excesses of the Yong Court.[70] Chief Justice Chan retired from office when he reached 75 years of age in 2012, and Sundaresh Menon was appointed as his successor. While it may be premature to state that Singapore is on the threshold of a constitutional renaissance, there are promising signs that the judiciary has once again regained an interest in engaging in a dialogue with the government on rights and constitutionalism.[71]

IV. Conclusion

I have explored the background to and the immediate aftermath of the three constitutional crises in Hong Kong, Malaysia, and Singapore. Inevitably, these crises have cast a pall over the state of constitutional review in the above-mentioned jurisdictions. While it is not uncommon for judges in all countries to act prudentially when they seek to avoid legislative or electoral outrage, this concern about political reprisals is particularly accentuated or pronounced in these three territories. All of them have a semi-permanent form of government in power; and where a dominant disciplined political party/coalition is in control, the less space their courts have to operate. As Professor Tom Ginsburg has observed, the extent of political diffusion within the legislative/executive structures determines how successfully courts can assert their judicial power.[72] Where divided government exists, the 'policy space'[73] of the courts is greater as

[68] See Li-ann Thio, 'Trends in Constitutional Interpretation: Oppugning *Ong*, Awakening *Arumugam*?' [1997] *Singapore Journal of Legal Studies* 240 and Li-ann Thio, 'An "i" for an "I"?—Singapore's Communitarian Model of Constitutional Adjudication' (1997) 27 *Hong Kong Law Journal* 152.

[69] Andrew Phang, VK Rajah, and Sundaresh Menon were elevated to the Court of Appeal in 2006, 2007, and 2012 respectively.

[70] See Opening Address of Chief Justice Chan Sek Keong, Singapore Academy of Law Conference 2011: Developments in Singapore Law 2006–10 (24 February 2011).

[71] Michael Hor, 'Criminal Justice in the Chan Court: Change, Contestation and Conservatism in the Court of Appeal' in Yeo Tiong Min, Hans Tjio & Tang Hang Wu (eds), *SAL Conference 2011: Developments in Singapore Law between 2006 and 2010—Trends and Perspectives* (Singapore, Academy Publishing 2011) 147.

[72] Tom Ginsburg, *Judicial Review in New Democracies: Constitutional Courts in Asian Cases* (Cambridge, Cambridge University Press 2003) 19.

[73] Ibid. 81.

the opposing parties in the legislature have to co-operate to effectuate any disagreement with the judiciary. Bipartisan legislative agreement to overrule judges would be less likely and frequent in liberal democracies. In contrast, where legislative and executive power is consolidated by a single party/coalition, these dominant political parties/coalitions can display their displeasure more easily, as illustrated above, by ousting judicial review or even the judges themselves.

In constitutional systems where a dominant party/coalition is in control, a robust judicial reading of the Constitution may precipitate another constitutional crisis when the government responds by deploying constitutional or unconstitutional means to 'punish' the courts. For Hong Kong, this may take the form of a SCNPC Interpretation from Mainland China that would further weaken rights in the territory. As for Singapore, the ruling People's Action Party can easily obtain another constitutional amendment to oust judicial review once again. In Malaysia, where a constitutional amendment is currently out of reach for the dominant coalition in government, at least without the consent of the opposition parties, the relative attraction of an extra-legal response, like the ouster of judges, may grow.

Therefore, in light of the dangers that these constitutional crises may pose to the judicial protection of rights and constitutionalism, these territorial courts should instead apply more dialogic tools when enforcing constitutional rights. The type and nature of these dialogic tools will be the focus of my next chapter as I explore how dialogic review can actually take place in these jurisdictions. Suffice to say briefly herein, where courts enforce rights by applying norms/doctrines that may be *reversed* by the local legislatures, in the course of *ordinary* politics, or providing the legislature with ample constitutional *space* to achieve their comparable substantive goals, the dominant party/coalition would feel less compelled to overrule the judges by resorting to constitutional amendments (or extra-legal methods) that will do more long-term harm to the constitutional polity in question. By engaging in dialogic review, judges would worry less about political backlash, as the stakes are so much lower. If the legislature is displeased intensely by a judicial decision, their disapproval can be more easily channelled into *ordinary* law. The Constitution is left intact and the judges are left alone. Constitutional review does not operate in a political vacuum; where courts are significantly constrained by the preferences of other political actors, by doing less, judges can often achieve more.

5

Dialogue and Sub-Constitutional Doctrines

The term 'sub-constitutional' law was first coined by Professor Henry Monaghan[1] in an influential article where he argued that the United States Supreme Court, alongside the exercise of the *Marbury v Madison* style of judicial review, had also enforced a 'substructure of substantive, procedural, and remedial rules'[2] that were inspired but not mandated by the United States Constitution and this 'constitutional common law of individual liberty'[3] was therefore subject to statutory modification or reversal. In America, this sub-order of 'quasi-constitutional' norms includes proper findings-and-study requirements, time-driven second-look doctrines,[4] and clear-statement rules that impose certain substantive norms in the absence of clear statutory language to the contrary.[5]

The specific sub-constitutional tools applied by courts may differ across jurisdictions, but whenever a common law court is willing to vindicate constitutional liberties by adopting remedial, substantive, or procedural rules at a sub-constitutional level, the legislature will be able to engage with the judiciary on its understandings of rights, even in the absence of structural devices in the Bills of Rights that expressly allow the lawmakers to override the

[1] Henry Monaghan, 'Foreword: Constitutional Common Law' (1975) 89 *Harvard Law Review* 1, 2–3.

[2] Ibid. [3] Ibid. 3.

[4] Dan T Coenen, 'A Constitution of Collaboration: Protecting Fundamental Values with Second-Look Rules of Interbranch Dialogue' (2001) 42 *William and Mary Law Review* 1578. Proper findings-and-study rules is a judicial innovation that requires legislatures to provide evidence that they have closely studied and examined a certain issue, and considered other alternatives, before enacting the impugned law in response. Second-look doctrines are judicial mandated legislative re-consideration of archaic laws, but courts do not permanently disable such laws if the legislature returns and reinstates its original views.

[5] For an elaboration of these rules, see William Eskridge, Jr & Philip P Frickey, 'Quasi-Constitutional Law: Clear Statement Rules as Constitutional Lawmaking' (1992) 45 *Vanderbilt Law Review* 595. Examples provided include the presumptions that the Supreme Court, in the absence of clear statutory text, would assume Congress would not regulate the core functions performed by the individual states and that federal legislation should be interpreted in a way that is consistent with international law.

judicial conception of fundamental liberties. Therefore, sub-constitutional rules are essentially dialogic in nature.

With regard to the three Asian common law jurisdictions under discussion, I shall argue in this chapter that their domestic courts have nevertheless engaged in dialogic review via the application of sub-constitutional doctrines that include the observance or recognition of one or more of the following norms/practices: (1) provisional or advisory determinations in constitutional matters; (2) administrative review; (3) common law liberties or statutory rights that are reversible by the ordinary political process; (4) procedural constitutional rules; (5) rational basis review of legislative actions; and (6) delayed declarations of invalidity.

Section I of this chapter begins with an examination of the objections against the use of such sub-constitutional or constitutional common law as advanced by learned scholars such as Thomas Schrock,[6] Robert Welsh,[7] and Mark Tushnet,[8] and this author will herein seek to respond to their concerns. Section II continues with an elaboration on the six types of sub-constitutional procedural, substantive, and remedial practices identified above, and I shall illustrate how the common law courts of Hong Kong, Malaysia, and Singapore have applied one or more of such norms during public law adjudication. This chapter concludes with observations on how the increasing use of sub-constitutional law norms can shape the constitutional discourse within a democracy by allowing the judiciary to forge a meaningful partnership with the legislature on rights-protection.

I. Sub-Constitutionalism and its Discontents

Professor Henry Monaghan[9] was the first scholar to observe that the United States Supreme Court had imposed a 'substructure of substantive, procedural, and remedial rules'[10] that were derived from but not imposed by the American Constitution. Within the American context, such rules, as discussed by Monaghan, included the imposition on the police of a duty of reading to an accused his *Miranda*[11] rights and also the creation of a

[6] Thomas S Schrock & Robert C Welsh, 'Reconsidering the Constitutional Common Law' (1978) 91 *Harvard Law Review* 1117.

[7] Ibid.

[8] Mark Tushnet, 'Subconstitutional Constitutional Law: Supplement, Sham or Substitute?' (2001) 42 *William and Mary Law Review* 1871.

[9] Monaghan (n 1). [10] Ibid. 2–3.

[11] *Miranda v Arizona* 384 US 436 (1966) (United States Supreme Court).

Bivens[12] remedy, which allowed a person to claim for civil damages against federal officers who violated his or her Fourth Amendment right against unreasonable searches and seizures.

Professors William Eskridge Jr and Philip Frickey, in a joint article,[13] have since identified other forms of quasi-constitutional doctrines that the United States Supreme Court applies; in particular, the Supreme Court has enforced a series of clear-statement rules that presumptively protect certain substantive constitutional values, unless Congress legislates otherwise in clear terms.[14] In the same vein, Professor Dan Coenen has also identified what he terms 'structural' doctrines that allow the judiciary to scrutinize the processes by which impugned legislation is enacted or enforced, and such doctrines include proper findings-and-study requirements and time-driven second-look doctrines.[15] What all these clear-statement and structural rules have in common is that they do not bar the government from pursuing any particular substantive policy choice; they instead merely slow down the policy-making process as the political branches can still pursue the same goals if they do so explicitly or after observing certain procedural requirements.

The judicial recourse to this sub-order of 'quasi-constitutional'[16] law is significant as it not only enables the courts to participate actively in rights-protection, but also provides the judiciary with the means to involve the legislature in the continuing process of defining the contents and consequences of individual liberties.[17] Therefore, even though the judiciary concurrently retains the power to invalidate statutes for perceived constitutional violations, so far as it implements the guarantees of the Constitution by prescribing only interstitial rules that accommodate space for legislative/executive disagreements or responses, the courts, in this process, can open up a channel of dialogue with the political branches of government on rights-limitations. This is so as this 'constitutional common law'[18] is always subject to statutory modification or reversal.

Nevertheless, sub-constitutional review has its critics, and it is to them I now turn. Thomas Schrock and Robert Welsh, in a joint article, have argued against sub-constitutional rule-making, as they argue that this violates the

[12] *Bivens v Six Unknown Named Agents of the Federal Bureau of Narcotics* 403 US 388 (1971) (United States Supreme Court).

[13] William Eskridge Jr & Philip Frickey (n 5).

[14] Ibid. Examples provided include the presumptions that the Supreme Court, in the absence of clear statutory text, would assume Congress would not regulate the core functions performed by the individual states and that federal legislation should be interpreted in a way that is consistent with international law.

[15] Dan T Coenen (n 4). [16] Eskridge & Frickey (n 5). [17] Monaghan (n 1) 27.

[18] Ibid. 3.

'separation of powers' doctrine. According to the learned authors, the 'separation of powers' doctrine is premised on the understanding that 'a number of relatively autonomous power centres check each other by jealously guarding their own prerogatives';[19] and insofar as the judiciary wields sub-constitutional powers, it could presumably regulate subjects like criminal law, welfare service, public employment systems, and other lawmaking concerns that fall within precincts of the legislature. In essence, the learned authors are subscribing to a 'pure' theory of the 'separation of powers' doctrine. This purist theory has also been formulated by MJC Vile in the following well-known terms:

> It is essential for the establishment and maintenance of political liberty that the government is divided into three branches or departments; the legislature, the executive, and the judiciary. To each of these three branches there is a corresponding identifiable function of government, legislative, executive, or judicial. Each branch of the government must be confined to the exercise of its own functions, and not allowed to encroach upon the functions of the other branches.[20]

Therefore, according to Schrock and Welsh, the fact that the legislature can, via the ordinary political processes, 'protect itself against the judicial invasion of its sphere does not justify that invasion in the first place'.[21]

With respect, this author has grave reservations about whether the learned scholars' view of the doctrine of 'separation of powers' is an accurate depiction of how the American government or any other common law system operates in reality.[22]

Common law courts have always exercised the power to craft rules of general application when they develop the contours of the common law or engage in statutory interpretation.[23] With the rise of the administrative state, the administrative tribunals, staffed with persons with specialized training and expertise, have increasingly been tasked to adjudicate over a myriad of disputes between the public and executive-run agencies. It would thus be impractical and unfeasible to argue for a complete separation of functions between all the branches of government. This does not however mean that the doctrine of 'separation of powers' is constitutionally irrelevant. All that the 'separation of powers' doctrine requires is for a set of institutional arrangements to exist whereby each branch of government remains the *primary* and *superior*

[19] Schrock & Welsh (n 6) 1127.

[20] MJC Vile, *Constitutionalism and the Separation of Powers* (Oxford, Clarendon Press 1967) 13.

[21] Schrock & Welsh (n 6) 1128.

[22] See Geoffrey Marshall, *Constitutional Theory* (Oxford, Clarendon Press 1971).

[23] Roger Masterman, *The Separation of Powers in the Contemporary Constitution: Judicial Competence and Independence in the United Kingdom* (Cambridge, Cambridge University Press 2011) 15.

institutional actor in the discharge of the central constitutional function that it has been assigned. Courts legislate, but they do so incrementally, and the common law is subject to the revision of the legislature; the latter always remains as the primary engine of legislative change. Similarly, administrative tribunals may exercise the powers of adjudication but their decisions are subjected to review by an independent judiciary, which remains the *primary* and *superior* adjudicatory forum of government. As any judicial recourse to sub-constitutional rule-making is subject to legislative revision, and is therefore subordinate to legislative lawmaking, the 'separation of powers' doctrine, as it is practised by common law systems in reality, is not violated.

Schrock and Welsh have also cast doubt on whether the judicial enforcement of sub-constitutional rules is 'concerned with interpretation of the Constitution'[24] at all as they view the constitutional common law as no more than judicial attempts at 'cost-benefit analysis and frank experimentation'.[25] With respect, the authors' argument rests on two assumptions, both of which are fallacious. First, they are assuming that *Marbury*-style judicial review is legitimate because judges are merely applying the Constitution and no more. Yet, constitutional provisions, especially provisions on fundamental liberties, are usually drafted in open-textured and abstract terms. Judges, in seeking to vindicate the underlying principles, inevitably have to use doctrines or legal tests (not found in the text) to implement the Constitution, especially when its structure and the text provide few concrete answers to specific disputes.[26] Therefore, judges invariably have to exercise interpretive choice whenever they craft doctrinal rules, regardless of whether these rules are of a constitutional or sub-constitutional nature. In particular, the proportionality analysis, adopted by many common law courts when they review the necessity of legislative limitations on rights, is one such doctrinal device. Second, the authors are assuming that the judicial foray into any form of cost-benefit analysis is automatically illegitimate. However, the proportionality doctrine, a ubiquitous interpretive device, also involves a form of cost-benefit analysis as judges often have to weigh the institutional competence of the courts to intervene in polycentric issues against the severity of any rights-derogations and adopt a context-specific variable intensity of review over the legislative actions.[27] The learned authors caricature sub-constitutionalism as some form of lawless, cost-benefit exercise. But, in reality, judges, when crafting

[24] Schrock & Welsh (n 6) 1156. [25] Ibid.

[26] See Richard Fallon, *Implementing the Constitution* (Cambridge, Harvard University Press 2001).

[27] Julian Rivers, 'Proportionality and variable intensity of Review' (2006) *Cambridge Law Journal* 174.

sub-constitutional rules or formulating constitutional doctrines, are merely considering the 'systemic, including institutional, consequences as well as consequences of the decision in the case at hand',[28] alongside the text, tradition, history, and precedent of a particular constitutional clause.[29]

Finally, Schrock and Welsh argue that the use of sub-constitutional rules will lead courts to under-enforce constitutional norms. This is an interesting concern. Earlier, the authors were worried that judges would over-enforce constitutional rights and encroach upon legislative prerogatives. Now, they are concerned that judges would do too little and this would lead to an unwarranted dilution in rights-protection. Leaving aside the question of whether the learned scholars are seeking to have their cake and eat it too, this particular concern is also unjustified. When judges have a binary choice between invalidating a legislative provision and upholding it, they invariably take into account their institutional competence and the costs of judicial error when formulating the specific decisional rule that implements the operative constitutional provision.[30] Where the only legislative response available to reverse a wrongful invalidation is a constitutional amendment, prudent judges, faced with the epistemic uncertainties over the correctness of their decisions, may often choose to under-enforce constitutional rights and err on the side of upholding plausibly unconstitutional practices. However, if the courts have recourse to sub-constitutional norms, which in turn can be reversed by the ordinary political processes, the judiciary may be more robust in enforcing those constitutional rights, which may otherwise go unprotected at all,[31] as the legislature is given a collaborative role to respond to any adverse consequences.

Professor Mark Tushnet has also expressed some reservations about sub-constitutional rule-making to which I now turn. One must note that while Schrock and Welsh are categorically and adamantly opposed to the judicial enforcement of sub-constitutional norms, Tushnet is more sanguine about its legitimacy.[32] Nevertheless, he questions whether 'courts might strategically deploy these sub-constitutional doctrines to avoid the sting of the charge that they are foreclosing legislative choice while effectively doing so'.[33] In the same vein, William Eskridge Jr and Philip Frickey believe that sub-constitutional rules might provide the judiciary 'with a cover for a great deal more counter-majoritarian activism, overall, than would open

[28] Richard Posner, *How Judges Think?* (Cambridge, Harvard University Press 2008) 238.

[29] Stephen Breyer, *Active Liberty: Interpreting a Democratic Constitution* (New York, Oxford University Press 2008) 28.

[30] See Kermit Roosevelt, 'Constitutional Calcification: How the Law Becomes What the Court Does' (2005) 91 *Virginia Law Review* 1649.

[31] Coenen (n 4) 2884. [32] Tushnet (n 8). [33] Ibid. 1871–2.

invalidation through judicial review'.[34] In short, these authors believe that the freedom of the legislature to respond and disagree with the sub-constitutional rules may prove to be illusory; and judicial supremacy may still prevail.

One must note, however, that the judicial enforcement of sub-constitutional norms is premised on a dialogic model of judicial review whereby the judiciary serves as an interlocutor of rights in a constitutional democracy by allowing legislators to have their way if they so choose, such that the lawmakers must openly deliberate, take political responsibility, and comply with the requisite procedural safeguards before pursuing their substantive choice of action. If the legislature is unable to harness the ordinary political processes to override a judicial sub-constitutional determination of rights, this only demonstrates that the court's decision is not so egregious (if at all) for such legislative consensus to be reached. So far as the burden is now on the legislature to displace the new judicially imposed default position on rights, this result is just an inevitable trade-off for a system of human rights enforcement by an independent branch of government.

The central benefits associated with sub-constitutional rule-making is that it allows the judiciary to place plausibly unpopular human rights concerns on the legislative agenda for the lawmakers' deliberation and response, while not foreclosing the legislature's ability to make a comparable substantive choice after a full consideration of the constitutional norms at play. The burden of inertia that must be overcome, before a ruling government can be provoked to actively advance human rights concerns, is often very prohibitive. This is especially so in instances where the rights of the minority conflict with the preferences of a sizable segment of the society, such that the vested interest of any administration committed to preserving its incumbency would be to maintain the status quo until the pressures for change outweigh the convenience of leaving things as they are.[35] Therefore, when judges vindicate constitutional values during public law adjudication with the use of *substantive* sub-constitutional norms, the benefit of legislative inertia is bestowed upon the aggrieved minority, as the onus is now on the legislature to openly debate and disagree with the courts if it so chooses. Where the sub-constitutional rule imposed is *procedural* in nature, the political branches are merely required to observe certain form-based rules of propriety or fairness before they act again. As the ordinary political processes retain control of any *substantive* legislative result and these sub-constitutional rules do not dictate the final outcome of any legislative deliberation, any concern about an overzealous judiciary thwarting democratic will is thus unwarranted.

[34] Eskridge & Frickey (n 5) 637.
[35] Po Jen Yap, 'Defending Dialogue' [2012] *Public Law* 527, 541.

II. Sub-Constitutional Doctrines in Common Law Asia

Unlike the various Commonwealth models found in the West, the Asian Constitutions of Hong Kong, Malaysia, and Singapore do not include any structural devices that enable the local legislatures within these territories to reverse or avoid a constitutional decision that they disagree with, except via a constitutional amendment. Nevertheless, in this section of my chapter, I shall show how the above-mentioned Asian common law courts, like their Western counterparts, have engaged in dialogic constitutional review. These Asian courts do so, however, via the application of sub-constitutional doctrines that include the observance or recognition of one or more of the following judicial norms/practices: (1) provisional or advisory determinations in constitutional matters; (2) administrative review; (3) common law liberties or statutory rights that are reversible by the ordinary political process; (4) procedural constitutional rules; (5) rational basis review of legislative actions; and (6) delayed declarations of invalidity. Each sub-constitutional doctrine will be discussed and illustrated with examples in turn.

A. Advisory Review

The first way by which courts engage in dialogic review is when they provide provisional or advisory determinations on particular constitutional questions. Provisional review is useful as it provides courts with an avenue to provide their independent, bona fide advice on a crucial constitutional matter; and the courts, in the process, can attempt to persuade the legislature to agree with their stance. When the judiciary engages in advisory review, the legislature is under no legal obligation to heed the court's advice and, so far as the legislature disagrees with the court's ruling, it may simply ignore those judicial suggestions.

The three Asian courts in the common law jurisdictions discussed all possess the power to engage in provisional/advisory review over constitutional matters in certain circumstances, and this right to provide a provisional constitutional determination is comparable to the Supreme Court of Canada's power to provide an advisory opinion under Section 53 of Canada's Supreme Court Act[36] or arguably even the United Kingdom courts' power to issue a declaration of incompatibility under Section 4 of the Human Rights Act

[36] James L Huffman, 'Advisory Opinions and Canadian Constitutional Development: The Supreme Court's Reference' (1990) 74 *Minnesota Law Review* 1251.

1998, which is of an advisory nature so far as the declaration does not affect the validity, continued operation, or enforcement of the impugned statutory provision in question.

In Malaysia, pursuant to Article 130 of the Federal Constitution, the King may request the Federal Court of Malaysia, the nation's court of final resort, to provide an advisory opinion on any question as to the effect of any provision of the Constitution though, in practice, the Federal Court has never been asked to exercise this advisory jurisdiction.

In the same vein, pursuant to Article 100 of the Singapore Constitution, the President of Singapore may refer to a tribunal consisting of not less than three Judges of the Supreme Court for its advisory opinion on any question as to the effect of any provision of the Constitution. To date, the President has only sought one such constitutional reference. In *Constitutional Reference No 1 of 1995*,[37] the Constitutional Reference Tribunal had to rule on the scope of the President's discretionary power to veto constitutional amendments that Parliament sought to pass. On the facts, the government was seeking to amend Article 22H(1) which then provided that the President may, acting in his discretion, withhold his assent to any Bill passed by Parliament (other than a Bill to which Article 5(2A) applied) if that Bill provided for the curtailment of the discretionary powers conferred upon him. Notably, Article 5(2A) provides that, unless the President concurs, any Bill that seeks to amend various constitutional clauses on fundamental liberties and general elections be supported by not less than two-thirds of the total number of votes cast in a national referendum. Significantly, Article 5(2A) was not in force at the time of the constitutional dispute and it still remains inoperative today. The Tribunal held that the President's veto powers under Article 22H(1) did not apply to any Bills which fell within the scope of Article 5(2A), and that the President's veto powers under Article 22H(1) 'could not enlarge itself by reason only of Art 5(2A) not being in force as, at the time of enactment, Art 22H(1) did not confer such a wide veto power on the President'.[38] Any proposed amendment to Article 22H(1) would thus only be subject to the usual constitutional amendment procedure,[39] and not a national referendum as required under Article 5(2A).

Unlike the Constitutions of Singapore and Malaysia, the Hong Kong Basic Law does not expressly confer upon the judiciary the right to exercise an advisory jurisdiction over constitutional matters. Nevertheless,

[37] [1995] 1 SLR 803 (Singapore Constitutional Reference Tribunal). [38] Ibid. 817.

[39] Pursuant to Article 5(2) of the Singapore Constitution, most constitutional provisions can be amended with the concurrence of at least two-thirds of the total number of elected legislators in Parliament.

the Court of Final Appeal (CFA) in *Democratic Republic of the Congo v FG Hemisphere*[40] had inferred an implied power to provide a provisional determination on constitutional matters falling under Article 158 of the Basic Law. Article 158 specifically provides that the Hong Kong courts are required, before making their final judgments, to seek an Interpretation from the Standing Committee of the National People's Congress (SCNPC) in Mainland China on any affairs falling within the responsibility of the Chinese Central People's Government. Nevertheless, the CFA held that Article 158 did not prevent the court from providing a provisional determination on the matter, subject to the Interpretation handed down by the SCNPC.[41] In that case, the CFA had to decide whether Hong Kong should observe the absolute doctrine of state immunity as practised in Mainland China or the restricted doctrine of state immunity as practised in Hong Kong prior to the hand-over. The CFA finally decided that this matter had to be resolved by the SCNPC as state immunity is an act of state,[42] a matter that falls within the legislative purview of the Central People's Government. Nevertheless, the court went on to provide a provisional assessment of why Hong Kong should observe the absolute doctrine of state immunity, arguably in the hope that this advisory opinion could subsequently guide the deliberation of the SCNPC on the matter.[43] This advisory, weak-form review is important because it paves the way for the CFA to offer its insights on those constitutional matters, which are technically out-of-bounds to the Hong Kong judiciary altogether, and nudge the SCNPC, where it so agrees with the CFA's conclusions, to endorse the reasoning offered in the provisional determination.[44]

B. Administrative Review

With the rise of the administrative state and the expansion of state powers via the creation of public bureaucracies, agencies, and tribunals whose exercise of powers can adversely and indelibly affect the citizenry's livelihood,

[40] (2011) 14 HKCFAR 95 (Hong Kong Court of Final Appeal). [41] Ibid. [398].

[42] Article 19(3) of the Basic Law provides: 'The courts of the Hong Kong Special Administrative Region shall have no jurisdiction over acts of state such as defence and foreign affairs.'

[43] See Albert Chen, 'The Congo Case: Introduction' (2011) 41 *Hong Kong Law Journal* 369, 371. See also Cora Chan, 'State Immunity: Reassessing the Boundaries of Judicial Autonomy in Hong Kong' [2012] *Public Law* 601.

[44] The Standing Committee of the National People's Congress handed down its Legislative Interpretation in August 2011, which was consistent with the provisional determination of the Hong Kong Court of Final Appeal. See *Democratic Republic of the Congo v FG Hemisphere Associates* (2011) 14 HKCFAR 395 (Hong Kong Court of Final Appeal).

administrative law principles have developed in tandem to ensure that the State observes basic ideas of fair play and good administration in such dealings.[45]

For jurisdictions with written constitutions that serve as the State's ultimate source of power, constitutional values, and concerns, as judicially conceived, more openly permeate the development of administrative principles, such that it would be erroneous and also impossible to posit a strict segregation between these two bodies of public law, as the varied strands of constitutional law and ordinary administrative law are inextricably interwoven.

Constitutional values can manifest in the administrative contexts in two ways. First, administrative constraints on the executive can be constitutionally *mandated*. Second, administrative law, as developed by the courts, can be constitutionally *inspired*. These constitutionally infused administrative principles can be termed sub-constitutional norms as the legislature retains a broad discretion to either reverse the judicial ruling or pursue the same substantive goals after observing certain procedural safeguards that the courts have imposed. As observed by Professor Gillian Metzger, the enforcement of constitutional concerns through 'ordinary administrative law preserves a degree of flexibility that better accommodates changing regulatory needs'[46] and the legislature's primacy in structuring government than 'more immutable constitutional law prescriptions do, and is also more likely to yield meaningful constraints'.[47]

Turning to the first interface between constitutional principles and administrative doctrines, we may note how common law courts have viewed some administrative constraints imposed on executive officials as constitutionally *required*.

The Singapore Court of Appeal decision in *Yong Vui Kong v Attorney General*[48] presents one such example. In that case, the Singapore judiciary had to decide *inter alia* whether the clemency power of the President over inmates on death row was justiciable; the Court of Appeal, in particular, had to decide whether the courts could review the Singapore ministerial cabinet advice to the President on how this clemency power should be exercised.

The Chief Justice, on behalf of a unanimous court, agreed that the courts would not review a clemency decision on the merits, but he went on to observe that there is nonetheless 'a constitutional duty on the Cabinet's part

[45] William Wade & Christopher Forsyth, *Administrative Law* (10th edn, Oxford, Oxford University Press 2009) 6–7.

[46] Gillian E Metzger, 'Ordinary Administrative Law as Constitutional Common Law' (2010) 110 *Columbia Law Review* 479, 485.

[47] Ibid. [48] [2011] 2 SLR 1189 (Singapore Court of Appeal).

to consider those materials *(relating to the clemency)* impartially and in good faith before it advises the President on the exercise of the clemency power'.[49]

According to Chief Justice Chan:

> It therefore follows that if, hypothetically speaking, conclusive evidence is produced to the court to show that the Cabinet never met to consider the offender's case at all, or that the Cabinet did not consider the... (clemency) materials placed before it and merely tossed a coin to determine what advice to give to the President... the Cabinet would have acted in breach... My conclusion that the clemency power is subject to judicial review may also be said to be a corollary of the right to life and personal liberty guaranteed by Art 9(1) of the Singapore Constitution, which provides that "[n]o person shall be deprived of his life or personal liberty save in accordance with law".[50]

Some critics may perhaps argue that the Singapore Court of Appeal has disabled executive/legislative prerogative to the extent that the Cabinet is now compelled to consider the clemency materials before it reaches a final decision. This may well be true, but this decision is still dialogic so far as the substantive norms so imposed do not interfere with the actual outcome that the Cabinet may reach during their deliberations, that is the Cabinet remains free to reject the applicant's appeal for clemency.

A similar position was reached by the Hong Kong Court of First Instance in *Ch'ng Poh v Chief Executive*.[51] Hartmann J (as he then was) so opined with regard to the Hong Kong Chief Executive's exercise of his prerogative of mercy:

> In my judgment, it would offend the Basic Law—and do so manifestly—if, for example, those advising the Chief Executive in respect of his discretion... were able with impunity to subvert the honesty of that advice on the basis of racial, sexual or religious grounds or were able with impunity to refuse to put before the Chief Executive evidential material which did not for whatever reasons suit their private ends... That is because the Basic Law, as a document of constitution that safeguards the rights and freedoms of all residents in Hong Kong in accordance with law (see: art. 4), does not permit such pollution of lawful process, executive or otherwise.[52]

To this end, the Hong Kong judiciary would intervene if the advice the Chief Executive received on how he or she should exercise the clemency power was compromised by bias[53] or relevant submissions were not accurately reported to him or her for deliberation.[54]

[49] Ibid. [82]. [50] Ibid. [83]–[84].
[51] [2003] HKEC 1441 (Hong Kong Court of First Instance). [52] Ibid. [37].
[53] Ibid. [66]. [54] Ibid. [94].

In the same vein, the Singapore Court of Appeal held in *Ramalingam Ravinthran v Attorney General*[55] that the Attorney General's exercise of his or her prosecutorial discretion was equally subject to judicial review. According to the unanimous court, the Attorney General's prosecutorial power was 'not immune to judicial correction where it has been exercised arbitrarily or in breach of constitutionally protected rights'[56] or 'for any extraneous purpose'.[57] While the Prosecution would be presumed to have been acting constitutionally, the court held that if the offender demonstrated, on the evidence before the court, that there was a *prima facie* breach of a fundamental liberty, the Prosecution would be required to justify its prosecutorial decision to the court or it would be found in breach of the fundamental liberty concerned.[58] This inherent limitation on the prosecutorial discretion was justified on the basis that the Singapore Constitution and the concomitant requirement of the rule of the law that 'all legal powers are subject to limits'.[59]

The judiciary in Malaysia has also expressed similar preferences for using the Constitution to restrain procedurally the conduct of executive officials. In *Hong Leong Equipment v Liew Fook Chuan*,[60] the Malaysian Court of Appeal held that the Minister of Labour and Manpower was constitutionally required to furnish reasons for his refusal to refer an industrial dispute to the Industrial Court for adjudication, even if the employment statute in question did not impose such a duty on him. According to Gopal Sri Ram JCA (as he then was):

> [A]s a general rule, procedural fairness, which includes the giving of reasons for a decision, must be extended to all cases where a fundamental liberty guaranteed by the Federal [Malaysia] Constitution is adversely affected in consequence of a decision taken by a public decision maker.[61]

The court justified this on the basis that a person's right to life and liberty as enshrined under Article 5(1) of the Malaysia Constitution[62] also encompassed one's right to his or her livelihood, and the State must observe procedural fairness in the discharge of its administrative functions as this constitutional clause implicitly required 'all state action to be fair and just'.[63] Herein, the Malaysian judiciary has deemed that executive officials are constitutionally

55 [2012] SGCA 2 (Singapore Court of Appeal). 56 Ibid. [17]. 57 Ibid. [51].
58 Ibid. [28]. 59 Ibid. [51].
60 [1996] 1 MLJ 481 (Malaysia Court of Appeal).
61 Ibid. 536–7. The Court conceded that in specific cases, national security, public safety, or other public interest considerations may exclude the application of such procedural fairness norms but such considerations were not applicable on the facts here.
62 Malaysia Constitution, Article 5(1) reads: 'No person shall be deprived of his life or liberty save in accordance with law.'
63 *Hong Leong Equipment* (n 60) 532.

required to observe certain procedural norms before they can make substantive decisions that impact the fundamental rights and liberties of the citizenry.

Constitutional values have also influenced and inspired the creation and development of other administrative law doctrines. Unlike the first interface between the two bodies of public law, the Constitution herein does not mandate the creation of these doctrines; instead, these doctrines are judicially devised so that certain constitutional law norms, for example separation of powers concerns, can be better vindicated.

A prime illustration is the judicial recognition of an administrative law doctrine in Malaysia that restrains the legislature from delegating 'excessive' legislative power to executive officials. In *Palm Oil Research & Development Board Malaysia v Premium Vegetable Oils*,[64] the Federal Court of Malaysia, the nation's court of final resort, had to decide, *inter alia*, whether certain subsidiary legislation was *ultra vires* the parent Act. On the facts, the statute in question empowered the Minister of Plantation and Commodities to impose a research cess on palm oil but the impugned subsidiary legislation enacted, pursuant to it, authorized the Minister to impose research cess on palm oil millers. According to Gopal Sri Ram, in his concurring opinion, there is a duty on the courts 'to ensure no excessive delegation take place';[65] therefore 'a provision in the statute conferring power on a member of the executive to enact subsidiary legislation must be construed strictly... particularly so where the subsidiary legislation is one that imposes a financial levy... upon the whole or any section of the public'.[66]

Herein, the narrow reading of the statutory authorization conferred upon the Minister to impose taxes was justified by the learned judge on the ground that this result would be more consistent with 'the doctrine of separation enshrined in the Federal Constitution'.[67] One must note that this judicial canon is sub-constitutional so far as it does not foreclose the legislature's choice of delegating specific taxing powers to executive officials; it merely requires the legislature to speak with clarity when it does so. In this way, this clear-statement rule can be properly understood as 'a species of judicial minimalism, indeed democracy-forcing minimalism, designed to ensure that judgments are made by the democratically preferable institution'.[68]

A more conscious recognition of how courts have assessed executive conduct in light of constitutional mandates and how courts have

[64] [2005] 3 MLJ 97 (Federal Court of Malaysia). [65] Ibid. [61]. [66] Ibid. [61].
[67] Ibid. [60].
[68] Cass Sunstein, 'Nondelegation Canons' (2009) 67 *University of Chicago Law Review* 315, 335.

developed administrative law doctrines in response to constitutional concerns will foster a culture of administrative constitutionalism whereby executive departments, agencies, and tribunals are encouraged to take into account constitutional values in their decision making.[69] Administrative review, imbued with constitutional ideals, is also dialogic so far as the legislature is not foreclosed from pursuing the same substantive goals if it so chooses, but lawmakers are compelled to observe certain fundamental procedural or substantive norms that promote good governance and fair play before they so act.

C. Common Law Liberties and Statutory Rights

The judicial recognition of common law norms that advances rights-protection and the robust interpretation of rights enshrined under statutory instruments presents another way which the courts can engage dialogically in a sub-constitutional fashion with the political branches of government. Both dialogic methods will be explored in turn.

Turning first to rights-adjudication under the common law, Professor Kent Roach has recognized that there are important continuities between the common law and dialogic constitutionalism.[70] Courts, in developing the common law, are commonly responding to legislative inertia, which can be viewed as an implied delegation of authority.[71] Nonetheless, this delegation of authority is revocable as the legislature can always reclaim the field by enacting ordinary legislation to overturn the judicial decision that is perceived to have gone awry. Therefore, so far as courts are willing to protect fundamental liberties with the use of common law principles that may be reversed by statute, dialogic review is engaged.

A prime example of how courts have developed the constitutional common law is the Singapore High Court decision of *Malcomson Nicholas Hugh Bertram v Naresh Kumar Mehta*,[72] where the common law tort of intentional harassment was first judicially conceived. On the facts, the defendant, a former employee of the two plaintiffs, had persistently harassed the latter by sending emails and mobile text messages to them over the course of one year. Despite the lacuna in the law as the Singapore legislature had at that time chosen not to provide for any statutory remedies against harassment, the Court herein held that 'the time has come in

[69] Metzger (n 46) 497.

[70] Kent Roach, *The Supreme Court on Trial: Judicial Activism or Democratic Dialogue* (Toronto, Irwin Law 2001).

[71] Kent Roach, 'A Dialogue about Principle and a Principled Dialogue: Justice Iacobucci's Substantive Approach to Dialogue' (2007) 57 *University of Toronto Law Journal* 449, 456.

[72] [2001] 4 SLR 454 (High Court of Singapore).

Singapore'[73] for the 'common law to respond to this need'[74] and vindicate the plaintiff's 'right to privacy'[75] by granting an injunction against the repetition of the above-mentioned conduct.

In the same vein, the Hong Kong courts have refined the existing contours of the common law to better reflect constitutional values. In *Cheng v Tse Wai Chun*,[76] the Hong Kong Court of Final Appeal (CFA) had to consider the applicability of the fair comment defence to the tort of defamation. Nevertheless, the CFA was cognizant that this tort necessarily implicated the freedom of expression, which the Chief Justice observed must be protected in its full vigour.[77] Therefore, the CFA unanimously decided that a comment which fell within the defence of fair comment would lose its immunity only by proof that the defendant did not genuinely hold the view he or she expressed.[78] Actuation by spite, animosity, intent to injure, or other motivation, even if it was the sole motive, did not of itself defeat the defence.[79]

This redefinition of malice for the purpose of negating the defence of fair comment was ground-breaking because, prior to this decision, the conventional wisdom in the Commonwealth suggested that the defendant would be deemed to have been actuated by malice if he or she had some improper or personal motive when he or she made the alleged defamatory statement. Nevertheless, the Chief Justice of Hong Kong justified this refinement to the tort of defamation on the following basis:

> In a society which greatly values the freedom of speech and safeguards it by a constitutional guarantee, it is right that the courts, when considering and developing the common law, should not adopt a narrow approach to the defence of fair comment... The courts should adopt a generous approach so that the right of fair comment on matters of public interest is maintained in its full vigour.[80]

One must however note that herein, even though the constitutional right to expression was engaged, the court vindicated this right with the use of common law principles, such that the legislature can reverse this modification to the law by statute, if it so chooses.

Aside from the robust development of the common law to reflect constitutional values, the Hong Kong courts have also engaged in sub-constitutional review when they interpret the Hong Kong Bill of Rights Ordinance[81]

[73] Ibid. 474. This Singapore decision was endorsed by the Hong Kong Court of First Instance as good law in *Lau Tat Wai v Yip Lai Kuen* [2013] 2 HKLRD 1197, and the Hong Kong judiciary therein also recognized a common law tort of harassment.

[74] Ibid. 472. [75] Ibid. 473.

[76] [2000] 3 HKLRD 418 (Hong Kong Court of Final Appeal). [77] Ibid. 344.

[78] Ibid. 360. [79] Ibid.

[80] [2000] 3 HKLRD 418 (Hong Kong Court of Final Appeal) 344.

[81] Bill of Rights Ordinance (Cap 383).

(BORO). Before China's resumption of sovereignty over Hong Kong in 1997, the BORO was passed in 1991 by the colonial government to 'bring home' the rights the British government acceded to in 1976 when it ratified the International Covenant on Civil and Political Rights and extended its application to Hong Kong.[82] This statute remains in force today in Hong Kong even though the Basic Law protects in parallel many of those same rights, for example the right to free expression, the right to assembly, and the right to equality. While most BORO rights are concurrently protected under the Basic Law as constitutional rights, the BORO also protects other rights that are not expressly protected in the Basic Law, for example the right to a fair hearing.[83] For these *exclusive* BORO rights, the protection of which are solely statutory in nature, the legislature retains the right to amend, via the ordinary processes, the scope and application of these rights, if it disagrees with any judicial determination. Therefore, where the courts adjudicate over these *exclusive* BORO rights, dialogic review is engaged.

The Hong Kong CFA decision in *Lam Siu Po v Commissioner of Police*[84] provides an illustration of how the judiciary engages in sub-constitutional review under the BORO. On the facts, a police constable argued that a blanket ban on professional legal representation at his disciplinary hearing by the relevant regulations violated Article 10 of the BORO, which *inter alia* enshrined his right to a fair hearing by an independent and impartial tribunal in the determination of his rights and obligations in a suit at law. Ribeiro PJ, on behalf of a unanimous court, decided that the judicial interpretation over Article 10 of the BORO should track European case law[85] on the comparable Article 6 of the European Convention on Human Rights,[86] which included generally the disciplinary hearings of civil servants within its protective ambit. On the facts, the CFA concluded that the disciplinary proceedings in the present case did amount to a determination of the constable's civil rights and obligations as the offence for which he was charged was 'normally terminatory';[87] and hence, he should have the right to a fair hearing. In determining what a fair hearing under Article 10 of the BORO would

[82] See Richard Swede, 'One Territory—Three Systems? The Hong Kong Bill of Rights' (1995) 44 *International and Comparative Law Quarterly* 358–78.

[83] Bill of Rights Ordinance (Cap 383), Article 10.

[84] [2009] 4 HKLRD 575 (Hong Kong Court of Final Appeal).

[85] See *Eskelinen v Finland* (2007) 45 EHRR 43 (European Court of Human Rights).

[86] Article 6(1) of the European Convention on Human Rights reads: 'In the determination of his civil rights and obligations or of any criminal charge against him, everyone is entitled to a fair and public hearing within a reasonable time by an independent and impartial tribunal established by law.'

[87] *Lam Siu Po* (n 84) [93].

require, the court opined that common law principles of procedural fairness would be applied. In the present case, the blanket exclusion of legal representation by the relevant subsidiary legislation was deemed unfair, in light of the severity of the charge and the potential penalty, and the impugned provisions were thus invalidated.[88] The CFA thus held that fairness would require the disciplinary tribunal to be given the discretion to permit legal representation in some circumstances.

In the same vein, the Hong Kong CFA in *Koon Wing Yee v Insider Dealing Tribunal*[89] held that the insider dealing proceedings heard by the Insider Dealing Tribunal involved the determination of a 'criminal charge', by reason of the Tribunal's power to impose fines for violations of the now-repealed Securities (Insider Dealing) Ordinance, even though the legislation in question classified these proceedings as civil in nature. Therefore, the accused was entitled to rights of criminal due process as conferred under Article 11[90] of the BORO when such proceedings were brought against them.

Lam Siu Po and *Koon Wing Yee* are significant illustrations that judicial review can operate dialogically under a statutory human rights scheme. So far as the CFA was only interpreting an exclusive BORO right, the legislature was free to disagree with either decision, via the ordinary processes, by amending the BORO and excluding civil servants or certain adjudicative tribunals from the statutory ambit. Therefore, where there is legislative inaction in the aftermath of these decisions, one can consider that the lawmakers have acquiesced to the continuing applicability of the principles judicially advanced. Yet, one must not undervalue the importance of such sub-constitutional rulings; a more robust judicial reading of rights bestows the benefit of legislative inertia upon the aggrieved political minority as they are now provided with a tangible remedy that takes the form of a recognized substantive/procedural right until and unless the legislature responds actively in disagreement.

D. Procedural Constitutional Rules

The judicial imposition of constitutional rules that are procedural in nature is another way by which the judiciary engages in dialogic review. In these circumstances, the impugned legislation is invalidated because there has been a procedural constitutional irregularity. Nevertheless, the legislature can still

[88] Ibid. [136]–[139].

[89] [2008] 3 HKLRD 372 (Hong Kong Court of Final Appeal).

[90] Bill of Rights Ordinance (Cap 383), Article 11 provides: 'Everyone charged with a criminal offence shall have the right to be presumed innocent until proved guilty according to law.'

pursue the same substantive ends again after complying with the constitutional procedures judicially conceived. In this way, procedural constitutional rules can be perceived as mere 'resistance norms'[91] that impose soft limits on the legislative right to achieve the legislature's substantive goals.[92]

One such example is when courts recognize and enforce implied constitutional procedural rights that are not expressly provided in the Constitution. This occurred in the Malaysian Federal Court decision of *Lee Kwan Woh v Public Prosecutor* where the nation's court of final resort adopted an expansive reading of Article 5(1) of the Malaysian Constitution, which provides that no person shall be deprived of his life or personal liberty save in accordance with law. Gopal Sri Ram FCJ, on behalf of the unanimous court, read Article 5(1) to mean that no one may be deprived of his life or liberty save in accordance with state action that was 'procedurally fair'.[93] In a criminal case, the Court held that this would mean that 'an accused has a constitutionally guaranteed right to receive a fair trial'.[94] On the facts, the trial judge denied the accused the opportunity of submitting that he had no case to answer at the close of the prosecution's case; and according to the Federal Court, this irregularity violated the implied constitutional right to a fair trial provided under Article 5(1).

This decision is noteworthy on two counts. First, the Federal Court had adopted a robust and extra-textual reading of the enshrined constitutional liberties by recognizing an implied right to a fair trial when the Malaysian Constitution does not expressly provide for this. Second, this activist judicial stance can nevertheless be considered dialogic so far as the State is not deprived of the right to prosecute and incarcerate an offender for any substantive offence it seeks to criminalize; the same substantive ends can still be pursued after the State complies with the judicially imposed procedural constitutional rules.

Another important illustration of a procedural constitutional norm follows from the constitutional requirement in Hong Kong that Ordinances infringing upon constitutional rights be 'prescribed by law'.[95] The Hong Kong courts have read this constitutional limitation to mean that any rights-infringing legislation must be adequately accessible to the public and

[91] See Ernest Young, 'Constitutional Avoidance, Resistance Norms, and the Preservation of Judicial Review' (2000) 78 *Texas Law Review* 1549.

[92] See also Aileen Kavanagh, 'Reasoning about Proportionality under the Human Rights Act 1998: Outcomes, Substance and Process', (2014) 130 *Law Quarterly Review* 235.

[93] *Lee Kwan Woh v Public Prosecutor* (2009) 5 MLJ 301 (Federal Court of Malaysia), 315.

[94] Ibid.

[95] Article 39 of the Basic Law provides: 'The rights and freedoms enjoyed by Hong Kong residents shall not be restricted unless as prescribed by law.'

sufficiently certain/precise so that the citizenry can regulate their conduct and affairs.[96]

Yet, one must note that this judicial limitation on legislative powers does not foreclose lawmakers from achieving the same legislative aim again. Constitutional invalidations on this basis can be perceived as a judicial remand to the legislature, such that lawmakers are forced to return to the drawing board and express their legislative views more clearly and explicitly before they seek to achieve a statutory result that threatens to intrude upon fundamental constitutional values.

The key case that illustrates this principle would be *Leung Kwok Hung v HKSAR*.[97] On the facts, the Hong Kong CFA had to consider the constitutionality of various statutory provisions that conferred on the Commissioner of Police the discretion to object to or impose conditions on a pre-notified public procession if he or she considered that such restrictions were necessary in the interests of public order (ordre public). The court eventually held that the legislative purpose of 'public order (ordre public)', which was statutorily undefined, was too wide and vague a term, such that no 'adequate indication of the scope of that discretion'[98] was conferred on a 'public official who was part of the executive authorities which of course stand in a fundamentally different position from that of an independent judiciary'.[99] Therefore, the nebulous term 'ordre public' was judicially severed and read out from the statute. One must note however that the CFA's ruling does not actually foreclose the legislature from pursuing the same substantive goals again; if the Legislative Council in Hong Kong so wanted, the lawmakers could have attempted to statutorily define 'ordre public' in clear explicit terms such that the conferral of this particular discretion on the police commissioner could arguably survive another constitutional challenge. But the Hong Kong legislature, after deliberation, responded by formally repealing the term 'ordre public' from the impugned statute in 2008.

Procedural constitutional rules therefore serve as a judicial brake on legislative excesses that may transpire when lawmakers are negligent or when they act in haste. Such sub-constitutional rules do not disable the government from achieving any particular substantive goals but merely slow down the processes by which the impugned legislative/executive decisions are taken, so that the re-formulated policies can adhere more closely to fundamental constitutional norms.

[96] *Shum Kwok Sher v Secretary of Justice* (2002) 5 HKCFAR 381 (Hong Kong Court of Final Appeal) 402.

[97] (2005) 8 HKCFAR 229 (Hong Kong Court of Final Appeal).

[98] Ibid. 264.

[99] (2005) 8 HKCFAR 229 (Hong Kong Court of Final Appeal).

E. Rational Basis Review

The application of rational basis review is another doctrinal tool by which courts impose soft constitutional limits on the legislature. In such instances, courts will defer to the legislative justification for any perceived rights-infringement, and uphold the impugned statute in question, whenever there is a rational basis for doing so.

This model of judicial deference is generally justified on the basis that the legislature or executive may have superior expertise and knowledge, vis-à-vis the judiciary, to assess certain polycentric issues that affect a large number of disparate interests, such that they are more likely than the judiciary, on epistemic grounds, to determine these constitutional questions correctly.[100] This is not to say that courts should always defer to legislative determinations of rights-compatibility; for indeed, where the rights-limitation in question is substantial or severe, a heightened level of judicial scrutiny is warranted, even if such an intrusion interferes with legislative or executive policy choices on these polycentric issues.[101] The central focus of my argument herein is not to offer a normative defence of judicial deference per se or to decide when deference is most appropriate.[102] Instead, my claim is more modest, for I am simply arguing that where courts have independently decided to apply rational basis review over certain legislative or executive actions, they are granting significant latitude to the political branches to pursue the constitutional course of action they want. In so doing, the judiciary is being sensitive to the role that the legislature or the executive can play in determining the optimum level of rights-protection in any legal system, such that a dialogic model of rights-protection can ensue.

A noteworthy illustration of rational basis review would be the Singapore Court of Appeal's decision in *Public Prosecutor v Taw Cheng Kong*.[103] On the facts, the accused argued that an anti-corruption statutory provision, which imposed extraterritorial criminal liability only on Singapore citizens, violated his right to equality under the Constitution. The Court of Appeal unanimously disagreed and held that when Parliament sought to impose criminal liability extraterritorially, it was 'rational to draw the line at citizenship and leave out non-citizens so as to observe international comity',[104] since state practices generally argue against the regulation of the

[100] See also Alison Young, 'In Defence of Due Deference' (2009) 72(4) *Modern Law Review* 554.

[101] See Rivers (n 27).

[102] See Young (n 100) and Aileen Kavanagh, 'Defending Deference in Public Law and Constitutional Theory' (2010) 126 *Law Quarterly Review* 222.

[103] [1998] 2 SLR 410 (Singapore Court of Appeal).

[104] Ibid. 434.

subjects of other sovereign powers outside one's jurisdiction.[105] In applying rational basis review over this differentiating legislation that implicated foreign relations, the court emphasized that the judiciary 'must not lose sight that Parliament, in enacting such laws, may be confronted with other practical constraints or considerations which the courts are in no position to deal with'.[106]

In the same vein, the Hong Kong courts have generally deferred to the legislature over the constitutionality of various differentiating measures present in social welfare legislations. In *Fok Chun Wa v Hospital Authority*,[107] the Hong Kong CFA upheld a governmental policy that denied non-Hong Kong residents subsidized medical services at public hospitals. The court noted that this differentiating measure on the basis of residency status did not strike at the heart of 'core values relating to personal or human characteristics (such as race, colour, gender, sexual orientation, religion, politics, or social origin)',[108] such that the court would only examine whether this policy was 'manifestly beyond the spectrum of reasonableness'.[109] On the facts, the court observed that the imposition of a residence requirement before one can be entitled to subsidized public health care was rational in view of Hong Kong's limited public resources. This level of judicial scrutiny was also justified on the basis that 'the executive and the legislature are better equipped than the courts'[110] in assessing the range of competing considerations on fiscal matters.

Courts, in framing doctrinal rules, often seek to 'minimize the sum of error costs and administrative costs',[111] that is they would seek to minimize both the costs of erroneous decisions, including their own, and the administrative costs of implementing a particular doctrinal rule. Rational basis review is an example of one such doctrinal rule, whereby courts take into account their institutional capabilities during constitutional adjudication and adopt a posture of deference when judges labour under conditions of epistemic uncertainty. Rational basis review is equally a dialogic tool, as whenever courts appreciate that the political branches, in light of their expertise or experience, are more qualified to determine certain polycentric constitutional questions correctly, the judiciary is effectively granting them significant leeway and discretion in the making of these substantive decisions.

[105] *Treacy v DPP* [1971] AC 537 (HL) 561. [106] *Taw Cheng Kong* (n 103) 437.

[107] *Fok Chun Wa v Hospital Authority* (2012) 15 HKCFAR 409 (Hong Kong Court of Final Appeal).

[108] Ibid. [77]. [109] Ibid. [76]. [110] Ibid. [81].

[111] David Strauss, 'The Ubiquity of Prophylactic Rules' (1988) 5 *University of Chicago Law Review* 190, 193.

F. Delayed Declarations of Invalidity

Even when courts deem certain legislative actions unconstitutional, judges can still engage in dialogic review when they issue delayed declarations of invalidity, instead of specific injunctions, as the constitutional remedy of choice. In particular, Professor Kent Roach has observed how the Supreme Court of Canada has increasingly suspended the immediate application of its declarations of invalidity, so that the government is given 'an opportunity to engage in policy-making, by deciding which of a range of multiple constitutional options would be implemented in light of the court's ruling'.[112] This judicial willingness to sanction delay and allow an unconstitutional state of affairs to persist serves twofold advantages. First, the suspension avoids any legal uncertainty or chaos that may result in the community, if there is an immediate vacuum or gap in the law, as the unconstitutional statute will remain in place until the suspension order expires or a remedial legislation is put in place. Second, a suspended declaration gives the legislature, rather than the courts, the opportunity to make the initial selection on how best to comply with the constitutional mandates among those competing alternatives available, such that due deference is paid to the primacy of the legislature's lawmaking role.[113]

While I concede that such temporary suspension orders are not dialogic so far as the courts have deemed certain legislative/executive actions out-of-bounds; nevertheless, so far as the judiciary consciously provides lawmakers with ample legislative space to re-decide for themselves how best to comply with the court's mandate, a constitutional dialogue can still ensue.

Of the three Asian common law jurisdictions, the Hong Kong judiciary is the only court to date that has formally issued a temporary suspension order. In *Leung Kwok Hung v Chief Executive of Hong Kong*,[114] the Court of Appeal invalidated a statutory provision that previously allowed the Chief Executive, whenever he or she considered that public interest so required, to order the interception or disclosure to the government of any telecommunications, and the Court also struck down an accompanying Executive Order that laid out the administrative procedures for the conduct of authorized covert surveillance. Upon further appeal, the CFA was solely asked to

[112] See Kent Roach, 'Remedial Consensus and Dialogue under the Charter: General Declarations and Delayed Declarations of Invalidity' (2002) 35 *University of British Columbia Law Review* 211, 212.

[113] See Bruce Ryder, 'Suspending the Charter' (2003) 21 *Supreme Court Law Review* (2d) 267, 285.

[114] [2006] HKEC 816 (Hong Kong Court of Appeal).

determine the appropriate remedy for addressing the unconstitutional state of affairs.[115] Concerned that an immediate invalidation of the impugned procedures would unduly hamper legitimate covert surveillance activities, the CFA, inspired by its Canadian counterpart, suspended its declaration of invalidity. Bokhary PJ, on behalf of the CFA, held that this judicial power to suspend the operation of a declaration arose from the inherent jurisdiction of the courts and was 'concomitant of the power to make the declaration in the first place'.[116] Equally significantly, the CFA refused to compel the government to bring into force a pre-existing but inoperative legislation that sought to regulate the interception of some forms of communications as the judges preferred to 'enable the authorities to decide what course they wish to take'.[117] Therefore, the suspension order not only provides latitude to the government in deciding how best to respond to the court's decision, it also gives time to the legislature to devise corrective legislation.

In the same vein, the Hong Kong Court of First Instance in *Chan Kin Sum v Secretary of Justice*[118] granted a suspension order after it invalidated a blanket legislative ban on the prisoners' right to vote as unconstitutional. The court acknowledged that the electoral disenfranchisement of prisoners prevented crime by sanctioning the conduct of convicted prisoners and provided incentives for the citizenry to exercise civic responsibility.[119] Notwithstanding the legitimate aims that the government was seeking to pursue, the court noted that the impugned legislative ban was disproportionate as all prisoners were barred from voting, regardless of the nature and severity of the offences or even the length of the custodial sentences.[120] Even prisoners on suspended sentences or released on parole were barred from voting. Nevertheless, the court was willing to suspend its declaration of invalidity for about seven months as the learned judge considered that the legislature would 'legitimately require and deserve a reasonable period of time to work out a replacement arrangement, whatever it may be'.[121] On the facts, the court refused to determine what type of voting restrictions would pass constitutional muster or 'where the cut-off line should be drawn and how it should be drawn'[122] as it is the function of the legislature and 'not the function of the courts to say

[115] *Koo Sze Yiu & another v Chief Executive of Hong Kong* [2006] 3 HKLRD 455 (Hong Kong Court of Final Appeal).

[116] Ibid. [35].

[117] Ibid. [59] (concurring opinion by Sir Anthony Mason, Non Permanent Judge).

[118] [2009] HKEC 393 (Hong Kong Court of First Instance).

[119] *Chan Kin Sum v Secretary of Justice* [2009] 2 HKLRD 166 (Hong Kong Court of First Instance) [88].

[120] Ibid. [112].

[121] *Chan Kin Sum* (n 118) [79].

[122] *Chan Kin Sum* (n 119) [165].

what would constitute reasonable restrictions in Hong Kong'.[123] This decision was therefore dialogic as the court had remanded the electoral issue to the legislature such that it could 'reply to the court's decision with one of a wide range of constitutional options available to it'.[124] In 2009, the Hong Kong Legislative Council, after deliberation, responded by repealing *all* restrictions on prisoners' right to vote, thus achieving a result that went beyond what was mandated in *Chan Kin Sum*.

Most recently, in the landmark decision of *W v Registrar of Marriages*,[125] a majority on the Hong Kong CFA ruled that the Registrar of Marriages, in applying the existing matrimonial legislation in Hong Kong that prohibited a post-operative male-to-female transsexual from marrying in the capacity of her acquired gender, had violated her constitutional right to marriage as protected under Article 37 of the Basic Law. Notwithstanding this constitutional finding, the CFA issued a temporary suspension order that gave the Hong Kong legislature one year to reform this area of law.[126] In particular, the CFA recognized that legislative intervention would be beneficial so that there could be comprehensive and holistic reforms following this decision 'in areas which include (apart from marriage and parenting) entitlement to benefits and pensions, discrimination, succession, the position of trustees administering trusts, sport, the application of gender-specific offences and recognition of foreign gender change and marriage'.[127]

The judicial grant of a suspension order may force the lawmakers to review a piece of legislation at a time, and within time limits not of its choosing. But this sub-constitutional ruling creates space for continued governmental and legislative policy-making, without purporting to mandate either the details of the legislative sequels or the processes that will be used to formulate those parliamentary replies.[128] As a result, the suspension of a declaration of invalidity remains an essential instrument of 'remedial dialogue'[129] between the judiciary and the legislature, and also the society at large.

III. Conclusion

In the above discussion, I have elaborated upon six different forms of sub-constitutional doctrines that the Asian courts can deploy. Each tool is dialogic as it allows the courts to play an active role in advancing human rights concerns, but it also preserves a substantial degree of legislative flexibility

[123] Ibid. [124] Roach (n 112) 219.
[125] [2013] 3 HKLRD 90 (Hong Kong Court of Final Appeal). [126] Ibid. [150].
[127] Ibid. [143]. [128] Roach (n 112) 221. [129] Ibid.

that better accommodates the political branches' primary role in governance than quasi-immutable substantive constitutional prescriptions do. But the tools also vary so far as they facilitate dialogue and operationalize a division of labour with the legislature in different ways.[130] In a sense, the dialogic nature of each sub-constitutional tool can be placed on a continuum that measures the 'robustness' of the judicial review associated with its deployment: the first dialogic tool, advisory review, embodies the least robust form of judicial review and the sixth technique, delayed declarations of invalidity, manifests the most robust type of dialogic review.

Advisory review is the weakest form of review as the legislature can simply ignore the provisional or advisory determinations of the judiciary, if the former so chooses. This tool is dialogic as lawmakers are under no legal compulsion to obey the court's mandate. Administrative review and the judicial enforcement of common law and statutory rights are more robust forms of review as the legislature has to overturn actively the court's determination by legislation. But these judicial techniques are still dialogic in nature, as the legislature may reclaim the field with the passage of an ordinary statute. These doctrines may impose additional enactment costs on the legislature if it disagrees with the judicial decisions in question; but after deliberation and careful consideration, 'the better-informed government decision-makers will only be willing to act when their true interest in the policy is sufficiently strong'.[131] The fourth tool, procedural constitutional rules, embodies an even more robust form of review as it involves the invalidation of a piece of legislation. But because this rule is procedural in nature, this technique is dialogic as courts are merely *slowing down* the legislative or executive decision-making processes as the political branches retain the right to pursue the *same substantive goals* as before, but they may do so only after they comply with certain crucial constitutional norms that underscore substantive principles of fair play and good administration. In other words, by deploying this tool, the judiciary is not precluding the legislature from achieving their primary statutory aims; the lawmakers can still legislate on the same substantive matter, but they may do so after observing certain procedural norms. The fifth tool, rational basis review, allows for courts to reject certain *substantive* determinations made by lawmakers. To the extent that this tool allows for courts to interfere with some substantive goals of the legislature, judicial review of this nature is more robust. But it would be myopic to dismiss the dialogic

[130] See also Dimitrios Kyritsis, 'Proportionality as a Constitutional Doctrine' (2014) 34 *Oxford Journal of Legal Studies* 395.

[131] Matthew Stephenson, 'The Price of Public Action: Constitutional Doctrine and the Judicial Manipulation of Legislative Enactment Costs' (2008) 118 *Yale Law Journal* 2, 11.

value of rational basis review by focussing only on laws that have been invalidated under this standard of review *ex post.* Instead, one must remember that where the judiciary is adopting an *ex ante* posture of deference to the legislative determination, such that the courts would only intervene when the legislature acts irrationally, lawmakers would have retained a lot of discretion to pursue the statutory goals they want in the first place. Dialogue occurs when judges decide modestly. Finally, the judicial issue of delayed declarations of invalidity may mean that the impugned legislation in question is unconstitutional, but so far as the legislature is provided with the opportunity and flexibility to choose from an array of statutory options when it seeks to rectify the flawed legislation, lawmakers are still given significant discretion and space to craft the new law they want. Therefore, while the six sub-constitutional tools may exist on different points on a single spectrum measuring the robustness of the judicial engagement, they are all dialogic in nature but to varying degrees; some tools allow the legislature to ignore/overrule the judicial ruling completely while others facilitate dialogue by granting the lawmakers significant room to legislate on comparable and/or related matters. Overall, all these sub-constitutional tools are dialogic as every one of them leaves legislative space, to varying degrees, for the lawmakers to respond actively, as opposed to merely yielding, to the judiciary's conception of rights. When courts deploy any of the above-mentioned judicial techniques, inter-branch dialogue can be upheld and fostered as the lawmakers are never wholly excluded from the legislative field, for they always retain significant latitude to harness the ordinary political process to pursue statutory goals that are related and/or comparable to their original ones. In this way, lawmakers are treated not as mere scribes of judges, but as participants in an enduring constitutional colloquy. And this is the essence of a constitutional dialogue between co-equal branches of government.

Moreover, as discussed in Chapters 3 and 4, the judiciary in each jurisdiction discussed above operates within a constitutional system dominated by a semi-permanent party/coalition in government. Therefore, the application of dialogic sub-constitutional tools is also the politically expedient way for the courts to engage in a valuable but less-confrontational conversation with the legislative and executive branches about the requisites of a constitutional democracy. The fundamental point is that, in deciding constitutional cases, the common law courts in Asia should and do create constitutional doctrines that take into account both the substantive values reflected in the relevant constitutional provisions and the institutional realities inherent within the legal system.[132]

[132] See also Strauss (n 111) 207.

Sub-constitutional rules foster dialogue with the political branches by appealing to a kind of judicial minimalism. Courts, in applying many of these rules, are seeking to leave open the more fundamental and difficult constitutional questions, and to decide these issues on narrower statutory, common law, or administrative grounds that do not foreclose legislative intervention; and this in turn promotes democratic accountability for the decisions reached.[133] Therefore, the use of these doctrines cultivates judicial modesty and moderation, and also safeguards the court's institutional legitimacy vis-à-vis the other political branches of government.[134] By remaining responsive to each other's unique contributions and the distinctive values that each branch of government brings to this joint project of governance,[135] the courts and the political branches of government are thus viewed as collaborators in a common enterprise to promote public welfare.

[133] Cass Sunstein, *One Case at a Time: Judicial Minimalism on the Supreme Court* (Cambridge, Harvard University Press 1999) 5.

[134] Stephenson (n 131) 39.

[135] Dimitrios Kyritsis, 'Constitutional Review in Representative Democracy' (2012) 32 *Oxford Journal of Legal Studies* 297.

6

Freedom of Expression

For centuries, political philosophers and legal scholars have advanced various separate but overlapping arguments for respecting the citizenry's right to free expression.[1] The argument from truth contends that a free and open public debate is essential to driving out falsehoods and misinformation in society. This 'truth-seeking' function of free speech is commonly associated with the writings of JS Mill who had argued that censorship inhibits the advancement of human knowledge as all censors are prone to err and the determinations of truth and falsity are thus better off left to the general public.[2] In the same vein, United States Supreme Court Justice Oliver Holmes had contended that 'the best test of truth is the power of thought to get itself accepted in the competition of the market'.[3] The argument from personal autonomy and self-realization contends that the freedom of expression is valued on the basis that it respects individuals by allowing them to form their own opinions about their beliefs/actions,[4] and this freedom helps them fulfil their life goals by developing their capacity for thought and judgement.[5] Finally, the argument from democracy contends that 'the principle of freedom of speech springs from the necessities of the programme of self-government'.[6]

[1] For a comprehensive overview of these rationales, see Eric Barendt, *Freedom of Speech* (Oxford, Oxford University Press 2005); Richard Moon, *The Constitutional Protection of Freedom of Expression* (Toronto, University of Toronto Press 2000).

[2] John Stuart Mill, *On Liberty*, ed. Elizabeth Rapaport (1st edn, Indianapolis, Hackett Publishing Company 1859). See also John Milton, *Areopagitica*, Order of the Long Parliament for the Regulating of Printing, 14 June 1643, A Speech for the Liberty of Unlicensed Printing: 'And though all the winds of doctrine were let loose to play upon the earth, so truth be in the field, we do injuriously by licensing and prohibiting to misdoubt her strength. Let her and falsehood grapple; who ever knew truth put to the worse, in a free and open encounter.'

[3] *Abrams v United States* 250 US 616 (1919) (United States Supreme Court) 630.

[4] Thomas Scanlon, 'A Theory of Freedom of Expression' (1972) 1 *Philosophy and Public Affairs* 204.

[5] Martin Redish, 'The Value of Free Speech' (1982) 130 *University of Pennsylvania Law Review* 591, 592. See also Jospeh Raz, 'Free Expression and Personal Identification' in Wil Waluchow (ed), *Free Expression: Essays in Law and Philosophy* (Oxford, Clarendon Press 1994) 13.

[6] Alexander Meiklejohn, *Free Speech and its Relation to Self-Government* (New York, Harper Brothers 1948) 27.

According to this argument, democracy requires its citizenry to be free to receive all information that may affect their voting choices; consequently, all speech relating to this right to collective self-determination must enjoy paramount protection.[7]

While these principal justifications for free speech are compelling, each theory, in itself, does not provide an adequate philosophical foundation for the legal developments and judicial ethos in the Asian common law jurisdictions under study, or, for that matter, in any legal system. This is because all three justifications for free speech are premised on assumptions that rarely hold true in the real world. True ideas may be vindicated in the long term. But, in the short run, the citizenry may be 'overwhelmed by the inexhaustible supply of freshly minted, often very seductive, false ideas',[8] and this is especially so if the average individual lacks the informational capacity or tools to differentiate truth from falsehood. The marketplace of information is also skewed in favour of those with the financial means and/or pecuniary incentives to buy access. Autonomy-based arguments are premised on the assumption that the freedom to speak is an aspect of the individual's autonomy that he or she retains upon entering the social world, but one must note that the value we attach to the freedom of expression makes sense only if we 'recognize that the creation of meaning (the articulation of ideas and feelings) is a social process, something that takes place between individuals and within a community';[9] and that this liberty cannot thus be wholly insulated from the demands of society's collective welfare and commitments. The argument from democracy is premised on the assumption that issues relating to the governmental processes form the core of the citizenry's concerns. Political expression is therefore prized above all other forms of expressions—notably scientific, artistic, or even intimate expressions, which may, in reality, be equally central to the aspirations of an individual.

In view of the adverse consequences that may follow from the citizenry's unbridled exercise of free speech, all governments have, to varying degrees, sought to regulate the level of free expression permissible in their respective states. Even within common law Asia, the jurisdictions are not the same, either with regard to the level of intrusiveness to which the governments have sought to limit free speech or in the intensity of review that their courts

[7] For an expression of this view, see Wojciech Sadurski, *Freedom of Speech and its Limits* (Dordrecht, Kluwer 1999) 20–1.

[8] Harry Wellington, 'On Freedom of Expression' (1979) 88 *Yale Law Journal* 1105, 1130.

[9] Richard Moon, *The Constitutional Protection of Freedom of Expression* (Toronto, University of Toronto Press 2000) 21.

apply when they examine the legality of governmental regulation over the citizenry's expression.

In these Asian territories under review, Hong Kong's position is most aligned with the practices commonly found in many Western democracies today. This liberal model of free speech is also one that is based in large part on 'a distrust of governmental determinations of truth and falsity, an appreciation of the fallibility of political leaders, and a somewhat deeper distrust of governmental power in a more general sense'.[10] In contradistinction to Hong Kong, Singapore's system of free speech advocates communal respect for politicians and public institutions as there is a perceived paramount community interest in protecting the institutional integrity of the state apparatus and the reputation of its leaders who are deemed to be trustworthy and honourable governors. This model of free speech also echoes a contemporary strain of cultural relativism in human rights discourse that rejects the perceived Western overemphasis on individual rights, as it is contrary to traditional Asian ideas of morality that prioritize a person's responsibility to his or her family and the community over the exercise of his or her individual liberties.[11] Finally, Malaysia, in view of the series of legislative and judicial innovations adopted in the last decade, as discussed below, can be placed on an intermediate point between the two models.

In this chapter, I shall examine the contemporary adjudicatory approach of the common law courts of Hong Kong, Malaysia, and Singapore in free speech disputes. In view of the prudential constraints that the judges face in these jurisdictions, as I have discussed more fully in Chapter 4, I shall argue that their courts can engage in soft dialogic review by protecting the right of free expression through the use of common law and/or administrative law doctrines. As discussed earlier in Chapter 5, these sub-constitutional rules, such as administrative review and the judicial enforcement of common law norms, appeal to a kind of judicial minimalism as courts, in applying these techniques, are seeking to leave open the more fundamental and difficult constitutional questions, and are deciding issues on narrower common law or administrative grounds that do not foreclose legislative intervention; and this, in turn, promotes democratic accountability for the judicial decisions reached.[12]

[10] Frederick Schauer, *Free Speech: A Philosophical Enquiry* (Cambridge, Cambridge University Press 1982) 86.

[11] See Parliament of Singapore, *Shared Values* (White Paper, Paper Cmd 1, 1991). For a discussion, see Li-ann Thio, *A Treatise on Singapore Constitutional Law* (Singapore, Academy Publishing 2012) 104–20.

[12] Cass Sunstein, *One Case at a Time: Judicial Minimalism on the Supreme Court* (Cambridge, Harvard University Press 1999) 5.

Specifically, I shall examine three different forms of free-speech disputes that have most commonly come before all three common law Asian courts. In Section I, I shall examine the law on defamation. Section II will continue with an analysis on the law on contempt of court. Finally, in Section III, I shall analyse the regulatory restrictions on public assemblies. In every section, I shall contrast and critique the legal position in each jurisdiction and examine how the courts can apply dialogic tools of administrative and 'common law' review to reform the law in each of these areas. Herein, the judicial use of these two sub-constitutional dialogic tools would be most appropriate to resolve the constitutional controversies in question as all these disputes pertain to a common law tort/offence or the exercise of power by administrative officials. Therefore, judges would be acting in a dialogic and minimalist fashion if they resolve the conflicts within the very same *situs* and forum that these disputes arose from, and avoid entrenching a constitutional rule that would disable the legislature from responding, short of a constitutional amendment.

I. Defamation

In every jurisdiction, its law on defamation seeks to balance the speaker's right to express himself or herself against his or her target's reputational rights. While one's reputational interest is not expressly recognized as a constitutional right in Singapore, Malaysia, or Hong Kong, it is generally accepted that its protection serves a legitimate public interest, as one's reputation is considered to be intimately connected with one's honour, dignity, and even one's economic value.[13] The common law courts of Singapore, Malaysia, and Hong Kong, however, all differ in the specific way they seek to balance the competing interests of free speech and reputational worth, and it is to these judicial approaches that we now turn.

We begin our analysis by first examining the state of affairs in Hong Kong and, in particular, the applicability of the *Reynolds* defence of 'qualified privilege' for reports on matters of public interest. This privilege was first mooted by the House of Lords in *Reynolds v Times Newspapers*[14] and it provided for a defence to an action in defamation if the defendants had engaged in responsible journalism. Specifically, Lord Nicholls in *Reynolds* identified

[13] Robert Post, 'The Social Foundations of Defamation Law: Reputation and the Constitution' (1986) 74 *California Law Review* 691.

[14] [2001] 2 AC 127 (HL). On the facts, the plaintiff, a former Irish Taoiseach, sued The Sunday Times for several allegedly defamatory statements published in a report.

ten non-exhaustive factors that courts would take into account when deciding whether the publisher of the impugned statements had acted responsibly:

> 1. The seriousness of the allegation…2. The nature of the information, and the extent to which the subject matter of a publication is a matter of public concern. 3. The source of the information…4. The steps taken to verify the information. 5. The status of the information…6. The urgency of the matter…7. Whether comment was sought from the plaintiff…8. Whether the article contained the gist of the plaintiff's side of the story. 9. The tone of the article…10. The circumstances of the publication (including its timing).[15]

The Hong Kong Court of Appeal in *Blakeney-Williams v Cathay Pacific Airways*[16] applied the *Reynolds* criteria. But it equally heeded the caution issued by the House of Lords in the post-*Reynolds* decision of *Jameel v Wall Street Journal Europe*[17] that the Nicholls ten-part test should not be seen as 'a series of hurdles to be negotiated by a publisher before he or she can successfully rely on qualified privilege';[18] otherwise, such a restrictive approach would defeat the spirit of *Reynolds*, the purpose of which was to usher in a new robust age of free speech for 'public interest' commentary. What had happened was that Cathay Pacific Airways had released several press statements accusing the plaintiffs of being bad employees and of not caring for the interests of the company and Hong Kong. The Hong Kong Court of Appeal decided that the defendant could not avail itself of the *Reynolds* defence as the airlines had not acted responsibly and fairly in making those defamatory statements, especially since the defendant was 'aware it had no concrete evidence to support any case of misconduct'[19] against the plaintiffs. Nevertheless, in recognizing the 'importance of the freedom of expression',[20] the Hong Kong Court of Appeal also held that 'the Reynolds defence was available not only to the press and broadcasting media but also to anyone who published through the mass media'.[21] Interestingly, the Court of Appeal purported to rely on the Privy Council's pronouncement in *Seaga v Harper*[22] for the above proposition;

15 Ibid. 205. 16 [2011] 1 HKLRD 901 (Hong Kong Court of Appeal).

17 [2007] 1 AC 359 (HL). In that case, the House of Lords agreed that *The Wall Street Journal* Europe could rely on the *Reynolds*-type defence of qualified privilege when it alleged that the bank accounts belonging to the claimants were being monitored by the Saudi Arabia central bank for potential terrorist ties. Specifically, the Law Lords emphasized that the defendant's failure to obtain the claimant's comments prior to the article's publication was not fatal to the defence as the subject matter therein was of great public interest, the publisher had sought to verify the accuracy of its contents, the article was unsensational in tone, and the general thrust of the article was true.

18 *Jameel* (n 17) 377 (Lord Bingham), 384 (Lord Hoffmann). See also *Blakeney-Williams* (n 16) [141].

19 *Blakeney-Williams* (n 16) [158]. 20 Ibid. [141]. 21 Ibid. [139].

22 [2008] 3 WLR 478 (Privy Council of Jamaica). On the facts, the Deputy Commissioner of Police in Jamaica sued the Leader of the Opposition for slander when the latter made defamatory statements about the former in the course of a public speech. The Privy Council however agreed

but, in reality, the Privy Council had actually laid down a proposition with a wider ambit—the Privy Council would allow the *Reynolds* privilege to 'extend to publications made by any person who publishes material of public interest in *any medium*'.[23] Arguably, under the rule in *Seaga*, even if a defendant's defamatory remarks were not reported by the mass media, he or she could still avail himself or herself of the *Reynolds* privilege.

In any case, credit must be given to Hong Kong for advancing the contours of the common law, by taking the lead in developing its tort of defamation in a more speech-friendly manner.[24] The landmark decision in question was the Court of Final Appeal case of *Cheng v Tse Wai Chun*.[25] The plaintiff in question, Tse Wai Chun, a solicitor, brought an action in libel against Albert Cheng and Lam Yuk Wah, two radio talk-show hosts who had allegedly defamed him on the airwaves. The defendants *inter alia* relied on the defence of fair comment but the plaintiff argued that this defence was defeated by malice. Prior to this ground-breaking decision, it was generally accepted by legal commentators that a defendant would be regarded to have been actuated by malice if he or she had some improper or ulterior motive when making the impugned statement.[26] Lord Nicholls (a Non-Permanent Judge on the Court of Final Appeal) in this ground-breaking case however disagreed:

> A comment which falls within the objective limits of the defence of fair comment can lose its immunity only by proof that the defendant did not genuinely hold the view he expressed. Honesty of belief is the touchstone. Actuation by spite, animosity, intent to injure, intent to arouse controversy or other motivation, whatever it may be, even if it is the dominant or sole motive, does not of itself defeat the defence.[27]

Given that the defendant has to prove that his or her comments must be ones which could have been made by an honest person[28] to avail himself or herself of the defence in the first place, it would appear that he or she would only lose the defence if the plaintiff can later prove that the defendant is subjectively dishonest, that is the defendant knows that his or her comments

with the trial judge that the defendant had failed to take sufficient care to check the reliability of his information, and thus was unable to rely on the *Reynolds* defence.

[23] Ibid. [11].

[24] This Hong Kong Court of Final Appeal decision and its reformulation on the test of malice have since been adopted by the English judiciary in *Branson v Bower (No 2)* [2002] 2 WLR 452 (QB).

[25] [2000] 3 HKLRD 418 (Hong Kong Court of Final Appeal). For an interesting discussion of this decision, see Jill Cottrell, 'Fair Comment, Judges and Politics in Hong Kong' (2003) 27 *Melbourne University Law Review* 33 and FA Trindade, 'Malice and the Defence of Fair Comment' (2001) 117 *Law Quarterly Review* 169–75.

[26] See Patrick Milmo & W V H Rogers, *Gatley on Libel and Slander* (9th edn, London, Sweet & Maxwell 1998) [16.2] and *Halsbury's Laws of England* (4th edn, Reissue) vol 28, p 78, para 149.

[27] *Cheng* (n 25) 438. [28] Ibid. 425.

are untrue, or is recklessly indifferent to the truth or falsity of his or her comments.[29]

According to Lord Nicholls, the rationale for liberalizing the 'fair comment' defence stems from the fact that politicians and social reformers will inevitably have ulterior motives or agendas in making comments of public interest and it will make no sense if 'a motive relating to the very feature which causes the matter to be one of public interest is regarded as defeating the defence'.[30] Therefore, the objective safeguards imposed by the fair comment defence, coupled with the need to have a genuine belief in what is said, would be adequate to keep the ambit of permissible comment within reasonable bounds.[31]

In his concurring opinion, the Chief Justice of Hong Kong held that in considering and developing the common law, 'it is right that the courts . . . should not adopt a narrow approach to the defence of fair comment'[32] as Hong Kong is 'a society which greatly values the freedom of speech and safeguards it by a constitutional guarantee'.[33]

Turning to Malaysia, the courts have been equally receptive to the liberalizing trends in free speech laws. The contemporary developments in Malaysia arose from a politically charged dispute between the plaintiff, Anwar Ibrahim, a former Deputy Prime Minister of Malaysia who had been dismissed by the defendant, then Prime Minister Mahathir. Specifically, Anwar sued Mahathir in defamation after the latter revealed in an interview that the former was fired because he had engaged in homosexual conduct. The High Court[34] found for the defendant, stating that he could avail himself of the defence of qualified privilege. Interestingly, the trial judge cited with approval both the High Court of Australia decision of *Lange v ABC*[35] and the New Zealand Court of Appeal decision of *Lange v Atkinson*.[36] One must however note that these cases in fact impose significantly different requirements that one has to satisfy before one can avoid liability in a defamation action; under *Lange v ABC*, the defendant must have acted reasonably when making the alleged defamatory statement(s);[37] under *Lange v Atkinson*, a defence would be available so long as one honestly believes in the truth of those statement(s), and it is irrelevant whether one has been negligent.[38] Unfortunately, the High Court did not seek to resolve this inconsistency, nor did it examine whether the defendant's

[29] *Cheng* (n 25) 429. [30] Ibid. 430. [31] Ibid. 430. [32] Ibid. 422.
[33] Ibid. 422.
[34] *Anwar bin Ibrahim v Mahathir bin Mohamad* [1999] 4 MLJ 58 (High Court of Malaysia).
[35] (1997) 189 CLR 520 (High Court of Australia).
[36] [1988] 3 NZLR 424 (High Court of New Zealand). [37] *Lange v ABC* (n 35) 574.
[38] *Lange v Atkinson* (n 36) 469–70.

making of the allegedly defamatory statement was in fact reasonable. On appeal, the Court of Appeal accepted the trial judge's ruling on the defence of qualified privilege, but only referred to *Lange v Atkinson* in doing so.[39] The Federal Court of Malaysia refused leave for further appeal but the Chief Justice on behalf of the unanimous court opined as follows in its refusal for leave:

> On qualified privilege, we also find the learned trial judge had applied the correct test and law to the facts and circumstances of the case. In fact the correct authority on qualified privilege in the context of the respondents' defence is Lange v Australian Broadcasting Corporation . . . and not Lange v Atkinson.[40]

Since the Federal Court decision in *Anwar v Mahathir*, the lower courts in Malaysia have diverged partially on the ambit of the qualified privilege defence. Some have strictly followed the Federal Court's observations and applied *Lange v ABC*.[41] Others have applied the House of Lords decision in *Reynolds* instead.[42] One must however note that on matters concerning political libel, there is no material difference between *Lange v ABC* and *Reynolds*. After all, the requirement of reasonableness imposed in *Lange v ABC* closely mirrors Lord Nicholls' *Reynolds* criteria.[43] As observed by the High Court of Australia in *Lange*:

> [A]s a general rule, a defendant's conduct in publishing material giving rise to a defamatory imputation will not be reasonable unless the defendant had reasonable grounds for believing that the imputation was true, took proper steps, so far as they were reasonably open, to verify the accuracy of the material and did not believe the imputation to be untrue. Furthermore, the defendant's conduct will not be reasonable unless the defendant has sought a response from the person defamed (if any) except in cases where the seeking or publication of a response was not practicable or it was unnecessary to give the plaintiff an opportunity to respond.[44]

[39] *Anwar bin Ibrahim v Mahathir bin Mohamad* [2001] 1 MLJ 305 (Malaysia Court of Appeal).

[40] *Anwar bin Ibrahim v Mahathir bin Mohamad* [2001] 2 MLJ 65 (Federal Court of Malaysia) [5].

[41] *Anwar v The New Straits Times* [2010] 2 MLJ 492 (High Court of Malaysia). On the facts, Anwar, the Leader of the Malaysian Opposition in Parliament sued the *New Straits Times*, a Malaysian daily, for alleging that he had close ties with a controversial American lobby group. The *Lange* defence failed on the facts.

[42] *Sivabalan a/L P Asapathy v The New Straits Times Press* [2010] 9 MLJ 320 (High Court of Malaysia); *YB Hj Khalid bin Abdul Samad v Datuk Aziz bin Isham* [2012] 7 MLJ 301 (High Court of Malaysia).

[43] See also Andrew Kenyon & Ang Hean Leng, 'Reynolds Privilege, Common Law Defamation and Malaysia' [2010] *Singapore Journal of Legal Studies* 256.

[44] *Lange v ABC* (n 35) 574.

Nevertheless, it is conceded that the *Reynolds* defence is wider so far as it applies to all communications of public interest while the *Lange* defence is only applicable to communications about 'government and political matters'.[45]

In contradistinction to Hong Kong and Malaysia, we turn to Singapore and, in particular, its Court of Appeal decision of *Review Publishing Co v Lee Hsien Loong*,[46] which remains the last word on the subject matter in Singapore. On the facts, various Singapore Cabinet Ministers, which included the Prime Minister of Singapore, sued Far Eastern Economic Review and its publisher, Review Publishing Company, in defamation for publishing certain statements that implied the ministers were corrupt in the discharge of their public office. The Court of Appeal had to decide, *inter alia*, whether the *Reynolds* defence was applicable in Singapore. On the facts, the Court of Appeal opined that the rationale behind the *Reynolds* privilege stemmed from 'a right based on a constitutional or higher legal order foundation';[47] and since Article 14 of the Singapore Constitution only accorded the right of free speech to Singapore citizens, the foreign defendants could not avail themselves of the *Reynolds* defence, even if it was applicable.

Nevertheless, the Court of Appeal went on to provide various significant observations on how the common law of defamation may develop in Singapore in the future. First, the court noted that any development that is based on a 'liberalizing intention' will only benefit Singapore citizens.[48]

Second, the court acknowledged that it was open to the judiciary to develop the common law of defamation and the Constitution does not preclude the courts from doing so.[49] This observation may seem unremarkable but it is actually an important concession from the court. Previously, the Singapore Court of Appeal, in an earlier defamation case of *Jeyaretnam Joshua Benjamin v Lee Kuan Yew*,[50] refused to accept *New York Times v Sullivan*[51] and *Lingens v Austria*[52] as good law in Singapore on the basis that, *inter alia*, the framers of the Singapore Constitution intended for the 'continuation of the laws existing at the time of independence as the Constitution and laws of Singapore ... thus against this background ... it is implicit that the right of free speech under Art 14 is subject to the

[45] Ibid. 571. [46] [2010] 1 SLR 52 (Singapore Court of Appeal).

[47] *Reynolds* (n 14) 208 (Lord Steyn). [48] *Review Publishing* (n 46) [268].

[49] Ibid. [270]. [50] [1992] 1 SLR 791 (Singapore Court of Appeal).

[51] (1964) 376 US 254 (United States Supreme Court). In *Sullivan*, the United States Supreme Court held that a public figure can only successfully sue under the tort of defamation if he can prove that the defendant had acted with actual malice.

[52] (1986) 8 EHRR 407 (European Court of Human Rights). In *Lingens*, the European Court of Human Rights held that a public figure must display greater tolerance for public criticism and the impugned law that required defendants to prove the truth of both assertions of fact and opinion,

common law of defamation'.[53] It is not patently obvious what the Court of Appeal in *Jeyaretnam Joshua Benjamin* was suggesting herein, but arguably it was adopting an originalist understanding of the Singapore Constitution: the local judiciary would not develop the common law of defamation in Singapore in tandem with the United States Supreme Court or the European Court of Human Rights as the pre-existing parameters of this tort (and its defences) were 'undoubtedly intended by the framers of [Singapore's] Constitution';[54] and therefore, whatever practices that were constitutional at the time of Singapore's independence must be deemed constitutional today. However compelling this originalist argument may be, it flies in the face of Article 162 of the Singapore Constitution, which expressly provides that all pre-existing laws must be construed as from the commencement of the Constitution with 'such modifications, adaptations, qualifications and exceptions as may be necessary to bring them into conformity' with it. Therefore, the Court of Appeal in *Review Publishing* must be right that the Singapore courts are empowered to modify and develop the parameters of the common law tort of defamation so as to ensure its compliance with the citizenry's constitutional right to free expression.

Third, so far as the Singapore court intends to develop the common law of defamation, the Court of Appeal held that it must do so 'in keeping with Singapore's prevailing political, social, and cultural values';[55] and the onus is on the proponents of change to 'produce evidence of a change in [Singapore's] political, social and cultural values in order to satisfy the court that change is necessary so as to provide greater protection against the existing law of defamation'.[56] In essence, what the court meant by this was that it would observe any liberalizing political trends initiated by the ruling government[57] to decide whether the judiciary should move in tandem to accord more latitude on the citizenry to speak freely on matters of public interest.

Finally, and most interestingly, the Court of Appeal observed that the *Reynolds* privilege can be applied in Singapore but not as a complete defence that excuses the defendant from all liability. Instead, the court so opined:

The Reynolds rationale can equally be given effect by holding the defendant liable for defamation but adjusting the quantum of damages payable, with the exact amount to be paid in each case being calibrated by the court in proportion to the degree of care which the defendant has taken (or failed to take) to ensure that what he publishes is "accurate and fit for publication".[58]

and which provided that it was no defence to prove that the statement was made without malice, was thus deemed an unnecessary restriction of the right to free expression.

[53] *JBJ v Lee Kuan Yew* (n 50) [58].
[54] Ibid.
[55] *Review Publishing* (n 46) [270].
[56] Ibid. [273].
[57] *Review Publishing* (n 46) [274].
[58] Ibid. [297].

In other words, even if the defendant could not avail himself or herself of a complete defence if he or she satisfies the 'responsible journalism' test laid out in *Reynolds*, the fulfilment of these criteria would be a mitigating factor when the court assesses the quantum of damages payable to the plaintiff.

This novel application of the *Reynolds* privilege in Singapore would have marked a modest advancement in the country's rights discourse but for the Court of Appeal's subsequent pronouncement in *Lim Eng Hock v Lin Jian Wei*,[59] a decision handed down about a year after *Review Publishing*, which practically took all the wind out of its sails.

In *Lim Eng Hock*, the Court of Appeal had to consider the quantum of damages payable in a defamation suit and it went on to opine the following:

> Public leaders are generally entitled to higher damages also because of their standing in Singapore society and devotion to public service. Any libel or slander of their character with respect to their public service damages not only their personal reputation, but also the reputation of Singapore as a State whose leaders have acquired a worldwide reputation for honesty and integrity in office.[60]

Previously, in *Jeyaretnam Joshua Benjamin v Lee Kuan Yew*, the Court of Appeal rejected the public figure doctrine recognized in *New York Times v Sullivan* and *Lingens* as the judiciary was adamant that persons holding public office in Singapore were 'equally entitled to have their reputations protected as those of any other persons'.[61] Now, in *Lim Eng Hock*, the Court of Appeal not only would not accord individuals greater latitude to criticize public officials, it has now turned this 'public figure' doctrine on its head[62] by conferring upon these officials a windfall when they successfully establish a claim in defamation.[63]

Interestingly, in defence of its decision, the Court of Appeal in *Lim Eng Hock* held that the quantum of damages awarded to date to these Singapore public officials 'cannot be said to be unreasonable or excessive'[64] if one compared the damages awarded in Singapore with that in England.[65] Yet, this comparison with the awards in England is misconceived. In England, so far

59 [2010] 4 SLR 357 (Singapore Court of Appeal).

60 *Lim Eng Hock* (n 59) [12].

61 *JBJ v Lee Kuan Yew* (n 50) [62].

62 See Tsun Hang Tey, 'Singapore's Jurisprudence of Political Defamation and its Triple-Whammy Impact on Political Speech' [2008] *Public Law* 452.

63 See *Lim Eng Hock* (n 59) [15], [16].

64 Ibid. [22]. In Singapore, the Prime Minister has been awarded up to S$500,000 in damages for a single defamation suit. Members of Parliament have been awarded up to S$210,000 in damages for a single defamation suit.

65 In *Lim Eng Hock* (n 59) [19], the Singapore Court of Appeal noted that in England, Jeffrey Archer had been awarded 500,000 pounds in damages for defamation, while George Galloway, a Member of Parliament, had been awarded 150,000 pounds in a separate libel suit.

as the defendant can establish that he or she satisfies the *Reynolds* 'responsible journalism' test, he or she would have a complete defence to an action in defamation. Therefore, in a sense, the claimant in England is fully entitled to the high sums awarded precisely because the defendant has failed to exercise due care when making the defamatory statement(s). However, in Singapore, the defendant can still be liable in defamation even if he or she has exercised the requisite standard of care imposed under *Reynolds.* Hence, it would be patently unfair for the Singapore judiciary to impose a comparable level of damages for defamation as that awarded in England when the threshold for succeeding in a libel suit is so much lower in Singapore.

If we read *Review Publishing* alongside *Lim Eng Hock*, we may notice a curious state of affairs. The defendant may now have his or her quantum of damages payable reduced if he or she satisfies the *Reynolds* criteria; but if the claimant in question is a public leader, these damages would be concurrently enhanced. As far as the right to free speech is concerned, it would seem that the court gives and the court has taken away.

In view of the above comparative analysis on the law of defamation, it is evident that Singapore is an outlier. The restrictive approach of the Singapore courts to public interest commentary is reflective of the ruling government's ethos towards the press. Unlike the Hong Kong press, which is subject to very limited governmental regulation,[66] the Singapore government exercises extraordinary control over the print media. In Singapore, the Newspaper and Printing Presses Act requires a person to first obtain a licence before he or she can print, publish, or circulate a newspaper in Singapore and this licence can be refused or withdrawn by the Minister of Information and the Arts (retitled Minister of Communications and Information in 2012) at his or her discretion.[67] Furthermore, any newspaper that publishes in Singapore must create two classes of shares, an ordinary share and a management share. Each management shareholder has 200 times the voting rights of an ordinary shareholder[68] over any resolution relating to the appointment/dismissal

[66] In Hong Kong pursuant to the Registration of Local Newspapers Ordinance Cap 268 (ROLNO), every local newspaper must be registered with the Registrar of Newspapers, but there is no governmental vetting in the registration process except to the extent that the name of a proposed newspaper cannot be identical to that of another newspaper already registered. There is generally no restriction on the proprietor of a local newspaper from acquiring an interest in any company without the approval of the relevant authority, or vice versa, nor does the ROLNO restrict foreign share-holding in a local newspaper. As for Malaysia, the Printing Presses and Publications Act (Laws of Malaysia Act 301) requires anyone who prints, imports, publishes, or circulates any newspaper in Malaysia to obtain a licence. This licence may be refused or revoked by the Minister of Home Affairs but his decision is subject to judicial review. Unlike Singapore, there is no statutory requirement on a newspaper to create management shares.

[67] Singapore's Newspaper and Printing Presses Act (Cap 206), ss 21, 22.

[68] Singapore's Newspaper and Printing Presses Act (Cap 206), s 10(11).

of a director or any staff member of the newspaper company, and the former share type can only be owned by Singapore citizens or corporations that have been approved by the same Cabinet Minister.[69] Singapore's heavy-handed approach towards press regulation[70] in particular and public expressive conduct in general is emblematic of the ruling party's belief that 'the concept of government by honourable men who ... have the trust and respect of the population fits [Singapore] better than the Western ideas that a government should be given as limited powers as possible, and should always be treated with suspicion unless proven otherwise'.[71]

The Singapore judiciary has equally endorsed these sentiments. As observed by the Court of Appeal in *Review Publishing*:

> [T]here is no room in our political context for the media to engage in investigative journalism which carries with it a political agenda ... Our local political culture places a heavy emphasis on honesty and integrity in public discourse on matters of public interest, especially those matters which concerns the governance of this country.[72]

To this end, the Singapore judiciary has been quick to discount the relevance of the *Reynolds* privilege to Singapore as this privilege was developed against the backdrop of the European Convention on Human Rights, of which Singapore obviously is not a signatory.[73] Yet, as discussed above, it is not just the Western liberal democracies that have evolved in this liberalizing fashion, as even semi-authoritarian democracies, like Malaysia and Hong Kong, have found the *Reynolds* privilege applicable to their local circumstances. Particularly, while the Malaysian courts have equally required 'a high standard of caution to be exercised by the media as responsible media',[74] they have nonetheless considered it appropriate for Malaysia to 'move with the times'[75] and have recognized the *Reynolds* privilege as 'a reasonable and proportionate response to the need to protect reputation while sustaining the public exchange of information that is vital to modern Malaysian society'.[76] Given that Singapore is such an outlier in its protection of free speech among not

[69] Ibid. s 10(1)(c).

[70] See Tsun Hang Tey, 'Confining the Freedom of the Press in Singapore: A 'Pragmatic' Press for 'Nation Building?' (2008) 30 *Human Rights Quarterly* 876; Jothie Rajah, *Authoritarian Rule of Law: Legislation, Discourse and Legitimacy in Singapore* (Cambridge, Cambridge University Press 2012) 117–51.

[71] Singapore, *Shared Values* (White Paper, Paper Cmd 1, 1991) para 41. See also Thio Li-ann, 'Between Apology and Apogee, Autochthony: The "Rule of Law" Beyond the Rules of Law in Singapore', [2012] *Singapore Journal of Legal Studies* 269.

[72] *Review Publishing* (n 46) [272].

[73] See ibid. [261].

[74] *YB Hj Khalid bin Abdul Samad* (n 42).

[75] *Sivabalan A/L P. Asapathy* (n 42) [37].

[76] Ibid.

just Western common law jurisdictions but also Asian ones, the onus surely must be on its courts to justify why Singapore's socio-political conditions justify the rejection of the *Reynolds* defence, rather than have the proponents of change 'satisfy the court that change is necessary'.[77]

The Singapore judiciary may perhaps believe that the country is exceptional in its heavy emphasis on the honesty and integrity of public discourse, and therefore fears that a more robust protection of free speech would allow false aspersions to affect the public officials' discharge of their duties[78] or 'deter sensitive and honourable men from seeking public positions of trust and responsibility, and leave them open to others who have no respect for their reputation'.[79] This might well be true, but as Professor Michael Hor has observed:

> This rather bleak picture of would-be politicians and holders of public office scurrying away from the light of adverse publicity is a startling indictment of [Singapore's] "honourable men". One would have thought that they would be made of sterner stuff. Moreover, the picture is not complete. It fails to show that if less than honourable men gain public office, the public may never know their true colours without a firm protection of speech concerning public affairs.[80]

Furthermore, it is not self-evident how the recognition of the *Reynolds* defence would lead to dishonest or irresponsible journalism taking root in Singapore. This qualified privilege is premised on the assumption that the speaker must have acted responsibly in verifying the truth of his or her statements before publication and according his or her target a right of reply. Moreover, the recognition of this defence is unlikely to affect the reputations of public leaders adversely since local commentators have observed that all the defendants in the key (and controversial) defamation cases decided in Singapore within the last decade would have failed to avail themselves of this defence anyway, even if it was applied on the facts.[81]

[77] *Review Publishing* (n 46) [273].

[78] *Goh Chok Tong v JBJ* [1997] 3 SLR 46 (High Court of Singapore) [25].

[79] See *JBJ v Lee Kuan Yew* (n 50) [64], citing Philip Lewis, *Gatley on Libel and Slander* (8th edn, London, Sweet & Maxwell 1981) 206.

[80] Michael Hor, 'The Freedom of Speech and Defamation: *JBJ v Lee Kuan Yew*' [1992] *Singapore Journal of Legal Studies* 542, 555.

[81] David Tan, 'The Reynolds Privilege in a Neo-Confucianist Communitarian Democracy: Reinvigorating Freedom of Political Communication in Singapore' [2011] *Singapore Journal of Legal Studies* 456. The Court of Appeal in *Review Publishing* (n 46) [258] also accepted that the *Reynolds* defence was unlikely to succeed on the facts as the impugned article did not contain the claimants' side of the story nor did the publishers seek the claimants' comments before publication.

As recognized by Professor Frederick Schauer, the political branches of government are comparatively poorer at regulating speech than they are at regulating other forms of conduct, as they have a personal interest in preserving the existing governmental structures and have the most to lose from attacks against their authority.[82] Therefore, the onus surely must be on the judiciary to initiate reforms that seek to extend the scope of free speech, as the other branches of government would have few incentives to do so on their accord. The development of common law norms thus provides a significant opportunity for the courts to advance rights-protection in a dialogical fashion. In this regard, the courts may have catalysed change or upset the status quo, but one must note that the legislature is not disabled from harnessing the ordinary political process to displace this common law *Reynolds* defence if it disagrees so adamantly with the judiciary. All the judiciary would have done, by recognizing this defence, is that they have foisted the burden of inertia on the legislature such that the onus is now on Parliament to actively reverse course and depart statutorily from the common law norms if it so chooses. In the absence of any explicit statutory derogation, the legislature can be presumed to have acquiesced to this judicially imposed default rule.

To this end, the Singapore judiciary should follow in the footsteps of its Malaysian and Hong Kong counterparts, and embrace the *Reynolds* qualified privilege defence. So far as the government adamantly disagrees with this development, the law is easily revocable as the legislature can always reclaim the field by enacting ordinary legislation to overturn the judicial decision. In this way, the courts and the political branches of government may be viewed as joint-collaborators in the general promotion of public welfare; any rights-disagreement between the institutions must not be regarded as a cacophonous power struggle,[83] but rather as a dynamic colloquy that celebrates the inter-branch coordinate construction of constitutional liberties.

Furthermore, even if the Singapore courts are convinced that the country's unique socio-political culture does justify some departure from Malaysia or Hong Kong law, it could perhaps accept the *Reynolds* defence in principle but 'accord different emphasis to each of the *Reynolds* factors—for example, an allegation of corruption against a senior public official, which is a very serious charge, must be counterbalanced by, *inter alia*, thorough steps taken to verify the information...and a publication of the plaintiff's side of the story'.[84] In

[82] Frederick Schauer, *Free Speech: A Philosophical Enquiry* (Cambridge, Cambridge University Press 1982) 81–2.

[83] Jeff King, 'Institutional Approaches to Judicial Restraint' (2008) 28 *Oxford Journal of Legal Studies* 409, 428

[84] Tan (n 81).

the alternative, the court could disregard the House of Lords' caution in *Jameel* and require the defendant to fulfil *all* of Lord Nicholls' *Reynolds* factors before he or she can successfully invoke the defence. The adoption of such proposals, though imperfect, would be a vast improvement from the current position in Singapore law, where the satisfaction of the *Reynolds* criteria is merely recognized as a mitigating factor when the court assesses the damages payable.

II. Contempt by Scandalizing the Judiciary

Traditionally, the common law has recognized two general categories of contempt of court. Back in 1900, Lord Russell observed in *R v Gray* as follows:

> Any act done or writing published calculated to bring a Court or a judge of the Court into contempt, or to lower his authority, is a contempt of Court. That is one class of contempt. Further, any act done or writing published calculated to obstruct or interfere with the due course of justice or the lawful process of the Courts is a contempt of Court.[85]

The former class belongs to the contempt category generally characterized as scandalizing a court or judge and the latter category of contempt includes (1) conduct that disrupts the court process itself, for example contempt in the face of court; or (2) acts that risk prejudicing or interfering with current/pending legal proceedings ('sub judice contempt'); or (3) disobedience of court orders as well as breach of undertakings given to the court.

It is this contempt by scandalizing the judiciary that raises the greatest free speech concerns. Unlike the latter category where the defendant's conduct directly impacts the administration of justice by affecting the *outcome* or *resolution* of specific (current or pending) legal disputes, scandalizing contempt is viewed as a public wrong merely because this conduct undermines the general public confidence in the administration of justice.

The authoritative decision in Singapore on scandalizing the judiciary would be the Court of Appeal decision in *Shadrake Alan v Attorney General*.[86] In that case, the court held that the British author of *Once a Jolly Hangman: Singapore Justice in the Dock* had made nine statements in his book that scandalized the court. This decision is particularly noteworthy for the following reasons.

First, the Singapore Court of Appeal accepted that for this form of contempt to be established, it would suffice if the defendant had intended the

[85] [1900] 2 QB 36 (QB) 40.

[86] [2011] 3 SLR 778 (Singapore Court of Appeal).

publication.[87] The defendant did not have to intend further to undermine the public's confidence in the administration of justice.

Second, the Court of Appeal established that the impugned statement must however pose a 'real risk' of undermining public confidence in the administration of justice before contempt can be found.[88] In so doing, the Court of Appeal overruled a long line of lower court decisions dating from the High Court case of *Attorney General v Wain Barry,* which accepted that the offending statements need only have the 'inherent tendency to interfere with the administration of justice'.[89]

Third, the Court of Appeal in *Shadrake* also established that 'fair criticism, may be better viewed as going towards the issue of liability, rather than constituting independent defences as such'.[90] In other words, the onus would now be on the Prosecution to prove beyond reasonable doubt that the impugned statement(s) did not constitute fair criticism, as opposed to the speaker bearing the burden of discharging this defence on a balance of probability.[91] More importantly, the Court of Appeal accepted that 'an imputation of judicial impartiality or impropriety is not *ipso facto* scandalizing contempt'.[92] In so doing, the Court of Appeal was implicitly overruling another long line of lower court precedents that decided that statements questioning the independence, impartiality and integrity of the courts could never amount to fair criticism.[93] This is an important and laudable development since most allegedly contemptuous statements, by their very nature, call into question the independence, impartiality, and integrity of courts; limiting the scope of fair criticism so narrowly would render this right nugatory.[94]

What is however unfortunate about *Shadrake* is the way the Court of Appeal applied the 'real risk' test. The Court of Appeal held that this inquiry is a simple one:

> [I]s there, having regard to the facts as well as surrounding context, a "real risk" that public confidence in the administration of justice is—or would be—undermined as a result of the impugned statement?[95]

Yet, in applying the test to the facts in question, the Court of Appeal seemed to have assessed the actual or potential impact of the impugned statements on the average reasonable reader by only looking at how unfair or untrue the statements were.[96] In other words, notwithstanding its protestations to

[87] *Shadrake Alan* (n 86) [23]. [88] Ibid. [57].
[89] *AG v Wain Barry* [1991] 1 SLR 85 (High Court of Singapore) [54].
[90] *Shadrake* (n 86) [15]. [91] Ibid. [78]. [92] Ibid. [84].
[93] See *AG v Lingle* [1995] 1 SLR 199 (High Court of Singapore) [13]; *AG v Hertzberg Daniel* [2009] 1 SLR 1103 (High Court of Singapore) [54].
[94] *Shadrake* (n 86) [84]. [95] Ibid. [30].
[96] Ibid. [100], [109], [121]–[122], [127], [130]–[131].

the contrary, the court was merely looking at the offending allegations in isolation from the other factual circumstances, beyond the assertions and innuendos of the publication.

In fact, the High Court in *Wain Barry* had examined the surrounding context beyond the actual publication when deciding whether the impugned statements were contemptuous. In particular, the High Court examined the repute of the publication in which the statements appeared, the standing and influence of the author/publisher, and the circulation of the publication.[97] These factors are highly relevant as contemptuous statements written by eminent authors in reputable publications with wide circulations are more likely to influence readers and have a more tangible risk of undermining the public's general confidence in the administration of justice than rants by unknown authors in obscure publications with limited circulation. On the facts in *Wain Barry*, the offending article was published in the *Asian Wall Street Journal*, a financial newspaper of international repute that enjoyed a wide circulation in Asia, and the author of the statements was none other than the President of Dow Jones himself. In sharp contrast, *Once A Jolly Hangman* was written by a little known British journalist, published by an obscure Malaysian publishing house and copies of the book were only sold for a brief period in Singapore.[98] Notwithstanding the vitriolic nature of the attacks against the judiciary, it is patently unclear how these impugned statements, in light of the surrounding context of its publication, would have a real risk of undermining the average reasonable person's confidence in the administration of justice in Singapore.

Turning to Hong Kong, we may observe another interesting state of affairs. The leading case on contempt by scandalizing the judiciary would be the Hong Kong Court of Appeal decision of *Wong Yeung Ng v Secretary of Justice*.

In that case, Mortimer V-P (who wrote the lead judgment) confirmed that in deciding whether such conduct was criminally actionable, the government must show that:

> [T]he statement (or conduct) was calculated to interfere with the administration of justice in its widest sense, that it involved a "real risk" that the due administration of justice would be interfered with and (the mental element) that there was an intention to interfere with the administration of justice, or recklessness by appreciating this possible consequence and ignoring it.[99]

[97] *Wain Barry* (n 89) [61]–[62].

[98] The Attorney General of Singapore had advised bookstores in Singapore that carried copies of the book to seek legal counsel and, as a result, copies of the book had been taken off the shelves. See *AG v Shadrake* [2011] 2 SLR 506 (High Court of Singapore) [31].

[99] [1999] 2 HKLRD 293 (Hong Kong Court of Appeal) 312.

This is a most interesting development. Most common law jurisdictions merely require the alleged offender to have intended the publication in question for the element of *mens rea* to be satisfied.[100] Now, in a significant and laudable departure from general Commonwealth trends, the court would actually require the offender to intend to interfere with the administration of justice or recklessly disregard the consequences of his or her actions.

In deciding whether the *actus reus* element was satisfied, that is whether there was a real risk that public confidence would be undermined by an alleged offender's conduct, the Hong Kong Court, unlike the Singapore Court of Appeal decision in *Shadrake*, also rightly looked to the surrounding context, outside of the publication itself, to make this determination. Relevant factors that the court examined included the timing of publication, size of the publication audience, and the likely nature, impact, and duration of the publication's influence.[101]

On the facts, the editor of the Oriental Daily News, a highly popular daily newspaper in Hong Kong with 2.3 million readers, was convicted on two counts of contempt of court for authorizing a series of abusive and scurrilous attacks (including racist slurs) over the course of three months against the Obscene Articles Tribunal, several named justices, and the Hong Kong judiciary at large. The attacks ultimately culminated in a round-the-clock pursuit of a particular judge for three days. The contempt in question was highly exceptional and egregious, and the court was undoubtedly right that such actions would have a real risk of undermining the public's confidence in the administration of justice.

Since *Wong Yeung Ng*, there have however been troubling signs that the Hong Kong judiciary has become somewhat uncomfortable with the *mens rea* requirement established by Mortimer V-P. In two subsequent Court of First Instance decisions, the judges expressly stated that the offence of contempt by scandalizing the court 'does not require proof of an actual intention to undermine public confidence in the administration of justice'[102] and merely that the 'publication was intentional'.[103] While this reversion to traditional orthodoxy may seem worrying, one must note that, on the facts, the scurrilous attacks against the judiciary were either made in court or made in connection with a pending or current legal proceeding.[104] Therefore, unlike

[100] See *Ahnee v DPP* [1999] 2 AC 294 (Privy Council); *Solicitor General v Radio Avon* [1978] 1 NZLR 225 (New Zealand Court of Appeal).

[101] *Wong Yeung Ng* (n 99) 329.

[102] *Secretary for Justice v Choy Bing Wing* [2005] HKEC 1971 (Hong Kong Court of First Instance) [48].

[103] *Secretary for Justice v Choy Bing Wing* [2011] HKEC 63 (Hong Kong Court of First Instance) [37].

[104] See *Secretary for Justice v Choy Bing Wing* (n 102) [70]; *Secretary for Justice v Choy Bing Wing* (n 103) [25].

the facts in *Wong Yeung Ng* where there was no attempt made to 'influence the outcome of particular proceedings either pending or in progress',[105] the later conduct in question may be better viewed as acts done calculated to obstruct or interfere with the due course of justice or the lawful process of the courts, the second type of contempt observed by Lord Russell in *R v Gray*,[106] as discussed above.

Finally, in Malaysia, we may once again observe a different stance taken by its judiciary. The authoritative case in question was *Attorney General v Manjeet Singh Dhillon*, and the dispute in question followed from the impeachment of Lord President Tun Salleh, as discussed earlier in Chapter 4. On the facts, the defendant, a member of the Malaysian Bar Council, had filed various affidavits in court, seeking a judicial order of committal to imprison the then Acting Lord President Abdul Hamid bin Omar for contempt of court. In his affidavits, the defendant alleged that the Lord President had, with improper motives, sought to prevent the Supreme Court from hearing an *ex parte* application of Tun Salleh who was then suspended from office, pending a Tribunal Inquiry.[107] The Attorney General instead brought proceedings against the defendant for contempt.

Justice Mohammed Yusoff, on behalf of the majority in the Supreme Court of Malaysia, agreed that the defendant was guilty of contempt of court. Interestingly, he observed as follows about the *mens rea* requirement:

> To find contempt, the court requires strict proof and before a contemner can be found in contempt, the act complained of must not only be wilful and calculated but must also be made with the intention of bringing the judge into contempt or casting suspicion on the administration of justice.[108]

As for the *actus reus* of the offence, the learned judge cited with approval[109] a dated Malaysian decision of *PP v The Straits Times*, which merely required that the alleged contemptuous statements in question 'tended to prejudice'[110] the administration of justice. Therefore, under Malaysian law, for the offence of contempt by scandalizing the judiciary to be satisfied, it would seem that the *mens rea* requirement is pitched at a high level while the *actus reus* element is significantly easy to satisfy.

In view of the comparative analysis on the law on contempt by scandalizing the judiciary discussed above, I shall make the following two suggestions.

First, for this form of contempt to be established, all of the three jurisdictions should require that there be a real risk that the impugned statement(s)

105 *Wong Yeung Ng* (n 99) 298.
106 *Gray* (n 85) 40.
107 See Chapter 4.
108 [1991] 1 MLJ 167 (Supreme Court of Malaysia) [105].
109 Ibid. [106].
110 [1949] MLJ 81 (Federal Court of Malaysia) 83.

in question would undermine the general public's confidence in the administration of justice. The common law on contempt 'operates against the broader legal canvass of the right to freedom of speech'[111] and an *actus reus* requirement that merely requires the allegedly contemptuous statement(s) to have a tendency (instead of a real risk) of undermining the public's perception of the judiciary would unduly stifle the citizenry's right to criticize any perceived judicial improprieties and hold judges accountable for their public actions. If we all believe that there is a public interest in having an open discussion on the court's performance of its judicial duties, surely any harm inflicted on the public interest from the impugned communication must be sufficiently serious and probable to justify the proscription of any such speech. Furthermore, to decide whether such a real risk is present, the courts must also look beyond the tone, veracity, and fairness of the publications in question, and examine the surrounding context of the entire publication—the timing of the publication, size of the publication audience, and the likely nature, impact, and duration of the publication's influence. After all, if one is indeed persuaded to assess the actual and potential impact these publications would have on the average reasonable member of the public, as the 'real risk' requirement would entail, the court cannot confine itself to merely examining the impugned statement(s) and the publication alone to decide whether the charge of contempt is made out.

Second, where the scurrilous attacks against the judiciary are not made in court or in connection with a pending or current legal proceeding, such that the outcome or resolution of particular proceedings is not affected by the allegedly contemptuous statement(s) in question, there is reason for the judiciary, in all three jurisdictions, to impose the *mens rea* requirement mooted by Mortimer V-P in *Wong Yeung Ng*, that is, the offender must actually intend to interfere with the administration of justice or he or she must appreciate this possible consequence but recklessly ignores it. While it is a proportionate response merely to require that the offender intend his or her publication if his or her conduct actually disrupts the court process itself or risks prejudicing current/pending legal proceedings, one must note that contempt proceedings brought for scandalizing the court, in circumstances where the resolution of specific proceedings is not affected, have been judicially recognized as 'virtually obsolescent'[112] in England and most common law jurisdictions, such that a reformulation of the *mens rea* requirement would show greater sensitivity to the needs of a deliberative democracy that allows the

[111] *Shadrake* (n 86) [17].

[112] *Secretary of State for Defence v Guardian Newspaper* [1985] AC 339 (HL), 347 (Lord Diplock).

citizenry to robustly debate and discuss the affairs of its public institutions, including the administration of justice.

After all, if the judiciary is to serve as the citizenry's guardian of rights, and its bulwark against legislative excesses, the court, of all the branches of government, must show the greatest tolerance to the criticisms of its own functioning. As eloquently observed by Justice Sachs in the South African Constitutional Court decision of *S v Mamabolo*:

> [The judiciary's] standing in the community can only be undermined if the public are led to draw the inference that in pursuance of the principle that an injury to one is an injury to all, the judicial establishment is closing ranks.[113]

If respect for the judiciary is to be regarded as integral to the administration of justice, such respect can only be genuine and real so far as it is earned from the public, by the quality of judgments delivered, rather than commanded by force of law.

III. Regulatory Restrictions on Public Assemblies

In a democracy, a person's right to assemble is an important and popular mode of the citizenry's expression and participation in the processes of government. It is a mode of political participation potentially 'supplementary to, or quite separate from, the formal ballot box, and within or outside the constraints of political parties or any form of organized politics'.[114] Demonstrations are generally cheap and effective in drawing the attention of crowds, and are thus especially suited for politically or economically disadvantaged minorities that do not have access to the mainstream media due to the lack of funds, expertise, or contacts, but nonetheless wish to disseminate their views widely. Public assemblies thus provide these groups with the visibility to gain access to the media through the publicity of their actions and the opportunity to persuade members of their immediate audience to participate in their causes. Thus, as observed by Professor Helen Fenwick, 'public protest can act both as a means of access to the media and as a substitute for fair media exposure'.[115]

Yet, public assemblies have the potential of disrupting public order (and even triggering violence), and all governments therefore seek to regulate this

[113] 2001 (3) SA 409 (South African Constitutional Court) [78].

[114] Janice Brabyn, 'The Fundamental Freedom of Assembly and Part II of the Public Order Ordinance' (2002) 32 *Hong Kong Law Journal* 271, 287.

[115] Helen Fenwick, 'The Right to Protest, the Human Rights Act and the Margin of Appreciation' (1999) 62 *Modern Law Review* 491, 493.

form of public expression in some form, so as to ensure public safety and minimize inconveniences imposed on others.

Of the three Asian jurisdictions under discussion, Singapore has the most intrusive model of regulation. The Public Order Act (POA), passed in 2009, requires an organizer of a public assembly, even if it is a demonstration by one person,[116] first to obtain a permit from the Commissioner of Police. An assembly is defined as a gathering to demonstrate support for or opposition to the views of any person(s) or government,[117] and thus the organization of social and recreational activities are exempted. The Commissioner may refuse or apply conditions to the organizer(s) of such assemblies if he or she, *inter alia*, has reasonable ground for apprehending that the proposed assembly or procession would occasion public disorder, damage public or private property, create a public nuisance, or give rise to an obstruction on any public road.[118] Decisions taken by the police can be appealed to the Minister of Home Affairs, and this is also further subject to judicial review. Nevertheless, indoor assemblies and outdoor demonstrations held by Singapore citizens in Speaker's Corner, a park, are exempted from these licensing requirements.

The Supreme Court of Singapore has not had the opportunity to consider the constitutionality of the POA or the legality of the enforcement regime. Nevertheless, the manner in which the judiciary reviewed the Miscellaneous Offences (Public Order and Nuisance) Act[119] (MOA), the precursor to the POA, would give us some clues to the plausible judicial approach and some pause for concern.

In *Chee Siok Chin v Minister for Home Affairs*,[120] three applicants commenced proceedings, seeking declarations that the Minister of Home Affairs and the Commissioner of Police had acted unlawfully in ordering them to disperse when they, alongside another individual, had engaged in a peaceful, four-person protest outside a governmental building. A central issue that arose was whether the MOA could curtail their right to assembly. The High Court acknowledged that every Singapore citizen has the right to assemble peaceably, but the learned judge noted that Article 14(2) of the Singapore Constitution also qualifies this right by allowing the government to impose 'such restrictions as it considers necessary or expedient in the interest of the security of Singapore or . . . public order or morality'.

116 Public Order Act (Cap 257A), Section 2(1).
117 Ibid.
118 Ibid. Sections 7(2), 8(4).
119 Miscellaneous Offences (Public Order and Nuisance) Act (Cap 184).
120 [2006] 1 SLR 582 (High Court of Singapore).

Specifically, the High Court observed as follows:

> It bears emphasis that the phrase "necessary or expedient" confers on Parliament an extremely wide discretionary power and remit that permits a multifarious and multifaceted approach towards achieving any of the purposes specified in Art 14(2) of the Constitution . . . there can be no questioning of whether the legislation is "reasonable". All that needs to be established is a nexus between the object of the impugned law and one of the permissible subjects stipulated in Art 14(2) of the Constitution.[121]

In other words, the court would only ascertain whether an impugned law fell within the purview of a legitimate purpose provided under Article 14(2) and it would not further examine whether this law was reasonable or necessary.

Furthermore, in deciding whether the police had legally exercised their discretion to disperse the protestors for perceived statutory violations, the court held that it would only examine whether there had been 'illegality, irrationality or procedural impropriety'[122] in the manner in which a decision was made; in so doing, the court emphasized that the proportionality doctrine has never been part of Singapore law in relation to the judicial review of the exercise of a legislative and/or an administrative power.[123] The court thus concluded that it was not irrational for the police to believe that the protestors' abusive language amounted to harassment, a statutory offence, such that the police were acting within their scope of powers when they asked the protestors to leave in lieu of arresting them. The applicants' application for a declaration against the government was therefore struck out by the court.

Pursuant to the then-operative MOA and its subsidiary rules, any person who wanted to organize a public assembly of five or more persons needed to obtain a permit from the police.[124] The High Court had consistently held that persons, who took part in such public assemblies, when they knew or reasonably knew that the assemblies in question were held without permits, would be liable for the offence.[125] The protestors' claim that the police would never have issued them a permit in the first place[126] or had wrongfully denied them a permit[127] was deemed irrelevant to their criminal proceedings, and the onus was thus on the protestors to seek their redress under administrative law if their application for a permit was rejected.[128] Interestingly, the

[121] *Chee Siok Chin* (n 120) [49]. [122] Ibid. [93]. [123] Ibid. [87].

[124] See Miscellaneous Offences (Public Order and Nuisance) (Assemblies and Processions) Rules, Rule 2(1).

[125] See Ibid. Rule 5.

[126] See *Chee Soon Juan v Public Prosecutor* [2011] 3 SLR 50 (High Court of Singapore).

[127] See *Yap Keng Ho v Public Prosecutor* [2011] 3 SLR 32 (High Court of Singapore).

[128] See *Chee Soon Juan* (n 126) [38]; *PP v Chong Kai Xiong* [2010] 3 SLR 355 (High Court of Singapore) [13].

Singapore Minister of Home Affairs had revealed in Parliament in February 2008 that the police would not grant permits for outdoor demonstrations and protests;[129] but to date, no one has challenged the police's exercise of these statutory powers of prior restraint, and in particular the implementation of the above policy, by way of judicial review.

Turning to Hong Kong, we may observe a more encouraging state of affairs. Public processions and meetings in Hong Kong are primarily regulated under the Public Order Ordinance (POO). Unlike Singapore, outdoor demonstrations are a regular feature of Hong Kong civic life. Organizers have to notify the police usually seven days in advance and the Commissioner of Police may object to or impose conditions on notified processions and meetings. One must note however that the POO only regulates public processions consisting of more than 30 persons on a public highway or thoroughfare or in a public park.[130] A public meeting of less than 50 persons or in private premises where the attendance at the meeting does not exceed 500 persons is not subject to the Ordinance. The Commissioner's decision to object to a public procession/meeting or to impose conditions may be appealed to an Appeal Board. Assuming the decision of the Commissioner is confirmed by the Appeal Board, the Commissioner's decision can still be subject to judicial review.

The landmark judgment in Hong Kong relating to the freedom of assembly would have to be the Hong Kong Court of Final Appeal (CFA) decision in *Leung Kwok Hung v HKSAR*.[131] The defendants had organized a public procession that had about 40–100 people taking part at any one time, without pre-notifying the police.[132] Specifically, for the purposes of our discussion, the CFA held that the judiciary would apply a proportionality analysis to challenges against specific administrative decisions made by the police to ban or impose conditions on notified public processions and meetings. In

[129] Singapore Parliamentary Debates, Official Report, 28 February 2008, vol 84, cols 1153–5.

[130] Public Order Ordinance (Cap 245), s 13.

[131] [2005] 3 HKLRD 164 (Hong Kong Court of Final Appeal).

[132] The demonstrators were arrested and they subsequently challenged the constitutionality of the POO on the basis that the statutory discretion conferred on the Police Commissioner to object to a notified public procession and/or to impose conditions, if he reasonably considered these methods to be necessary in the interests of 'public order (ordre public)', was too wide and uncertain. The majority on the CFA upheld the statutory notification requirement but accepted that the Commissioner's power to restrict peaceful assembly, for the statutory purpose of 'public order (ordre public)' was constitutionally too vague, such that no 'adequate indication of the scope of that discretion' was conferred on a 'public official who was part of the executive authorities which of course stand in a fundamentally different position from that of an independent judiciary' (at [76]). Therefore, the nebulous term 'ordre public' was judicially severed and read out from the statute while the term 'public order' was retained. Nevertheless, given that the defendants had not complied with the notification procedures, the severance of the constitutionally invalid provision did not affect their appeal, and their convictions were confirmed.

other words, with regard to every absolute ban or condition imposed by the Commissioner of Police, (1) the restriction must be rationally connected with one or more of the statutory purposes; and (2) the means used to impair the right of peaceful assembly must be no more than is necessary to accomplish the legitimate purpose in question.[133]

Turning to Malaysia, we may notice a significant change in the law relating to the right of assembly. In December 2011, the Peaceful Assembly Act (PAA) was passed and it now merely requires organizers of a public assembly to pre-notify the police ten days in advance of the event.[134] This legislation replaced the Police Act, which had required persons to first obtain a permit before a demonstration. Currently, the police may restrict or impose conditions on a notified assembly for the purpose of security or public order, including the protection of the rights and freedoms of other persons.[135] The PAA prohibits non-Malaysian citizens and children below the age of 15 from participating in the public assemblies. Decisions taken by the police can be appealed to the Minister of Home Affairs, and this is also further subject to judicial review.

In *Dr Mohd Nasir Hashim v Menteri Dalam Negiri Malaysia*,[136] the Court of Appeal upheld the constitutionality of an administrative policy, which required a political party seeking registration at a national level to include at least one member from seven states in the Federation of Malaysia within the party's committee. What is fascinating about this decision was the court's take on Article 10(2) of the Federal Constitution. Article 10(2) allows the federal government to limit a citizen's right to free expression, assembly, and association if the restrictions are 'necessary or expedient' in the interests of, *inter alia*, security or public order. Nevertheless, the Court of Appeal held that 'we can read the word "reasonable" before the word "restrictions" '[137] in Article 10(2) and the 'court is therefore entitled to strike down State action on the ground that it is disproportionate to the object sought to be achieved'.[138] This judicial approach stands in stark contrast from that taken by the Singapore High Court in *Chee Siok Chin,* as discussed above. This freedom-friendly reading of Article 10(2) has also been accepted by Gopal Sri Ram, on behalf of a unanimous Federal Court in *Sivarasa Rasiah v Badan Peguam Malaysia.*[139]

[133] *Leung Kwok Hung* (n 131) [96].

[134] Peaceful Assembly Act (Laws of Malaysia Act 736), Section 9(1).

[135] Ibid. Section 15(1).

[136] [2006] 6 MLJ 213 (Malaysia Court of Appeal).

[137] [2006] 6 MLJ 213 (Malaysia Court of Appeal) [9].

[138] Ibid. [8].

[139] [2010] 2 MLJ 333 (Federal Court of Malaysia) [5]. On the facts in *Sivarasa Rasiah*, the Federal Court upheld a federal law that prohibited a lawyer from serving on Malaysia's Bar Council if he or she was concurrently holding office in any political party or was a member of either House of Parliament or a State Legislative Assembly; this statutory restriction was deemed reasonable as it was in the public interest that lawyers serving on the Bar Council were independent of any political influence.

Henceforth, the Malaysian Courts would examine whether any legislative or administrative restriction on the citizenry's right of expression and assembly is reasonable and proportionate.[140]

It is noteworthy that the Malaysian Court of Appeal, in *Nik Nazmi bin Nik Ahmad v Public Prosecutor*,[141] has invalidated Section 9(5) of the PAA, which imposed criminal sanctions on organizers who fail to notify the police at least ten days before a proposed public assembly. While the court accepted that it was constitutional to impose a notification requirement on organizers, the judges took the view that non-compliance with the notice requirement should not automatically attract criminal sanctions as the police retained a host of criminal law powers to address disorderly and unlawful assemblies.

In view of the above comparative analysis on public assemblies, it would appear that Singapore is an outlier. Nevertheless, it is open to the judiciary to advance the right of the citizenry to assemble peacefully by asserting greater control over how its police implement the licensing scheme under the POA. In particular, so far as the police deny or impose conditions on a notified assembly, the Singapore court[142] should adopt the proportionality analysis observed by the Hong Kong and Malaysian judiciary to examine whether (1) these restrictions are rationally connected with one or more of the statutory purposes; and (2) the means used to impair the right of peaceful

[140] Subsequently in *Muhammad Hilman v Kerajaan Malaysia* (2011) 6 MLJ 507 (Malaysia Court of Appeal), the Court of Appeal relied on *Sivarasa Rasiah* to strike down a statutory provision in the University and University Colleges Act that prohibited tertiary students from supporting or opposing any political party, in or outside Malaysia, as this restriction was deemed to be an unreasonable restriction of their freedom of expression. In 2012, the Malaysian Parliament amended the legislation to allow students to join any political party, but those who do so are not allowed to hold leadership positions in the university's organizations or societies. In *Mat Shuhaimi bin Shafiei v Public Prosecutor* [2014] 2 MLJ 145, the Malaysian Court of Appeal upheld the Sedition Act as a reasonable restriction on free speech.

[141] [2014] 4 MLJ 157. The Malaysian High Court (Kuala Lumpur) in *Dato' Seri Anwar bin Ibrahim v Public Prosecutor* [2013] 3 MLJ 103 has recently upheld the statutory ban on 'street protests', i.e. mass marches in public, pursuant to Section 4 of the PAA, as a *reasonable* limitation of the constitutional right to free assembly.

[142] In *Chan Hiang Leng Colin v Minister for Information and the Arts* [1996] 1 SLR 294 (Singapore Court of Appeal), [38], the Singapore Court of Appeal had to decide whether a ministerial order that prohibited the importation, sale, and distribution of all publications by a Jehovah's Witnesses association was constitutional. In deciding whether this order was a violation of their constitutional right to religious freedom, the court observed that it was 'questionable whether proportionality exists as an independent ground for judicial review or whether it is simply an adjunct of irrationality'. Nevertheless, in a recent extra-judicial address entitled 'Judicial Review—From Angst to Empathy' (2010) 22 *Singapore Academy of Law Journal* 469, 478, the Chief Justice of Singapore emphasized that the 'Court did not foreclose the possibility of adopting the principle of proportionality in an appropriate case'.

assembly are no more than is necessary to accomplish the legitimate purpose in question.[143]

At the outset, I must emphasize that I am not arguing that proportionality should be adopted as a general head of judicial review over all exercises of legislative or executive power in all three jurisdictions, as Professor Paul Craig has suggested with regard to the United Kingdom.[144] My claim is far more modest. Instead, I am arguing that the proportionality analysis is the appropriate standard of review when the court examines the legality of the police's powers of prior restraint conferred under the above three statutory regimes regulating public assemblies.

Critics of the proportionality analysis often warn that the recognition of this doctrine would steer the judiciary closer toward merits-review over administrative decisions. There are two justifications commonly advanced as to why this is unwise, and I would argue why these objections are not persuasive, so far as proportionality review is applied to these particular statutory powers of prior restraint.

First, it is often argued that it is ill-advised for courts to second-guess the wisdom of legislatures or administrative tribunals, as the latter groups have special sources of knowledge or expertise.[145] This is an argument based on the relative institutional competence of the branches of government and the observation may be valid if courts are seeking to resolve 'polycentric questions affecting a large number of disparate interests',[146] for example social welfare entitlements, or issues relating to complicated factual determinations, for example matters relating to foreign affairs and national security. But it would be rather incredulous to claim that the operation of the licensing scheme for public assemblies is so complex that courts lack the training to assess whether the public order considerations in a particular case reasonably justify the police's refusal of a permit. Courts, in their daily administration of the criminal justice system, routinely deal with matters that are factually more complicated than these.

Second, it may be argued that the proportionality doctrine is normatively objectionable as courts owe a duty of deference to the decisions taken by the elected branches of government. This is an argument from

[143] See *Leung Kwok Hung* (n 131) [96].

[144] Paul Craig, 'Proportionality, Rationality and Review' [2010] *New Zealand Law Review* 265.

[145] Lon Fuller, 'The Forms and Limits of Adjudication' (1978) 92 *Harvard Law Review* 353, 394–404.

[146] Julian Rivers, 'Proportionality and Variable Intensity of Review' (2006) 65 *Cambridge Law Journal* 174, 176.

democratic legitimacy.[147] But one must note that the primary decision makers herein are the police, who are equally not accountable to the public directly for the decisions they make. The judiciary, on the other hand, is given a constitutional mandate to serve as guardians of the fundamental liberties enshrined. Therefore, vis-à-vis the police, the democratic pedigree of the courts surely is no less inferior. Furthermore, as far as Singapore is concerned, the POA does not even grant a subjective discretion on the police to make the requisite factual determinations; the legislation in fact requires the police to have 'reasonable ground'[148] for apprehending that the notified assembly would raise public order concerns. A *Wednesbury* standard of review that allows the police to do anything they want so long as their actions are not capricious or absurd therefore flies in the face of the legislative language and would in turn impede an objective evaluation of the statutory duty imposed on the police to act reasonably.

Finally, the application of the proportionality doctrine, within this species of administrative law, is prudential as it is also dialogic in nature. If the legislature disagrees with this heightened standard of review, the Singapore Parliament is perfectly entitled to amend the POA and reintroduce a lower standard of review. So far as the courts take the initiative to redraw the contours of administrative law, one must remember that its doctrines and ambits have always been a consequence of judicial innovation and legislative acquiescence.

IV. Conclusion

The freedom of expression is a sacrosanct right but it is equally recognized that there are other vital public interests and values, for example reputation and public order, the protection of which may justify its limitation in a democratic society. The onus thus falls on the judiciary to review the reasonableness of any perceived governmental restriction of this right but the courts can do so, as suggested above, by deploying dialogic sub-constitutional tools of administrative and common law review that accommodate legislative disagreements and political realities.

[147] See eg Tom Hickman, 'Problems for Proportionality' [2010] *New Zealand Law Review* 303, 314; Keith Ewing & Conor Gearty, 'Rocky Foundations for Labour's New Rights' (1997) 5 *European Human Rights Law Review* 146.

[148] Public Order Act (Cap 257A), Section 7(2).

The development of novel private law defences in defamation law and the recalibration of the constituent elements of contempt by scandalizing the judiciary are significant common law pathways by which constitutional norms can be integrated into the public discourse. In this way, the constitutional right to free expression is given 'indirect interpretive effect'[149] as the pro-active judiciary is taking the initiative to advance human rights concerns, but its interpretive choices remain 'conditional, dynamic, and contingent on on-going politics'[150] as the common law principles pronounced are always subject to statutory reversals.

Similarly, so far as the judiciary allows administrative doctrines to be informed by constitutional principles and norms, administrative agencies and executive officials, for fear of judicial reversals, would be incentivized to take constitutional values seriously when they make decisions. Furthermore, administrative constraints on the government that take the form of a heightened 'proportionality' review, especially in matters where judges do not need to make complex factual determinations or where judicial intervention would have minimal 'allocative impact'[151] on public resources, are also less intrusive on the policy-making prerogatives of the political branches than the constitutional invalidation of legislation would be.[152]

As discussed earlier in Chapter 4, all these courts co-exist with a semi-permanent government/legislature in their respective jurisdictions. Where the legislature is exempt from the usual pressures and constraints imposed by electoral competition, it will more likely rein in the courts when it is displeased with a judicial decision. But if a constitutional amendment, or the ouster of judges, is the only way by which the legislature may display its disagreement, it may be prudent and wise for judges to avoid heading for the constitutional precipice by entrenching a 'maximalist'[153] constitutional rule. Instead, where the dispute relates to merely a common law or administrative law matter, the dialogic path would be to resolve the conflict within the very forum it arose. Wherein the conflict arose, therein it can be resolved. The implementation of sub-constitutional doctrines, such as common law or administrative rules, may suffice, in the

[149] Helen Hershkoff, '"Just Word": Common Law and the Enforcement of State Constitutional Social and Economic Rights' (2010) 62 *Stanford Law Review* 1521, 1582.

[150] Ibid.

[151] See Jeff King, 'The Justiciability of Resource Allocation' (2007) 70 *Modern Law Review* 197, 208.

[152] Gillian E Metzger, 'Ordinary Administrative Law as Constitutional Common Law' (2010) 110 *Columbia Law Review* 479, 485.

[153] Sunstein (n 12) 20.

first instance, for courts to stake out their positions on rights-protection, such that it leaves space for the legislature to reclaim the field with the passage of an ordinary statute, if it so wants. In the final analysis, the development of common law and administrative law pathways allows courts to implement constitutional mandates while providing the political branches with a meaningful role in reshaping the ambit of these requirements if they so choose.

7
Freedom of Religion

Within common law Asia, there are neither theocracies nor strict church-state separationist regimes. Instead, we can find a diverse range of models that exhibit varying relationships of religion-state co-operation and accommodation that have evolved as a result of the respective jurisdictions' specific constitutional arrangements and traditions.

In Hong Kong, the Basic Law protects a person's freedom of religious belief and his or her freedom to preach and participate in religious activities in public.[1] Furthermore, the Basic Law expressly enshrines the right of religious organizations, according to their previous practice, to continue to run seminaries, schools, hospitals, and other social services.[2] In a similar vein, the Singapore Constitution equally protects a person's right to profess, practise, and propagate his or her religion,[3] though religious groups have been conferred the explicit right to manage their own religious affairs and establish and maintain institutions for religious or charitable purposes.[4] It is however noteworthy that the Singapore Constitution obliges the legislature to adopt legislation to provide for Muslim religious affairs,[5] which has taken the form of the Administration of Muslim Law Act[6] that enlists syariah (Muslim religious) courts in the administration of Muslim personal law. The Malaysia Constitution, on the other hand, expressly provides that Islam is the official religion of the state, though all religions may be practised in peace and harmony throughout the Federation.[7] Furthermore, while everyone has the right to profess and practise his or her religion, the Malaysia Constitution expressly allows federal or state law to restrict any religious propagation among Muslims.[8] Moreover, a constitutional amendment was passed in 1988 to provide that the civil courts shall have no jurisdiction in respect of any matter within the jurisdiction of the syariah courts.[9]

[1] Hong Kong Basic Law, Article 32. [2] Ibid. Article 141.
[3] Singapore Constitution, Article 15(1). [4] Ibid. Article 15(3).
[5] Ibid. Article 153. [6] Administration of Muslim Law Act (Cap 3).
[7] Malaysia Constitution, Article 3(1). [8] Ibid. Article 11(4).
[9] Malaysia Constitution, Article 121(1A).

It is therefore unsurprising that common law courts in Asia have sought to address the competing demands of God and Caesar in their respective jurisdictions in different ways. Indeed, a close survey of the three territories would allow us to identify three different judicial models of religious liberty.

First, we may observe the formal model of religious liberty. According to this model, a person's right to practise his or her religion does not relieve him or her of the obligation to comply with a secular law that is formally authorized by the appropriate branch of government. Where the religious deprivation is duly enacted by the constitutionally authorized body, the courts will not further examine whether the impugned law is reasonable or proportionate. This is the position taken in a line of Singapore appellate cases.[10] Second, according to the categorization model, courts would seek to categorize the contested activity as religious or non-religious in nature; and, where the disputed activity is deemed to be non-religious in nature, the believer's expressive conduct would not receive any constitutional protection at all. This is the view held by the Singapore[11] and Hong Kong's[12] courts of final resort. Finally, according to the balancing model of religious freedom, in deciding whether an impugned secular law is constitutional, courts will seek to balance the importance of the secular objectives pursued by the state legislation against the burdens imposed on the affected believer if he or she has to comply with the law in question. This is the general position taken by the Malaysian courts, though it is subject to one important caveat. The Malaysian courts generally apply this proportionality/balancing approach in matters where the syariah courts have not been conferred adjudicatory jurisdiction; in matters deemed Islamic in nature, the Malaysian civil judiciary often defers to the religious courts.

In this chapter, I shall essentially argue that the balancing model of religious liberty is the only constitutionally meaningful and substantively defensible vision of religious liberty. Section I of this chapter begins by providing an overview of the three models of religious liberty. Section II continues by arguing why, aside from the balancing model, the other two models are fatally flawed judicial attempts to protect a person's constitutional right to practise his or her religion. Section III, in view of the prudential constraints imposed on the judiciary as discussed in Chapter 4, proceeds by identifying the soft dialogic tools by which common law courts in Asia can seek to

[10] *Chan Hiang Leng Colin v Public Prosecutor* [1994] 3 SLR 662 (High Court of Singapore).

[11] *Nappalli Peter Williams v Institute of Technical Education* [1999] 2 SLR 569 (Singapore Court of Appeal).

[12] *Catholic Diocese of Hong Kong v Secretary of Justice* (2011) 14 HKCFAR 754 (Hong Kong Court of Final Appeal).

vindicate this balancing model. Particularly, with respect to Malaysia, I will show how its secular civil courts can dialogically engage with the state legislatures over constitutional matters that engage Islamic issues.

I. Overview of the Three Models of Religious Liberty

Section I maps out the three judicial models of religious liberty that are applied by the appellate courts of Singapore, Malaysia, and Hong Kong when they seek to constrain the ability of the state to limit the citizenry's right to profess and practise their religion. By differentiating between these three models, we should be able to appreciate the interpretive options open to the territorial secular courts, such that we can understand why the balancing model is preferred over the other models of religious liberty, as discussed more fully in Section II of this chapter.

A. Formal Model

According to the formal model of religious liberty, any statutory enactment that restricts an individual's right to practise his or her religion would be constitutionally valid so long as the impugned limitation is duly authorized by formal legislation. The courts herein would not further examine whether this statutory restriction is necessary, reasonable, or proportionate.

This formal understanding of religious liberty was endorsed by Chief Justice Yong of Singapore in *Chan Hiang Leng Colin v Public Prosecutor*.[13] In that case, the appellants, a group of Jehovah's Witnesses, argued *inter alia* that the blanket legislative ban on all publications by their religious society was an unconstitutional violation of their right to profess their religion. Nevertheless, the court flatly disagreed, observing that 'religious beliefs ought to have proper protection, but actions undertaken or flowing from such beliefs must conform with the general law relating to public order and social protection'.[14] Given that the secular state insists on compulsory military conscription for all able-bodied males to safeguard the sovereignty of the nation, any publications propagating any religious practices, including the pacifist beliefs of the Jehovah's Witnesses that 'tend to run counter to these objectives must be restrained'.[15] In other words, all religious practices must conform to formal laws validly passed. There would be no judicial need to examine the reasonableness of these legislative measures.

[13] *Colin Chan* (n 10). [14] Ibid. 684. [15] Ibid.

B. Categorization Model

According to the categorical approach to religious liberty, courts would seek to classify the nature of the disputed activity between the individual and the state; where the contested activity is deemed to be non-religious in nature, his or her act would receive no constitutional protection at all.

In the Singapore Court of Appeal decision of *Nappalli Peter Williams v Institute of Technical Education*,[16] the appellant teacher was dismissed from his employment for refusing to abide by the employment circular, which required him to recite the National Pledge and sing the National Anthem in school. The appellant equated any participation in the pledge recitation or anthem ceremony with partaking in a religious ceremony, an act inconsistent with his Jehovah's Witnesses faith. Nevertheless, the Court of Appeal disagreed, observing that these secular activities did not bear any religious significance at all. Instead, according to Chief Justice Yong:

> It seemed clear to us that the appellant's interpretation of the pledge and anthem ceremony as a religious ceremony was a distortion of secular fact into religious belief. It is not accepted as a religious belief and is not entitled to protection under the Constitution of Singapore.[17]

This judicial classification of a prohibited activity is also evident in Hong Kong. In *Catholic Diocese of Hong Kong v Secretary of Justice*,[18] the Hong Kong Court of Final Appeal (CFA) had to decide *inter alia* whether a statutory amendment, which required all public-aided schools to appoint independent members to each school's management committee, violated the Catholic Church's constitutional right to run schools according to its previous practice, as protected under Article 141(3) of the Basic Law.

The CFA responded with an interesting gloss on Article 141(3). The court held that Article 141(3), read purposively, only protected religious organizations' right to run schools 'in so far as it involves the exercise of their right to freedom of religious belief and religious activity'.[19] Therefore, legislative policies imposed on religious schools 'which have no religious content, for instance, as to the teaching of second languages, providing more physical education or information technology classes, or providing student travel or textbook subsidies, would not engage the [constitutional] protections'[20] at all.

This categorical approach to religious liberty requires courts to classify the nature and character of the contested activity. Where the prohibited practice

[16] *Nappalli Peter Williams* (n 11).
[17] [1999] 2 SLR 569 (Singapore Court of Appeal) [28].
[18] *Catholic Diocese* (n 12).
[19] Ibid. [78].
[20] Ibid. [79].

is deemed to be non-religious in nature, the individual/entity would receive no constitutional protection at all.

C. Balancing Model

According to the balancing approach, the courts would seek to balance the individual's right to practise his or her religion against the secular objectives of the legislation. In particular, the courts would examine whether the impugned measures undertaken by the government are reasonably necessary to achieve the stipulated legislative goals.

Within common law Asia, the Malaysia courts have generally adopted this balancing approach. In *Meor Atiqulrahman bin Ishak v Fatimah Bte Sihi*,[21] the Federal Court of Malaysia had to decide whether a school regulation that prohibited all students from wearing the turban (an Islamic headdress) violated the pupils' right to profess their religion. In deciding whether the restriction was constitutional, the court held that it would examine (1) whether the prohibited practice was an integral part of the religion professed;[22] (2) the extent and severity of the prohibition;[23] and (3) the governmental justifications for the prohibition.[24] On the facts, the Federal Court upheld the turban ban as the wearing of this religious headdress was not a mandatory component or even integral to the Islamic faith,[25] students were prohibited from wearing the turban only during school hours and only in those secular publicly funded schools,[26] and the government had a legitimate interest in fostering racial and religious harmony amongst the citizenry by instilling discipline and inculcating certain shared values during their formative years.[27]

In applying the above-mentioned legal principles laid out in *Meor Atiqulrahman*, the Court of Appeal in *Menteri Dalam Negeri v Titular Roman Catholic Archbishop of Kuala Lumpur*[28] has however upheld a ministerial order that prohibited the Catholic Church in Malaysia from using the term 'Allah' in its weekly newsletter to members. But one must note that the unanimous court had done so because Christians around the world were

[21] [2006] 4 MLJ 605 (Federal Court of Malaysia). In the same vein, in *Minister for Home Affairs v Jamaluddin bin Othman* (1989) 1 MLJ 418 (Supreme Court of Malaysia), the Supreme Court of Malaysia held that the state could not detain an individual without trial under the Internal Security Act as the mere participation in religious meetings and the conversion of six Malays to Christianity, could not, by themselves, be regarded as a threat to the nation's security.

[22] Ibid. [17]. [23] Ibid. [19]. [24] Ibid. [20]. [25] Ibid. [39].

[26] Ibid. [41].

[27] [2006] 4 MLJ 605 (Federal Court of Malaysia) [45], [46]. For a critique of the lower courts' decisions, see Li-ann Thio & Jaclyn Neo, 'Religious Dress in Schools: the Serban controversy in Malaysia' (2006) 55 *International and Comparative Law Quarterly* 671.

[28] [2013] 6 MLJ 468 (Malaysia Court of Appeal).

themselves divided over whether the term 'Allah' was an appropriate and correct translation to reference the Christian God, and therefore its use was not an essential and integral part of the Catholic faith.[29]

This balancing approach requires the judiciary to weigh the governmental interests against the individual's right to practise his or her religion. In other words, the courts would ensure that the state derogation on rights, in view of its goals, would not be disproportionately excessive. While Malaysia has not been consistent in upholding this balancing model of religious liberty, as we will explore later in Section II of this chapter, it remains the only jurisdiction within the Asian territories surveyed to have expressly endorsed this model of adjudication.

II. Evaluating the Three Models

A. Formal Model

According to the formal model of religious liberty, citizens are entitled to profess and propagate their religions so long as their conduct is compliant with any state law. The judiciary would not examine whether any governmental restriction is reasonable or proportionate; it would merely ensure that the state is acting pursuant to lawful authority when restricting the individual's right to practise his or her religion.

In Magistrate's Appeal of *Colin Chan*,[30] Chief Justice acknowledged that the Jehovah's Witnesses had the constitutional right to practise their religion and 'ought to have proper protection, but actions undertaken or flowing from such beliefs must conform with the general law relating to public order and social protection'.[31] In other words, so long as there is a validly enacted piece of legislation or administrative regulation that seeks to deprive individuals of their right to religious liberty, their constitutional freedom is *ipso facto* so limited by the derogating law.

The learned Chief Justice appeared to justify this positivistic stance on the basis that Article 15(4) of the Singapore Constitution expressly states that an individual's constitutional right to his or her religious liberty 'does not authorize any act contrary to any general law relating to public order, public health or morality', and therefore, any religious acts must comply with

[29] Ibid. [136] (Zawawi Salleh JCA). The Federal Court of Malaysia has refused to grant the applicant leave to appeal against the Court of Appeal's decision. See *Titular Roman Catholic Archbishop of Kuala Lumpur v Menteri Dalam Negeri* [2014] 4 MLJ 765.

[30] *Colin Chan* (n 10).

[31] Ibid. 684.

and defer to general law. The view of Chief Justice Yong appeared to be that any governmental regulation passed in the interests of any of the stipulated objectives would fall within the protective ambit of Article 15(4) and would therefore be constitutional. With respect, such a reading of Article 15(4) is misconceived. Article 15(4) is a specific limitations clause that allows Parliament to restrict and regulate religious acts in interests of public order, public health, and/or morality. This does not however mean that any legislation passed pursuant to these statutory ends is therefore constitutional and may automatically trump a conflicting religious expression. Otherwise, this constitutional exception would, in essence, swallow up the constitutional rule that safeguards a fundamental freedom and make a mockery of the framers' intent of placing it beyond the reach of majoritarian politics.[32] Under a constitutional arrangement where parliamentary supremacy is expressly jettisoned, judges are tasked to devise doctrinal tests that seek to reconcile the expression of a constitutional freedom with any conflicting statutory goals; they should not exalt the governmental goals of public order or national security, and immunize all legislation from constitutional attacks.

B. Categorization Model

The categorical approach merely requires courts to classify the contested activity as religious or secular in nature. Where the contested activity is characterized as non-religious in nature, the individual's expressive conduct is not subjected to any constitutional protection.

In the Singapore decision of *Nappalli Peter Williams*,[33] the Court of Appeal did not perceive the national anthem ceremony to be religious in nature, and therefore did not regard the applicant's refusal to participate as an expression of his religious belief. In the same vein, in *Catholic Diocese of Hong Kong v Secretary of Justice*, since the Catholic Church's appointment of members to the management committees of its affiliated schools was not deemed to be a religious matter, the CFA reasoned that no constitutional violation of its religious freedom was demonstrated on the facts.

With respect, this categorization model is not without its difficulties. First, it is not easy to determine a priori whether a disputed activity is religious or secular in nature. By way of example, if the state were to require publicly aided schools to teach evolution or stem-cell research in science classes or instruct

[32] For a comprehensive discussion of the decision of *Colin Chan*, see Thio Li-ann, 'The Secular Trumps the Sacred: Constitutional Issues Arising from *Colin Chan v Public Prosecutor*' (1995) 16 *Singapore Law Review* 26.

[33] *Nappalli Peter Williams* (n 11).

on the use of contraception in health classes, it is unclear whether such matters can be definitively or easily categorized as religious or non-religious in nature.

Second, in applying this categorization model, the Asian courts under discussion appear to only examine whether the contested activity in question is religious or secular in nature, and fail to examine whether the governmental regulation actually impinges on the individual's religious belief. In *Nappalli Peter Williams,* the Singapore Court of Appeal focussed only on the secular nature of the activity (the national anthem ceremony) in which the applicant refused to participate; but surely, the crux of the issue was not whether the activity in question was a religious one but whether the actor was motivated by his religious belief when he refused to sing the national anthem.[34] By way of an example, while an abortion is a secular medical procedure, a doctor may equally be motivated by his or her religious belief when he or she refuses to perform a surgery of this nature. Similarly, the Hong Kong CFA had opined that governmental policies 'which have no religious content'[35] would not engage any constitutional protection, but in so doing, the CFA failed to consider whether the Catholic Diocese had any religious concerns when it was seeking to retain full control over the membership of the management committees in its affiliated schools.

This categorization model of rights-protection is therefore deeply flawed as herein, the judiciary only scrutinizes the contested activity to see whether it has any religious elements or whether the state is targeting any religious group in so acting. Unfortunately, this approach fails to consider the more crucial question of whether the disputed activity, even if it is wholly secular in nature, affects and impinges upon the religious belief of the individual if he or she is compelled to comply with the governmental regulation. Such scenarios most commonly arise when believers are seeking exemptions from secular laws of general application, for example where conscientious objectors are protesting against compulsory military service or religious minorities are seeking exemptions from state imposed dress codes. Therefore, a coherent model of religious rights-protection must instead be one whereby courts seek to weigh the value of the individual's religious expression against the importance of any ostensibly conflicting statutory goals, and this balancing approach must take place even where these governmental objectives are wholly secular in nature.

[34] For a critique of this case, see Thio Li-ann, 'Courting Religion: The Judge Between Caesar and God in Asian Courts' [2009] *Singapore Journal of Legal Studies* 52, 67–70.

[35] *Catholic Diocese* (n 12).

With regard to the Hong Kong case in *Catholic Diocese of Hong Kong v Secretary of Justice*,[36] one may however note that a balancing approach to rights-adjudication would probably not have led to a different result. On the facts, the government required the management committees in all public-aided schools, including religious ones, to have at least 40 per cent of their managers independently appointed. While such measures arguably violate the religious freedoms of the Catholic Church as this may allow the appointment of board members who do not wholly share the vision and/or ethos of the Catholic Church, this restriction is proportionate as the appointment of independent managers to the management boards would increase the transparency of school policies and therefore enhance the accountability of their members, while allowing the Catholic Church to retain its majority in every school management board such that it would still have control over the running of its schools according to its previous practice.

C. Balancing Model

According to the balancing approach, courts would weigh the significance of the individual's religious practice against the importance of any ostensible conflicting state objective. In many liberal democracies, this balancing test most commonly takes the form of a proportionality framework[37]—the judiciary would ensure that (1) the state is pursuing legitimate objectives; (2) the governmental measures undertaken are rationally connected to the stated policy objectives; and (3) the right-derogation is no more than necessary to achieve those stated goals.[38]

Nevertheless, such a balancing approach to rights-derogation is not without its sceptics, and their criticisms usually come in two forms. The first form, commonly termed the 'internal critique of balancing',[39] questions whether incommensurable interests can be identified, valued, and compared. According to Stavros Tsakyrakis, balancing concerns 'the assumption of a common metric in the weighing process',[40] and it says 'nothing about how

[36] *Catholic Diocese* (n 12).

[37] See Alec Stone Sweet & Jud Mathews, 'Proportionality Balancing and Global Constitutionalism' (2008) 47 *Columbia Journal of Transnational Law* 72.

[38] See *Prince v President of the Law Society of the Cape of Good Hope* 2002(2) 794 SA (South African Constitutional Court); *Multani v Commission scolaire Marguerite-Bourgeoys* [2006] 1 SCR 256 (Supreme Court of Canada).

[39] T Alexander Aleinikoff, 'Constitutional Law in the Age of Balancing' (1987) 96 *Yale Law Journal* 943, 972.

[40] Stavros Tsakyrakis, 'Proportionality: An Assault on Human Rights?' (2009) 7 *International Journal of Constitutional Law* 468.

various interests are to be weighted, and this silence tends to conceal the impossibility of measuring incommensurable values by introducing the image of a mechanistic, quantitative common metric'.[41] According to the second form, commonly termed the 'external critique of balancing',[42] critics question whether balancing is a legitimate method of adjudication as it appears to replicate the tasks of a legislature and allows the courts' cost-benefit analysis to supplant the legislature's determination.

Turning first to the 'internal critique', Virgilio Afonso da Silva has since provided a robust reply to this ground of objection. According to him, the presence of incommensurable values does not preclude the possibility of balancing rights; on the contrary, weighting rights is a procedure that increases comparability among principles.[43] Where two constitutional interests collide, even though these values may be incommensurable, courts may establish a relation of precedence between them such that judges can 'compare the numerous possibilities of protecting and realizing such rights in a concrete situation and to weigh among them'.[44] Therefore, balancing is not about courts deciding between the protection of religious liberty and legitimate state goals in the abstract; instead, balancing is about comparing and considering trade-offs in concrete situations such that rational choices can be made between possible alternatives.

Consider this example: the state wants to admit 500 students into its publicly funded medical schools a year. Part of the medical training would include lessons on the termination of unwanted pregnancies. If the state does not exempt students with ethical concerns about abortions from this component of the course, 200 students, whom the state would otherwise admit, would not enrol into the medical programmes and the state would have to admit less qualified candidates. If the state provides exemptions to these religiously motivated students, the state discovers that it would have fewer but sufficient doctors, trained to perform abortions, entering the medical profession such that the quality and efficiency of public medicine is not compromised. Is it thus not rational for the state to make cross-categorical comparisons and consider the trade-offs from making or refusing exemptions? As David Luban observes, 'ounces and inches can't be compared; but percentage gains and losses can'.[45] Naturally, there will not always be situations where a small sacrifice in the fulfilment of one right/interest would automatically lead to larger gains in another, as the balancing

[41] Ibid. [42] Aleinikoff (n 39) 984.

[43] Virgilio Afonso da Silva, 'Comparing the Incommensurable: Constitutional Principles, Balancing and Rational Decision' (2011) 31 *Oxford Journal of Legal Studies* 273, 276.

[44] Ibid. 286.

[45] David Luban, 'Incommensurable Values, Rational Choice, and Moral Absolutes' (1990) 38 *Cleveland State Law Review* 65.

of interests may indeed lead to a stalemate, that is a parity of values between plausible alternatives. But this 'rough equality among alternative decisions'[46] is the *consequence* of balancing the competing rights/interests at stake and not the reasons against balancing rights in the very first place.

Critics of balancing may respond by questioning whether courts have the right to recalibrate the competing rights and interests at stake after the legislatures have already openly debated and determined the appropriate balance.[47] What reasons, they argue, would the courts have for supplanting the legislative balance with a judicially conceived one? In the same vein, Justice Scalia, on behalf of the majority of the United States Supreme Court in *Employment Division v Smith*,[48] has argued that courts should not have to decide when religious claims of various strengths should triumph over state interests of variant strength[49] as this is a matter for the political process. Scalia's concern brings us to the heart of the external critique of balancing, that is even if balancing can be done, why should it be done by judges and not the elected representatives of the people?

One must note that while this argument appears to be a specific argument against balancing, it is in essence an argument against judicial review in general. After all, whenever courts invalidate a statute passed by Parliament, regardless of whether this is a consequence of rights-balancing, judges are supplanting the legislative will with their own. But as we have explored in Chapter 2, so far as courts engage in a constitutional colloquy with the political institutions on rights by applying judicial techniques of interpretation that permit statutory responses and disagreements from the political branches of government on the interpretation of constitutional values, any concern that this judicial discourse will serve as a *de jure* veto on politics is misplaced. The central justification for judicial balancing (or review) is that the initial legislative balance may result in rights-violations as a result of legislative inadvertence or neglect, and a judicial recalibration can thus play a positive role in placing such issues on the legislative agenda for the lawmakers' re-deliberation and response. While critics may be right to question the epistemic superiority of judges to make the final determination on the appropriate balance of rights, their argument against judicial balancing loses force when Parliament can harness the ordinary political process subsequently to respond and overrule this judicially conceived balance.

Stavros Tsakyrakis has however argued that judicial balancing 'obscures the moral considerations that are at the heart of human rights issues, and it thus

[46] Afonso da Silva (n 43) 277. [47] Aleinikoff (n 39) 984–5.
[48] 494 US 872 (1990) (United States Supreme Court).
[49] Ibid. 890. See also Kent Greenawalt, *Religion and the Constitution* (Princeton, Princeton University Press 2006) 79.

deprives society of a moral discourse that is indispensable'.[50] In other words, judicial review becomes an amoral endeavour when judges investigate only whether a legislative measure is appropriate or too far-reaching, and not whether it is right or wrong. With respect, this observation of judicial balancing is misconceived. When judges decide that a small amount of a constitutional good has to be sacrificed so that a larger amount of another public good can be realized, they are in essence making moral choices between conflicting alternatives. In vindicating a particular constitutional value, so far as judges prefer one statutory option over another, they are also in essence making a moral judgment on the legislative measures pursued.[51] While one may not necessarily agree with the moral choices judges make, one cannot discount the moral significance and consequence that each judicial decision entails.[52]

Within the jurisdictions under review in common law Asia, the Malaysian courts are alone in endorsing this balancing model of religious liberty. In particular, the Federal Court's application of the balancing test in *Meor Atiqulrahman*,[53] as discussed above, is an exemplary illustration of how courts should seek to reconcile an individual's religious rights against the state's secular objectives.

Unfortunately, the Malaysian judiciary has not been consistent in upholding this balancing model, and it is to this that we now turn. Several months after *Meor Atiqulrahman* was decided, the Federal Court of Malaysia handed down its highly controversial decision in *Lina Joy v Federal Territory Islamic Council & Director-General of the National Registration Department*.[54] In that case, the applicant, Lina Joy, had wanted the National Registration Department (NRD) to delete Islam as her designated religion in her national identity card as she had converted to Christianity. The NRD, however, refused to comply as it wanted her to first produce documentary proof that the syariah courts had approved of this change in religious status. One must nevertheless note that, within Malaysia, only Negeri Sembilam and Sarawak have allowed Muslims to officially convert out of their faith.[55] In other Malaysian states and also within the Federal Territories, no procedures are provided for apostasy; and in a few states, apostasy is even a crime.[56] To

[50] Tsakyrakis (n 40).

[51] Kai Moller, 'Proportionality: Challenging the Critics' (2012) 10 *International Journal of Constitutional Law* 709, 726

[52] Luban (n 45) 78–9.

[53] [2006] 4 MLJ 605 (Federal Court of Malaysia).

[54] (2007) 4 MLJ 585 (Federal Court of Malaysia).

[55] Mohamed Azam Mohamed Adil, 'Law and Apostasy and Freedom of Religion in Malaysia' (2007) 2(1)(6) *Asian Journal of Comparative Law* 23, 27.

[56] Apostasy is a crime in Perak, Pahang, Terengganu, Malacca, and Sabah. In Sabah and Kelantan, those who leave the faith are not considered criminal offenders but they are given mandatory counselling in a faith-rehabilitation centre. Ibid. 21–4.

complicate matters further, this case was decided against the backdrop of an Islamic revival within Malaysian society whereby the ruling government and a key opposition party, the Islamic Party of Malaysia (PAS), were and are still competing to make Islam more prominent within the national discourse.[57]

A central issue before the Federal Court was thus whether Lina Joy's right to her religious freedom was violated by these state restrictions. The Federal Court, by a 2-1 majority, eventually ruled against the applicant. Chief Justice Ahmad Fairuz, on behalf of the majority, held that an individual's constitutional right to religious freedom 'cannot be construed... with such a wide meaning to the extent that it annuls all laws that require a Muslim to perform an Islamic obligation or that restrict them from performing a matter that is prohibited by Islam'.[58] The court offered two reasons for this holding: (1) Islam is the only religion mentioned by its name in the Constitution as it is the religion of the Federation; and (2) the Constitution expressly empowers the individual state legislatures to legislate on matters relating to the Hukum Syarak (Islamic law and teachings) over persons who profess Islam as their religion.[59] More importantly, the Federal Court noted that Article 121(1A) of the Constitution ousted the jurisdiction of the federal courts over 'any matter within the jurisdiction of the Syariah courts'; and although the syariah courts in many Malaysian states and within the Federal Territories had not been expressly conferred jurisdiction over apostasy matters, the Federal Court held that it was logical for those syariah courts to have implied jurisdiction over this matter, as it was one that concerned the application of Islamic law.[60]

Professor Thio Li-ann has argued that the Malaysian civil courts should not have abdicated their responsibility of deciding the apostasy issue for 'renunciation has civil law dimensions as it involves constitutional liberties'.[61] Yet by its very nature, the syariah courts are tasked to adjudicate over religious matters and their decisions would always affect and impinge on the scope of a Muslim's religious freedom. Taking Professor Thio's argument to its logical conclusion, a Muslim will always be able to plead that his or her constitutional right to religious freedom has been infringed by the syariah

[57] See Andrew Harding, *The Constitution of Malaysia: A Contextual Analysis* (Oxford, Hart Publishing 2012) 229–33.

[58] (2007) 4 MLJ 585 (Federal Court of Malaysia) [17.4]. The majority's judgment was only written in the Bahasa Malaysian language. An unofficial English translation of the majority judgment was made available by The Becket Fund and may be viewed in Tan & Thio, *Constitutional Law in Malaysia and Singapore* (Singapore, LexisNexis 2010) 1286–9.

[59] *Lina Joy* (n 58).

[60] Ibid. [15], [16].

[61] Thio Li-ann, 'Apostasy and Religious Freedom: Constitutional Issues Arising from the *Lina Joy* Litigation' (2006) 2 *Malayan Law Journal* 1.

courts and can always seek a civil remedy to circumvent a religious court ruling. Such an approach is untenable as it would render the Article 121(1A) amendment nugatory and deprive it of all effect.

On the other hand, one should not also take the other extreme position whereby the Malaysian civil courts are deprived of any jurisdiction to decide on any matters that ostensibly relate to the Islamic faith. For one, this is not the usual position that the civil courts have taken, even after Article 121(1A) was passed in 1988. Indeed, only several months before its decision in *Lina Joy*, the Federal Court decided on its own in *Meor Atiqulrahman*[62] that the state could prohibit the wearing of the Islamic headdress in public secular schools and the judges never considered whether the matter should be referred to the syariah courts for determination. Therefore, Article 121(1A) cannot also be read to deprive all Muslims of any constitutional protection or a civil remedy whenever their religious practices, even tangentially, are implicated in the dispute.

III. Dialogic Tools to Implementing the Balancing Model of Religious Freedom

In the earlier sections, I have argued that the balancing model of religious freedom is the only constitutionally meaningful safeguard for religious freedom. Accordingly, in deciding whether a state restriction is constitutional, courts should endeavour to weigh the significance of the individual's religious practice against the importance of any ostensible conflicting legislative objectives. This general proposition is subject to one caveat. In Malaysia, the application of the balancing model of religious rights must not render the Article 121(1A) constitutional amendment otiose and redundant.

In this section of my chapter, I shall seek to show how the common law courts in Asia can apply dialogic sub-constitutional tools in upholding the balancing model of religious freedoms, such that the state can respond, engage, and/or disagree with the judicial conception of rights. As discussed in Chapter 4, legislative backlash is a political force that the courts cannot disregard. If courts are perceived to have ruled too broadly and aggressively, the legislature may take hostile steps to resist the ruling (via a constitutional amendment) or remove the judges. Such consequences would significantly affect national politics and undermine

[62] [2006] 4 MLJ 605 (Federal Court of Malaysia).

the very human rights causes that advocates of a particular judicial ruling are seeking to promote.[63] In view of this prudential constraint, two such sub-constitutional tools are particularly apposite. The first, a jurisdictional clear-statement rule, a *common law* right, requires individual Malaysian states in the Federation to confer jurisdiction expressly by an ordinary legislation on the syariah courts before the jurisdiction of the civil courts is ousted; and the second, administrative review, allows judges to resolve administrative law disputes within the same situs from which the conflicts have arisen.

A. Jurisdictional Common Law Clear-Statement Rule

In Malaysia, as discussed above, the general religious rights clause is subject to a constitutional ouster clause that bars the civil courts from adjudicating over matters that fall within the jurisdiction of the syariah courts. Unfortunately, the Constitution does not enumerate the affairs that the religious courts may have jurisdiction over. Nevertheless, the Ninth Schedule of the Constitution (commonly termed the State List) provides that the individual states, within their respective states, would have the right to legislate over matters concerning *inter alia* Islamic law and personal and family law of Muslims, the constitution, organization, and procedure of syariah courts that shall have jurisdiction over Muslims only, and the control of propagating doctrines and beliefs among Muslims.

Therefore, before the Malaysian civil courts defer to the syariah courts, it would be open to the civil judges to require that the religious courts be conferred express jurisdiction by a relevant piece of state legislation to adjudicate over the matter, and determine that this matter is one that the state governments are authorized to legislate over. One may remember that the converse approach was taken by the Federal Court in *Lina Joy* where the majority held that syariah courts have implied jurisdiction over apostasy as it was one that concerned the application of Islamic law, even though the Federal Territories and most Malaysian states have not expressly conferred jurisdiction upon the religious courts over the above-mentioned matter.

Yet, the judicial imposition of a jurisdictional common law clear-statement rule would hardly be novel in Malaysia as this is the general approach taken by the civil courts on most matters, save apostasy. Indeed, just two months after

[63] Cass Sunstein, *A Constitution of Many Minds: Why the Founding Document Doesn't Mean what it Meant Before* (Princeton, Princeton University Press 2009) 125.

Lina Joy was decided, the Federal Court in *Latifah bte Mat Zin v Roasmawati*[64] re-affirmed this jurisdictional clear-statement rule:

[T]he Legislature of a State, in making law to "constitute" and "organize" the syariah courts shall also provide for the jurisdiction of such courts within the limits allowed by item 1 of the State List, for example, it is limited only to persons professing the religion of Islam . . . the State Legislature may choose one or some or all of the matters allowed therein to be included within the jurisdiction of the syariah courts. It can never be that once the syariah courts are established, the courts are seized with jurisdiction over all the matters mentioned in item 1 automatically.[65]

Subsequently, in *Abdul Kahar bin Ahmad v Kerajaan Negeri Selangor*,[66] the Federal Court was even more emphatic that only the civil courts were exclusively authorized to interpret the constitution and that it was for the civil courts to decide when the syariah courts had exclusive jurisdiction over a religious matter. In that case, Selangor's state Islamic council had sought to argue that the syariah courts had the power under Article 121(1A) to decide whether any state legislation passed to implement Islamic law within the state was in accordance with the Federal Constitution. The Federal Court unanimously rejected this proposition and stated unequivocally that the 'interpretation of the Federal Constitution is a matter for this court, not the Syariah Court'[67] and that the 'jurisdiction of the Syariah courts are confined to the limited matters enumerated in the State List [in the Ninth Schedule of the Federal Constitution] *and* enacted by the respective state enactments'.[68] In other words, the issue must be one in which the respective state government has conferred by legislation adjudicatory jurisdiction upon the syariah courts, and it was up to the civil courts exclusively to decide whether their own jurisdiction has been ousted.

Professor Ran Hirschl has observed that the 'blurred jurisdictional matrix'[69] in Malaysia has given rise to a jurisdictional war of courts. But, as Malaysian civil courts seek to navigate this legal quagmire, they do not always have to determine definitively, at the outset, whether a Muslim's constitutional right to religious liberty should always be subjected to a ruling

[64] [2007] 5 MLJ 101 (Federal Court of Malaysia). On the facts in *Latifah*, the Federal Court had to decide in a succession dispute whether the federal law on probates should apply or the Islamic law on gifts ('hibah').

[65] [2007] 5 MLJ 101 (Federal Court of Malaysia) [43].

[66] [2008] 3 MLJ 617 (Federal Court of Malaysia). On the facts, the applicant had sought to challenge the constitutionality of Selangor's Syariah Criminal Offences Enactment but herein, the Federal Court only decided the preliminary question of whether the syariah courts could, pursuant to Article 121(1A), determine the constitutionality of this legislation.

[67] Ibid. [8]. [68] Ibid. [10].

[69] Ran Hirschl, *Constitutional Theocracy* (Cambridge, Harvard University Press 2010) 134.

from the religious courts. Instead, the civil courts could simply impose a jurisdictional clear-statement rule that requires the individual state, on a matter it is empowered under the State List to legislate over, to confer expressly adjudicatory jurisdiction on the syariah courts by legislation.[70] In instances where the syariah courts have not been conferred adjudicatory jurisdiction, the civil courts should simply apply the balancing model of religious liberty to decide whether an individual's (Muslim or otherwise) religious freedom has been constitutionally limited by the state, as the Federal Court has so done in the earlier decision of *Meor Atiqulrahman*.

In view of the above analysis, we may now re-examine the Federal Court decision in *Lina Joy*.[71] While apostasy is a matter of Islamic law, which the state governments are authorized to legislate on, one must also note that the state governments in most Malaysian states and the federal government vis-à-vis the Federal Territories have chosen not to expressly confer adjudicatory jurisdiction over apostasy upon their syariah courts. Therefore, in the absence of an express delegation of authority to the syariah courts, the Federal Court should have ruled that the civil courts were free to adjudicate over this religious matter. Indeed, this was the position advanced by the dissenting judge, Justice Richard Malanjum, in *Lina Joy*, who so rightly observed:

> And in the matters of fundamental rights, there must as far as possible be express authorization for curtailment or violation of fundamental freedoms. No court or authority should be easily allowed to have implied powers to curtail rights constitutionally granted.[72]

This judicial approach which requires the individual Malaysian states to confer expressly adjudicatory jurisdiction on their syariah courts, before the civil courts' jurisdiction is ousted, may arguably lead to inconsistent and conflicting decisions within the Federation,[73] but this is not necessarily a vice as some scholars have argued. The very essence of federalism is that individual states are empowered to diverge from one another on legislative matters that fall within their purview. So far as the Malaysian states choose not to be uniform in conferring adjudicatory jurisdiction on their syariah courts, this should be viewed as a valid demonstration of state autonomy and not be derided as jurisdictional anarchy.

[70] For a survey on the practices of the civil courts, see Thio Li-ann, 'Jurisdictional Imbroglio: Civil and Religious Courts, Turf Wars and Article 121(1A) of the Federal Constitution' in Andrew Harding & H P Lee (eds), *Constitutional Landmarks in Malaysia: 1957–2007* (Kuala Lumpur, LexisNexis 2007).

[71] (2007) 4 MLJ 585 (Federal Court of Malaysia).

[72] Ibid. 636.

[73] Pawancheek Marican, 'Murtad (Apostasy) and Article 121(1A) of the Federal Constitution' [1998] 2 MLJ lxxvii.

Furthermore, the judicial imposition of this jurisdictional common law clear-statement rule is dialogic in nature as it does not permanently foreclose the legislature from conferring adjudicatory jurisdiction on religious matters such as apostasy on the syariah courts if it so chooses. A common law clear-statement rule merely compels the government to speak clearly before it intrudes upon an individual's constitutional right to religious liberty, thereby not creating an absolute prohibition against a desired governmental action.[74] This clear-statement rule is also democracy-enhancing as the state and/or federal legislatures have to deliberate openly, decide explicitly, and take electoral responsibility for any decision(s) to oust the civil courts' jurisdiction and prerogative to protect religious freedoms in Malaysia.

B. Administrative Review

The rise of the 'administrative common law'[75] ameliorates the constitutional tensions of a burgeoning bureaucratic state as courts are empowered to superintend the operation and review the decisions of executive's ministries and agencies. Nevertheless, as administrative review is subject to legislative reversal, it remains a central mechanism through which common law courts in Asia can defend a balancing model of religious liberty, while accommodating the state's changing regulatory needs.

The development of the administrative common law may be loosely tethered (if at all) to any pre-existing statutory text; but so far as it is required or influenced by constitutional mandates and norms, administrative review is vital in checking the excesses of ministerial officials and advancing substantive values of fairness and good administration. Nevertheless, where the judiciary, via administrative review, is merely remanding executive decisions for any perceived failure to take into account constitutional concerns, judges do not oust the legislature's primacy in structuring government as immutable constitutional prescriptions would.[76]

Turning back to the constitutional disputes on religious liberty in Singapore, we may now examine how the judges could have observed a balancing model of religious freedoms via the use of administrative review.

[74] John Manning, 'Clear Statement Rules and the Constitution' (2010) 110 *Columbia Law Review* 399, 402.

[75] Gillian Metzger, 'Embracing Administrative Common Law' (2012) 80 *George Washington Law Review* 1293.

[76] Gillian Metzger, 'Ordinary Administrative Law as Constitutional Common Law' (2010) 110 *Columbia Law Review* 479, 485.

Central to the Singapore government's animus against the Jehovah's Witnesses is the religious group's intransigent refusal to undertake military service, which is mandatory on all able-bodied men in Singapore. Their religious group has been banned in Singapore since 1972 and it is believed that dozens of its male believers are court-martialled and detained yearly for refusing to undertake national service. The Singapore government has consistently refused to make any religious exemptions for any conscientious objectors to the military draft, especially since the island state has a small population of five million,[77] and the grant of any religious exemptions is perceived to have an adverse impact on the operational capabilities of its army. While some scholars have argued that it would be a more proportionate response for the government to offer conscientious objectors the option between a term of military service and a longer term of civilian service,[78] the Singapore judiciary is adamant that such issues are non-justiciable.

As observed by the Singapore Court of Appeal in *Chan Hiang Leng Colin v Minister for Information and the Arts*:[79]

> [I]t is not for the courts to say how many men must refuse to do National Service before the Government can legitimately consider that the refusal constitutes a threat to national security. Nor is it for the courts to say what effect allowing even only a handful of conscientious objector exemption from National Service will have on the morale of those doing National Service or whether it will encourage others to refuse to do National Service... the issue is not justiciable.[80]

Whether we agree or disagree with the judicial observations above, the issue of whether military conscription is a necessary burden for every man to bear, in his discharge of the shared obligation of citizenship, is not the legal question that the Singapore courts had to resolve then.

At the heart of those litigations were far less controversial disputes. In *Colin Chan*, the applicant was merely seeking to quash a ministerial order that banned the import, sale, and distribution of all publications by the International Bible Students Association (IBSA), an affiliate group of the Jehovah's Witnesses; and in *Nappalli Peter Williams*,[81] the applicant was merely challenging the governmental policy that required all teachers in public schools to sing the National Anthem at the school's flag-raising ceremony.

[77] Department of Statistics Singapore, Latest Data <http://www.singstat.gov.sg/ > accessed 15 March 2015.

[78] Kent Greenawalt, *Religion and the Constitution* (Princeton, Princeton University Press 2006) 53.

[79] [1996] 1 SLR 294 (Singapore Court of Appeal).

[80] Ibid. 305–6.

[81] *Nappalli Peter Williams* (n 11).

These disputes raise the legitimacy of various administrative regulations/orders which the courts can easily review, even if they only apply traditionally accepted canons of administrative law. In both cases, the Singapore courts could have subjected the impugned subsidiary legislation or ministerial policy to *Wednesbury*[82] review. One may note that the Singapore Court of Appeal did apply *Wednesbury* review in *Colin Chan*, but it gave a rather bizarre spin on this 'irrationality' test. In deciding whether the blanket ban on all publications by the IBSA was irrational so far as the Minister had used a sledgehammer to crack a nut, the Court of Appeal so observed:

> [The applicant] must show... that no reasonable Minister would use the proverbial sledgehammer to crack the figurative nut. And he must do so within the restriction that issues such as the size of the nut, the thickness of its shell, the force required to crack it, how many attempts one has to crack it, the consequences of failing to crack it, and the adequacy or otherwise of any other alternative such as a smaller nutcracker, are non-justiciable.[83]

With respect, this is a perverse distortion of the *Wednesbury* test, and it is no wonder that the applicant's constitutional challenge failed. If the Singapore judiciary had merely observed traditional *Wednesbury* orthodoxy, it would be patently obvious that the ministerial ban was irrational as the blanket prohibition extended even to innocuous publications such as the King James version of the Bible, which other Christian denominations could freely import and distribute in Singapore. In the same vein, if the *Wednesbury* review had been applied in *Nappalli Peter Williams*, it would have been self-evident that in any free and democratic state, the government would have no legitimate interest at all in compelling its religious-minded teachers, otherwise dedicated and devoted educators, to echo sentiments they do not share and verbalize words they do not mean. Allowing the Jehovah's Witnesses to remain in respectful silence during such ceremonial state events would speak volumes about the country's toleration for religious minorities and serve as a clarion call for communal cohesion.

IV. Conclusion

The formalist understanding of religious liberty is devoid of any normative constitutional content as it merely confers a right to an individual if his or her religious practices are consistent with any state law. The categorization

[82] *Associated Provincial Picture Houses Limited v Wednesbury Corporation* [1948] 1 KB 223 (CA).
[83] *Colin Chan* (n 79) 309.

model of rights fares no better; so far as judges are tasked merely to classify a contested activity as religious or not, this judicial approach fails to consider the more crucial question of whether compelled participation in the disputed activity, even if it is wholly secular in nature, impinges upon the religious belief of the individual. Only the balancing model of rights, which allows courts to assess the reasonableness of a rights-restriction by weighing the significance of the individual's religious practice against the importance of any ostensible conflicting state objective, can serve as a meaningful constitutional safeguard against any state-sanctioned deprivation of religious liberty.

Nevertheless, even as judges observe the balancing model of religious liberty, the courts can implement this with the use of two dialogic sub-constitutional doctrines that I have discussed in Chapter 5. This would include administrative review and, for Malaysia, the judicial enforcement of a common law right (that is the jurisdictional clear-statement rule) that can be displaced by ordinary legislation.

As we have examined in Chapter 4, an aggressive and unpopular constitutional ruling may precipitate another judicial crisis and lead ultimately to the demise of the rule of law. These Asian judges should not simply decide as they deem fit and let the chips fall where they may. On issues pertaining to religion, it is not uncommon for the government and/or the people to hold particularly strong views, such that it is prudent for courts to shape legal doctrines that are responsive to dialogue beyond the judiciary. This is especially so for Islamic nations like Malaysia. It is not inconceivable that there would be massive outrage and significant repercussions if the Malaysian judges were to rule outright that Muslims have the constitutional right to renounce their faith at will. Common law clear-statement rules are dialogic precisely because they invite other states in the Malaysian Federation to participate in a multi-sited conversation on the scope of a Muslim's religious freedom. The Federal Court of Malaysia, in the first instance, does not need to foreclose this constitutional conversation for the entire nation. So far as there is state-level experimentation and differences across Malaysia, democracy is enriched and dialogue is alive. As for the use of administrative review in Singapore, its application would be particularly apt as all those constitutional disputes in question arose from within the administrative law forum. Furthermore, the Singapore Parliament would retain the choice of overturning any judicial determination with an ordinary statute if it so chooses. Administrative review embodies the essence of inter-branch dialogue as it is a form of adjudication that regularly invites judges, executive officials, and the legislature to develop and contest public law norms and meanings.

These sub-constitutional methods allow judges to provide a robust reading of rights while not excluding or foreclosing the political branches of government from responding to the judicial decisions and engaging the courts in a constitutional conversation on the protection of religious liberty. By leaving room for democratic deliberation and popular resistance to the court's interpretive mandate, all three branches of the government (the executive, the legislature, and the judiciary) are able to expose one another's weaknesses, hold one another's excesses in check, and gradually forge a consensus on constitutional values.[84] Therein lies the legitimacy and vitality of any constitutional instrument intended to endure for ages to come.

[84] Neal E Devins & Louis Fisher, *The Democratic Constitution* (Oxford, Oxford University Press 2004) 239.

8

Right to Equality

Almost every modern Constitution contains a general equal protection clause that seeks to guard against arbitrary or discriminatory state practices. In most western democracies, this constitutional guarantee of equality is judicially understood to embody a substantive ideal—courts are required to identify *prima facie* prohibited bases of legislative differentiations and where they do exist, the onus is on the government to demonstrate how these differentiations are justifiable.[1]

Unfortunately, within common law Asia, many of the territorial courts do not uphold this substantive model of equality. Neither are they constant in upholding a particular model of equality. In fact, a review of the constitutional practices of Malaysia, Singapore, and Hong Kong reveals four judicial approaches to equality.

First, we may observe a formal model of equality where the courts merely require equal treatment for all persons who are situated within the same legislative category. This is merely a principle for consistency. Second, a corollary of the formal principle, we may find the rational connection model. This model provides that a statutory provision would be deemed arbitrary if the legislative distinctions do not have a rational connection to the object sought to be achieved by the law in question. Third, the 'forbidden personal characteristics' model is, in essence, the substantive model of equality commonly applied in the West—courts seek to identify *prima facie* forbidden grounds of statutory differentiations based on an individual's personal traits, that is personal characteristics for which individuals have been historically subjected to stereotype and/or prejudice, that require state justification. Finally, the 'fundamental rights' model of equality assumes that all legislative differentiations that affect an individual's exercise of his or her fundamental rights are *prima facie* discriminatory unless justified.

[1] *Withler v Canada* [2011] 1 SCR 396 (Supreme Court of Canada); *United States v Virginia* 518 US 515 (1996) (United States Supreme Court); *Carson v Secretary of State for Work and Pensions* [2006] 1 AC 173 (HL).

One must note at the outset that the Asian territorial courts do not always observe the same model of equality. Malaysia, in particular, vacillates between the different judicial models. Nonetheless, it is reasonable to state that some Malaysian courts subscribe to the formal model;[2] the Singapore courts[3] and a few Malaysian decisions[4] endorse the rational connection approach; the 'forbidden personal characteristics' model represents the Hong Kong approach,[5] and finally, one line of Malaysian cases espouses the 'fundamental rights' model of equality.[6]

In this chapter, I shall advance two main claims. The first claim is that the 'forbidden personal characteristics' model of equality serves as the only logical and meaningful constitutional standard of equality for courts in these Asian jurisdictions to apply. The second claim is that common law courts in Asia should develop a 'sliding scale' of review to determine whether the equality infringement on the basis of a personal traits-differentiation is justified. This sliding scale would permit courts to assign different categories/types of traits-differentiation to varying standards of judicial scrutiny, and the standard of review may differ over time and space.

This chapter consists of three main parts. Section I begins with a description of the four models of equality as exemplified by case law. Section II examines how, apart from the 'forbidden personal characteristics' model of equality, the other three judicial models of equality are inherently defective as constitutional safeguards against discriminatory state action. Finally in Section III, I explain and defend why courts should apply a sliding scale of review over legislative differentiations on the basis of an individual's personal traits. Specifically, I shall argue that prudence may counsel in favour of judicial restraint when courts are faced with legislative differentiations on grounds where the polity is in a state of moral flux. In such circumstances, where judges adopt a posture of deference and uphold the impugned legislation so long as there is a rational basis for the legislative decision, a constitutional dialogue on rights with the legislature may ensue. After all, the notion of deference suggests that the courts are abiding by a determination that they might not have reached if the judges had decided the same question

[2] *Danaharta Urus v Kekatong* [2004] 2 MLJ 257 (Federal Court of Malaysia); *Public Prosecutor v Khong Teng Khen* [1976] 2 MLJ 166 (Federal Court of Malaysia).

[3] *Public Prosecutor v Taw Cheng Kong* [1998] 2 SLR 410 (Singapore Court of Appeal); *Yong Vui Kong v Public Prosecutor* [2010] 3 SLR 489 (Singapore Court of Appeal).

[4] *Public Prosecutor v Harmenderpall Singh* [2007] 3 MLJ 433 (Malaysia Court of Appeal); *Datuk Haji bin Harun Idris v Public Prosecutor* [1977] 2 MLJ 155 (Federal Court of Malaysia).

[5] *Secretary of Justice v Yau Yuk Lung* [2007] 3 HKLRD 903 (Hong Kong Court of Final Appeal); *Fok Chun Wa v Hospital Authority* (2012) 15 HKCFAR 409 (Hong Kong Court of Final Appeal).

[6] *Sivarasa Rasiah v Badan Peguam Malaysia* [2010] 2 MLJ 333 (Federal Court of Malaysia).

independently for themselves. As discussed more fully in Chapter 5, rational basis review is a dialogic sub-constitutional tool as lawmakers are granted significant discretion to pursue the statutory goals they want if courts only interfere with their legislative determinations when lawmakers act *irrationally*.

I. Overview of the Four Models of Equality

Section I maps out the four models of equality that are applied by the appellate courts in Malaysia, Singapore, and Hong Kong when they interpret the general equal protection clauses of their respective constitutions. At the outset, it may be useful to restate the respective general equal protection clauses enshrined in the Constitutions of these jurisdictions that guard against discriminatory state practices.

Malaysia: 'All persons are equal before the law and entitled to the equal protection of the law.'[7]

Hong Kong: 'All Hong Kong residents shall be equal before the law.'[8]

Singapore: 'All persons are equal before the law and entitled to the equal protection of the law.'[9]

This section of this chapter focusses on how the courts have interpreted their respective general equal protection clauses and, in particular, on how they have sought to constrain the ability of their respective governments to differentiate between groups of people. By differentiating between these four judicial models of equality, we can better appreciate the interpretive options that are available to the courts in each jurisdiction, and this comparative exercise will also permit us to appreciate the reasons for endorsing one model over another as discussed in Section II of this chapter.

A. Formal Model

Pursuant to the formal model of equality, any legislative differentiation would pass constitutional muster so long as the state treats all persons within that particular legislative classification alike. Hence, the state may classify persons along any legislative baselines so long as it treats all people within each legislative class the same way and does not single out any person within the same classification for discriminatory treatment. This is, in essence, a principle of

[7] Malaysia Constitution, Article 8(1).
[8] Hong Kong Basic Law, Article 25.
[9] Singapore Constitution, Article 12(1).

consistency. The state is required to treat all persons that it has classed in the same category consistently and in the same way.

This formal model has been endorsed by the Federal Court of Malaysia recently in *Danaharta Urus v Kekatong*.[10] In that case, an applicant challenged a legislative provision that barred the courts from granting an injunction against Danaharta, the nation's asset management company, which was statutorily authorized to buy over bad loans from financial institutions (together with any charged securities, where available) and to dispose of these charged assets by private treaty expeditiously without a court order. In particular, the applicant, Kekatong, the defaulter of a loan acquired by Danaharta, argued that this legislative provision violated his constitutional right to equality as Danaharta itself or other defaulters of loans not acquired by Danaharta were not barred from seeking injunctive relief in court. The Federal Court unanimously disagreed, stating that this statutory denial of injunctive relief applied to all persons in the same position as the applicant, that is all persons whose assets and liabilities have been acquired by Danaharta, and therefore, there would be a violation of the right to equality 'only if a legislation does not apply to a person who is similarly circumstanced as the other persons in the classification—and not to someone… outside of it'.[11]

Pursuant to this formal model of equality, the court must ascertain whether the state has treated all persons within a particular legislative category alike. The court does not examine the reasonableness of the legislative classifications. Ergo, all forms of legislative classifications are permissible; it is immaterial whether they further the aims of the legislative policy in question. In essence, under the formal model of equality, the court is only concerned with discriminatory administrative decisions taken under the statute in question and not with the discriminatory nature of the impugned legislation.

B. Rational Connection Model

According to the rational connection model of equality, the court examines the constitutional propriety of the impugned statutory classifications. However, the reasonableness of the legislative classes is determined by whether the classifications have a rational connection with the legislative policy in question. So long as the legislative classes further a state interest, the legislative provision in question is constitutionally valid. This model of equality, also known as the doctrine of rational classification, has its origins in American constitutional jurisprudence.[12]

[10] *Danaharta Urus* (n 2). [11] Ibid. [59].

[12] See Gregory S Chernack, 'The Clash of Two Worlds: Justice Robert H. Jackson, Institutional Pragmatism, and Brown' (1999) 72 *Temple Law Review* 51, 103.

Although American courts no longer exclusively apply the doctrine of rational classification, this model of equality continues to find favour with Singaporean and Malaysian courts.

The Malaysian Court of Appeal in *Public Prosecutor v Harmenderpall Singh*[13] had applied this rational connection test in determining whether a differentiating legislative measure was a violation of the right to equality. On the facts, the accused was charged under Section 41 of the Road Transport Act[14] (RTA), an offence-creating provision for reckless driving which resulted in death, and his licence was suspended pending trial. He argued that his right to equality was violated as an individual charged under Section 42 of the same Act, an offence-creating provision for reckless driving that did not result in death, would not have his or her licence suspended pending trial. The Court of Appeal disagreed, arguing that the objective of the RTA was to 'offer protection to third party against risks arising from the use of motor vehicle'[15] and that 'this standard of using the death factor'[16] had a rational connection to this legislative policy.

In the same vein, in *Public Prosecutor v Taw Cheng Kong*,[17] the Singapore Court of Appeal had to decide whether an extraterritorial legislative provision that applied only to Singapore citizens violated Article 12(1) of the Singapore Constitution that guarantees to all persons equal protection of the law. The impugned statutory provision provides that a Singapore citizen who had committed an offence under the Prevention of Corruption Act may be dealt with in respect of that offence as if it had been committed in Singapore, even if he or she was outside of Singapore.[18] There was no equivalent legislative provision that applied to non-Singapore citizens. The Court of Appeal opined that in determining whether the differential treatments between citizens and non-citizens were reasonable, the court would look to:

(a) whether the classification was founded on intelligible differentia and
(b) whether the differentia bore a rational relation to the object of the provision—in other words, a nexus must be established.[19]

The court eventually concluded that there was a rational nexus between the legislative differentia, that is citizens and non-citizens, and the object of the law, which was to suppress corruption in Singapore while observing 'international comity and the sovereignty of other nations'[20] that discouraged the

[13] *Public Prosecutor v Harmenderpall Singh* [2007] 3 MLJ 433 (Malaysia Court of Appeal).
[14] Road Transport Act (Laws of Malaysia Act 333).
[15] *Harmenderpall Singh* (n 13) [71].
[16] Ibid.
[17] [1998] 2 SLR 410 (Singapore Court of Appeal).
[18] Singapore Prevention of Corruption Act (Cap 241), s 37(1).
[19] *Taw Cheng Kong* (n 17) [61].
[20] Ibid. [75].

regulation of other sovereign powers' subjects outside one's own territory. The constitutional validity of the legislative provision was thus upheld on this basis.

Similarly, the Singapore Court of Appeal in *Yong Vui Kong v Public Prosecutor*[21] upheld the constitutionality of a legislative provision, against an equality challenge, which imposed the mandatory death penalty on persons who trafficked 15g or more of diamorphine, a controlled drug, in Singapore.[22] In applying the rational classification test, the Court of Appeal concluded that the 'quantity of addictive drugs trafficked is... broadly proportionate to the harm likely to be posed to society by the offender's crime',[23] and thus the statutory 15g differentia bore a rational relation to the social object of stamping out the illicit drug trade in Singapore.

More recently, in *Lim Meng Suang v Attorney General,*[24] the Singapore Court of Appeal upheld Section 377A of the Singapore Penal Code,[25] which criminalizes any act of gross indecency between men, even where the conduct is consensual and performed in the privacy of one's home, against an equal protection challenge. According to the Court of Appeal, the impugned legislative provision did not violate the applicants' (two gay partners) constitutional right to equality as the object of Section 377A was as stated by the then Attorney General CG Howell when he introduced the law into Singapore in 1938, that is to criminalize grossly indecent acts between men even in private; and there was thus a complete coincidence between the differentia underlying the classification prescribed by Section 377A (the statutory distinction drawn between males who perform sexual acts with males and the legislative exclusion of male-female/female-female sexual acts) and the purpose of the impugned provision.[26]

The rational connection model of equality only examines whether there is a logical nexus between the legislative differentia and the statutory policy in question. The court does not further examine whether the legislative policy itself is reasonable or legitimate. Hence, purely arbitrary legislative classes that do not further the aims of the legislative objective will be deemed null and void. Taken to its logical conclusion, the court would even sustain legislative policies that are invidiously irrational or unjust, so long as there is some nexus between the object sought to be achieved and the classifications.

[21] [2010] 3 SLR 489 (Singapore Court of Appeal).

[22] The Singapore Court of Appeal in *Nguyen Tuong Van v Public Prosecutor* [2004] SGCA 47 (Singapore Court of Appeal) had previously also applied the rational connection test to uphold this law against an equality challenge.

[23] *Yong Vui Kong* (n 21) [112].

[24] [2014] SGCA 53

[25] Penal Code, (Cap 224), Section 377A.

[26] *Lim Meng Suang* (n 24) [153].

C. 'Forbidden Personal Characteristics' Model

The 'forbidden personal characteristics' model of equality is a version of substantive equality whereby the court seeks to import a moral precept that identifies the type of legislative classifications that are *prima facie* forbidden. This model instructs that some differences based on an individual's personal traits should be treated as accidental and be ignored in the legislative allocation of benefits and burdens. Unlike the two earlier discussed judicial models of equality, the courts herein would identify personal characteristics that are *prima facie* forbidden grounds for legislative differentiations, unless the state can provide due justifications for their existence.

This model of equality is the judicial approach adopted by the House of Lords[27] (and now Supreme Court of the United Kingdom) and the Supreme Court of Canada.[28] Within common law Asia, this is also the judicial approach adopted by the Hong Kong Court of Final Appeal (CFA). In *Secretary of Justice v Yau Yuk Lung*,[29] the CFA had to decide whether a statutory provision, which only criminalized homosexual buggery committed otherwise than in private, was a violation of the accused's constitutional right to equality. This was a differentiating measure as the statute does not impose any criminal liability on heterosexuals who commit the same or comparable sexual conduct in public.[30] Even though the Hong Kong Basic Law does not expressly enumerate what legislative bases of differentiations are prohibited, the CFA opined that the Constitution would implicitly prohibit any discrimination that is statutorily barred by the Hong Kong Bill of Rights Ordinance[31] (BORO), a statute passed in 1991 by the colonial government to 'bring home' the rights the British government acceded to in 1976 when it ratified the International Covenant on Civil and Political Rights and extended its application to Hong Kong.[32] This statute remains in force and, in particular, Article 22 of the BORO expressly prohibits any 'discrimination on any ground such as race, colour, sex, language, religion, political or other opinion, national or social origin, property, birth or other status'. Even though sexual orientation is not a ground expressly prohibited under the BORO, the CFA agreed that it fell within the statutory phrase 'other status' and that any legislative differentiation on this ground was

[27] *Carson v Secretary of State for Work and Pensions* [2006] 1 AC 173 (HL).

[28] *Withler v Canada* [2011] 1 SCR 396 (Supreme Court of Canada).

[29] *Secretary of Justice v Yau Yuk Lung* [2007] 3 HKLRD 903 (Hong Kong Court of Final Appeal).

[30] One must note that it was and remains a common law offence for any person (heterosexual or homosexual) to commit an act of a lewd or obscene nature which outrages public decency.

[31] Bill of Rights Ordinance (Cap 383).

[32] See Richard Swede, 'One Territory—Three Systems? The Hong Kong Bill of Rights' (1995) 44 *International and Comparative Law Quarterly*, 358–78.

also *prima facie* forbidden under the BORO and the Basic Law. Subsequently, in *Fok Chun Wa v Hospital Authority*,[33] the CFA explained that these enumerated and analogous BORO grounds of legislative differentiation strike at the 'heart of core-values relating to personal or human characteristics'[34] that involve 'the respect and dignity that society accords to a human being',[35] and the courts would 'extremely rarely (if at all) find this acceptable'.[36]

This 'forbidden personal characteristics' model has the capacity to remedy discrimination that arises not only from legislation that expressly distinguishes between persons, on *prima facie* forbidden grounds, in the distribution of benefits but also facially neutral laws of general application, that is laws that do not categorize people into groups but have discriminatory impact on such persons. In Canada, for example, the Supreme Court in *Eldridge v British Columbia*[37] agreed that the legislative failure to provide interpreter services for hearing impaired persons at hospitals violated the disabled's right to equality, even though, on its face, the Medicare system did not single out hearing-impaired persons for differential treatment.

Similarly, in Hong Kong, the Court of Appeal in *Leung v Secretary of Justice*[38] invalidated a law that restricted both homosexual and heterosexual acts of buggery to persons who were at least 21 years old on the ground that this legislation had a discriminatory impact on gay men. The court opined that although this penal prohibition applied to both homosexuals and heterosexuals, a female could nevertheless legally consent to vaginal intercourse at the age of 16, such that it 'remains discriminatory when persons of a majority class are permitted the right to sexual expression in a way natural to them'[39] while persons of a minority class are denied the same right to sexual intimacy.

D. 'Fundamental Rights' Model

Finally, the 'fundamental rights' model of equality is one in which the courts would deem any legislative differentiation, on whatsoever ground, *prima facie* forbidden if the differentiating measure would affect the individual/group's exercise of a fundamental right and the onus is always on the state to justify the reasonableness of such measures.

In *Sivarasa Rasiah v Badan Peguam Malaysia*,[40] the Federal Court of Malaysia was faced with a constitutional challenge against a statutory

[33] [2012] 15 HKCFAR 409 (Hong Kong Court of Final Appeal). [34] Ibid. [77].
[35] Ibid. [36] Ibid. [37] [1997] SCR 624 (Supreme Court of Canada).
[38] [2006] 4 HKLRD 211 (Hong Kong Court of Appeal).
[39] *Leung v Secretary of Justice* (n 38) [48].
[40] *Sivarasa Rasiah v Badan Peguam Malaysia* [2010] 2 MLJ 333 (Federal Court of Malaysia).

provision that barred advocates from serving on the governing body of the Malaysian Bar if they were either members of Parliament or office-holders in any political party. The court noted that the impugned legislation had distinguished between advocates who held office in a political party and those who did not. Interestingly, to survive an equality challenge, the only test the court applied was whether the legislative state action was disproportionate to a sufficiently important object it sought to achieve.[41] The court did not examine whether the legislature was distinguishing persons on the basis of personal traits; instead, this legislative distinction was *prima facie* a violation of a person's right to equality and had to be justified. On the facts, while the applicant's right to run for office (and hence his freedom of association) was infringed upon, the court held that this differentiating measure was proportionate as Parliament had a legitimate interest in keeping the Bar Council free from political influence, and the applicant (and others in his position) retained their right to attend and speak out at the Bar general meetings if they so wanted to influence any Bar resolutions.[42]

This judicial model of equality deems all legislative classifications that affect an individual's fundamental right suspect and would subject all forms of such statutory differentiations to the court's scrutiny under the equal protection clause. This is an expansive understanding of the mandate imposed under the constitutional right to equality as the state is required to justify all varieties of legislative distinctions drawn, regardless of whether these differentiations are premised on an individual's personal traits and characteristics that reflect societal stereotypes or historical prejudices.

II. Evaluating the Four Models

A. Formal Model

Pursuant to the formal model of equality, all individuals must be treated alike to the extent that they are alike. However, the formal model simply presumes that people may be equal or unequal by virtue of certain attributes they have or lack, but it fails to articulate a moral standard for determining what traits are relevant in this constitutional calculus. It also provides no

[41] Ibid. [30]. [42] *Sivarasa Rasiah* (n 40) [33].

criteria to assess the propriety of any statutory differentiations of persons. Seen in this light, as Professor Peter Westen has observed:

> Equality is an empty vessel with no substantive moral content of its own. Without moral standards, equality remains meaningless, a formula that can have nothing to say about how we should act.[43]

After all, everyone is similar and different from one another in an infinite number of ways. Unless some restrictions are placed on the types of character traits that can be morally relevant for differential treatment, the principle of equality becomes tautological and meaningless.

Consider, for instance, a hypothetical legislative provision that states, 'no divorced females may be appointed as judicial officers in the legal service'. This rule clearly singles out divorced females for differential treatment by prohibiting their appointment as judges. According to the formal principles of equality laid out by the Malaysian Federal Court in *Danaharta Urus v Kekatong,* there will be a constitutional violation of the right to equality 'only if a legislation does not apply to a person who is similarly circumstanced as the other persons in the classification—and not to someone... outside of it'.[44] Ergo, since divorced females form a separate class of persons apart from men and non-divorced females, the mandate of equality is satisfied so long as all divorced females are treated in the same way under this legislative policy.

Under the formal model of equality, the court is merely required to ensure that the state has treated all persons within a particular legislative category in the same way. All members of a class are similarly situated in this respect and consequently, any legislative classes however drawn would be deemed reasonable.[45] By not scrutinizing whether the legislature's rationale for making such statutory distinctions is in itself reasonable, all forms of legislative classifications are arguably constitutionally permissible, regardless of how irrational, silly, or arbitrary they may be.

Consider, for instance, another hypothetical statutory provision: 'No person with myopia shall be allowed to attend public school.' Again, there are two distinct legislative classes—persons with myopia are distinguished from those with perfect vision for differential treatment. According to the formal model of equality, the state is only required to deny all short-sighted persons public education and grant all persons with perfect vision access to public schools. Hence, the judiciary would only interfere if some students with myopia are admitted into public schools while other similarly situated persons are excluded. It seems then that under the formal model of equality, every legislative differentiation

43 Peter Westen, 'The Empty Idea of Equality' (1982) 95 *Harvard Law Review* 537, 547.

44 *Danaharta* (n 2) [60].

45 Joseph Tussman & Jacobus tenBroek, 'The Equal Protection of the Laws' (1949) 37 *California Law Review* 341, 345.

would satisfy the constitutional mandate of equality as the judiciary would only intervene when discriminatory administrative decisions are made and not when discriminatory legislation is enacted. In effect, this formal model of equality exempts every piece of legislation from scrutiny under the equal protection clause. This would be indeed a very odd state of affairs; the operative effect of an equal protection clause on legislation surely cannot be the same as if such a constitutional clause never existed.

Perhaps the most explicit judicial rejection of the formal model has been voiced by Canadian Supreme Court Justice McIntyre in *Andrews v Law Society of British Columbia*:[46]

> [M]ere equality of application to similarly situated groups or individuals does not afford a realistic test for a violation of equality rights. For, as has been said, a bad law will not be saved merely because it operates equally upon those to whom it has application.[47]

If the similarly situated test was applied formalistically, '[i]t could be used to justify the Nuremberg laws of Adolf Hitler. Similar treatment was contemplated for all Jews'.[48]

The formal model of equality is not insignificant so far as it is a model for consistent state action and ensures that the ruling government, at the very minimum, observes a thin conception of the rule of law. Nevertheless, this model is seriously defective as a constitutional safeguard as it does not supply 'the crucial criteria that are required to determine who is similarly situated to whom, and what kinds of difference in treatment are appropriate to those who are not similarly situated'.[49] In excluding any judicial consideration of the nature, purpose, content, and/or impact of the law, this formal model of equality is merely a mandate for administrative consistency as it is practically inoperative against any discriminatory legislation.

B. Rational Connection Model

Unlike the tautological and vacuous nature of the formal model, the rational connection model of equality is an improvement as judges would herein measure the nexus of the legislative classifications against the object of the law. In other words, the relevant legislative classes must bear a rational connection to the statutory goals.

The judicial model of equality is marginally better than its formal predecessor, but it is open to legislative manipulation. By framing the purpose of the law narrowly, the legislature would always be able to establish a logical

[46] [1989] 56 DLR 1 (Supreme Court of Canada) 12. [47] Ibid. [10]. [48] Ibid.

[49] Peter Hogg, *Constitutional Law of Canada* (4th edn, Scarborough, Carswell 1997) 1242.

nexus between the legislative classes and the statutory purpose. For instance, if the Singapore Parliament decides to pass a piece of legislation with the purpose of 'excluding women from public office', the legislative classifications, that is men and women, would invariably bear a rational nexus to the object sought to be achieved. As SM Huang-Thio indicated, '[i]n this way, discriminatory provisions can be validly enacted so long as the purpose of the law is formulated in narrow terms'.[50]

Furthermore, the rational connection model is also defective so far as '[i]t is always possible to define the legislative purpose of a statute in such a way that the statutory classification is rationally related to it', because 'the reach of the purpose has been derived from the classifications themselves'.[51] In every case in which the courts would invalidate a statutory provision for failing the rational nexus test, it would be equally possible for the judiciary to define the purpose more broadly such that the court could deem a rational nexus established. In other words, pursuant to this rational connection model, courts can either sustain or reject the rationality of the legislation by manipulating the level of abstraction of the legislative object judicially discerned.

In *Taw Cheng Kong v Public Prosecutor*, the High Court of Singapore held that the objective of the extraterritorial legislative provision in question was 'to address acts of corruption taking place outside Singapore but affecting events within it'.[52] The High Court's definition of the legislative purpose led the learned judge to observe that the impugned statutory provision caught a class of people not contemplated by the legislature, that is Singaporean citizens who lived and worked abroad and who have committed corrupt acts abroad that had no impact on Singapore. Thus, the High Court held that citizenship was 'not a useful criteria for determining guilt'[53] because the 'strength of the nexus between the objective and the classification is not sufficiently strong to justify the derogation'[54] from the constitutional mandate of equality.

The Court of Appeal disagreed, holding that the intent of Parliament was to increase the effectiveness of corruption prevention while observing international comity that argued against the regulation of non-citizens outside one's jurisdiction. Any legislative differentiation between citizens and non-citizens was thus rationally connected to the furtherance of this legislative aim. One can thus observe how a court defines or formulates the legislative purpose invariably allows it to decide whether the impugned statutory classifications are rational. In essence, the rational connection model of equality is not a

[50] SM Huang-Thio, 'Equal Protection and Rational Connection' [1963] *Public Law* 412, 428.
[51] 'Legislative Purpose, Rationality, and Equal Protection' (1972) 82 *Yale Law Journal* 123, 128.
[52] [1998] 1 SLR 78 (High Court of Singapore) [51]. [53] Ibid. [64]. [54] Ibid.

constitutional tool for testing the constitutional validity of a statute, but is merely a method for justifying or denying its legality.

Finally, in focussing only on the relationship between the purpose of the law and the legislative classification, this rational connection model, like the formal model, as commonly applied, fails to consider whether the object of the law is in itself legitimate and reasonable. For instance, consider again a hypothetical legislative provision that bars females from seeking public office. If the object of the law is framed as such, any gender classifications pursuant to this objective would still bear a rational nexus to the legislative purpose at hand and could be constitutionally sustained under the rational connection model of equality. Taken to its logical conclusion, this judicial model of equality that imposes no substantive limits on the statutory ends that a legislature may pursue would equally legitimize the apartheid regime in South Africa and the Nuremberg laws of Nazi Germany, since all the racial classifications would invariably bear a rational connection to the deplorable statutory goals.

Turning to the recent Singapore gay rights case of *Lim Meng Suang*,[55] the Court of Appeal explicitly held that the Singapore judiciary did not have the power to examine the legitimacy of the legislative object as this would 'confer on the court a licence to usurp the legislative function in the course of becoming (or at least acting like) a "mini-legislature"'.[56] The Court of Appeal was emphatic that the 'duty of a court is to interpret statutes enacted by the legislature; it cannot amend or modify statutes based on its own personal preference or fiat'.[57] While the Singapore Court was right that judges should not impose their personal whims during constitutional adjudication, this is not to say that they should therefore be bound by the statutory object. After all, under a constitutional arrangement where Parliamentary supremacy has been expressly jettisoned, the statutory object of the law is not sacrosanct. In implementing the open-ended contours of the equal protection clause, it is always for the Singapore courts to devise or reformulate doctrinal tests to determine whether an impugned law is constitutional, and judges should not merely exalt the statutory object during such adjudication. There is therefore no reason why the Singapore Courts should be hamstrung by the rational classification test, especially since the rational connection test itself, as conceded by the Court of Appeal in *Lim Meng Suang* was also 'formulated by the courts'.[58]

[55] *Lim Meng Suang* (n 24). See Yap Po Jen, 'Section 377A and Equal Protection in Singapore—Back to 1938?' (2013) 25 *Singapore Academy of Law Journal* 630.

[56] *Lim Meng Suang* (n 24) at [82].

[57] *Lim Meng Suang* (n 24) at [77].

[58] *Lim Meng Suang* (n 24) at [88]. Interestingly, the Court of Appeal in *Lim Meng Suang* held that certain legislative differentia may be so unreasonable as to be illogical and/or incoherent,

C. 'Forbidden Personal Characteristics' Model

The 'forbidden personal characteristics' model of equality is a substantive formulation of the equality ideal because it seeks to bar legislation whose purpose or effect discriminates against individuals on morally irrelevant grounds. The central idea that animates a substantive interpretation of equal treatment is that all persons should be treated on the basis that they are of equal moral status.[59] Professor John Rawls has written that this equality ideal encompasses a duty of mutual respect that is owed to all human beings as moral persons. Professor Ronald Dworkin had also argued that every person is entitled to 'equal concern and respect'.[60] To this end, some judges have devised a test that directly translates these substantive egalitarian norms into legal doctrines. In *Vriend v Alberta*, L'Heureux-Dubé J proposed, in a concurring opinion, that courts, in deciding whether any impugned legislative differentiation was *prima facie* forbidden, should look at whether the impugned law has deprived an individual or group 'in a way which negatively affects their human dignity and personhood, [and] does not treat these persons or groups with "equal concern, respect and consideration"'.[61]

While few would disagree, in the abstract, with these substantive egalitarian norms of human dignity and 'equal respect', for any judicial rule or standard to be workable in practice, it must however, be 'judicially manageable'. Professor Richard Fallon has argued that for a doctrinal test devised by the courts to be judicially manageable, the legal doctrine must (1) be intelligible (rationally comprehensible); (2) have 'analytical bite', that is the capacity to structure an analysis that could in principle lead to correct results; (3) have the ability to generate predictable and consistent results; and (4) be administrable without overreaching the court's empirical capabilities.[62] In view of the four criteria Fallon raised, one may indeed have concerns about whether a term as malleable and fluid as 'dignity' or 'equal concern and respect' can be

but the illogicality must be 'so extreme that no reasonable person would ever contemplate the differentia concerned as being functional as intelligible differentia' (at [67]). The Court of Appeal held that it was thus arguable that a hypothetical law, which banned all women from driving on Singapore roads, would not pass legal muster under the rational connection test (at [114]), but no such illogicality existed on the facts.

[59] Patrick Shin, 'The Substantive Principle of Equal Treatment' (2009) 15(2) *Legal Theory* 149, 155.

[60] Ronald Dworkin, *Taking Rights Seriously* (Cambridge, Harvard University Press 1977) 272–3. See also David Feldman, 'Human Dignity as a Legal Value' [1999] *Public Law* 682.

[61] *Vriend v Alberta* 1 SCR 493 (Supreme Court of Canada) [183].

[62] Richard Fallon, 'Judicial Manageable Standards and Constitutional Meaning' (2006) 119 *Harvard Law Review* 1274, 1285–92.

used as a self-standing criterion to decide whether the constitutional mandate of equality has been complied with. The legislature can arguably differentiate between persons in a myriad of ways; persons who are denied certain benefits that are conferred on others would almost always argue that their dignity or their right to equal respect has been violated by the state. Relying on the dignity discourse alone, the judiciary may not have a workable determinate standard and the requisite conceptual and empirical resources to determine when a perceived disrespect to an individual/group is a constitutional violation of equality. In short, while 'dignity' and 'equal concern and respect' may form the philosophical underpinnings and rationale for a substantive understanding of equality, these concepts *alone* are too general, too vague, and lack analytical bite to form an effective doctrinal test that helps courts decide whether the right to equality has been violated in specific instances; any recourse to dignity alone as a juridical concept then becomes a mere 'assertion, not an analysis'.[63]

Therefore, the only logical, meaningful, and judicially manageable interpretation of equality is one where courts have to first identify various presumptively forbidden grounds of discrimination that are based on differentiating descriptors/traits that evince any legislative display of unequal respect between individuals/groups. But for these traits to have determinate limits and analytical bite, we should restrict these presumptively forbidden differentiating descriptors to particular personal traits, that is personal characteristics for which individuals with these traits have been historically subjected to stereotype and/or prejudice.[64] This would include personal traits such as one's race, gender, disability, religion, and sexual orientation. This is also the general position taken by the courts in Canada,[65] United Kingdom,[66] and Hong Kong.[67]

[63] Donna Greschner, 'Does Law Advance the Cause of Equality?' (2001) 27 *Queen's Law Journal* 299, 312–13.

[64] Arguably, in the same vein, Professor Hugh Collins in 'Discrimination, Equality and Social Inclusion' (2003) 66 *Modern Law Review* 43 has argued that the conception of equality encapsulates a notion of social inclusion that seeks to identify whether a disadvantaged group, in practice, has been disproportionately excluded socially compared to the population as a whole and whether a legislative practice tends to reinforce the exclusion of an individual member of an excluded group or most members of the excluded group.

[65] *Withler v Canada* [2011] 1 SCR 396 (Supreme Court of Canada).

[66] *Carson v Secretary of State for Work and Pensions* [2006] 1 AC 173 (HL). *Clift v Secretary of State for the Home Department*, [2007] 1 AC 484 (HL). One must however note that on further appeal to the European Court of Human Rights (ECHR), the European Court in *Clift v United Kingdom* [2010] ECHR 1106, held that the European Convention's prohibition of discrimination was not limited to differential treatment based on characteristics which were personal in the sense of being innate or inherent.

[67] *Fok Chun Wa v Hospital Authority* [2012] 15 HKCFAR 409 (Hong Kong Court of Final Appeal).

In *Yau Yuk Lung*, the Hong Kong CFA has recognized the role that the dignity discourse plays in fleshing out the philosophical underpinnings of the constitutional right to equality. As observed by Chief Justice Li:

> Discriminatory law is unfair and violates the human dignity of those discriminated against. It is demeaning for them and generates ill-will and a sense of grievance on their part.[68]

Nevertheless, and more importantly, the CFA, as discussed earlier, has gone on and relied only on a 'forbidden personal traits' model of equality to determine whether there has been any actionable legislative discrimination.[69] With regard to Malaysia and Singapore, it is thus proposed that the courts should follow suit and endorse a 'forbidden personal traits' model of substantive equality.

Nevertheless, critics may argue that while this 'forbidden personal traits' model of equality could arguably address discriminatory treatment as a result of legislative animus against persons who have been historically subjected to stereotype and/or prejudice, it does not address purely arbitrary actions taken by the legislature that are not premised on any adverse historical stereotypes. Consider this law: All persons who are born in the month of August are not entitled to legal counsel when they face a criminal prosecution. This legislation clearly differentiates between persons on the basis of the month of the year they are born in. Yet, critics may argue that, pursuant to the 'forbidden personal traits' model of equality, this law would not violate the constitutional right to equality because persons born in August have historically not been subjected to any adverse stereotype and/or prejudice. Ergo, critics may argue that the 'forbidden personal traits' model of equality is defective and deficient so far as it fails to invalidate such arbitrary differential legislative treatments.

To address the above objection, we must first distinguish between comparative and non-comparative rights.[70] A comparative right, like the right to equality, is one whose content is dependent on how others in some comparison class are treated. A non-comparative right, like the right to legal counsel, is one that is not predicated on how another individual is treated. With regard to the arbitrary law discussed above, the statutory provision is in fact objectionable not because it distinguishes between persons on the basis of the month of their births; the law is unconstitutional because it deprives an individual of his or her right to counsel. This dispute raises, in essence, a

[68] *Yau Yuk Lung* (n 29).

[69] See Ibid.; *Fok Chun Wa* (n 67).

[70] Shin (n 59) 157.

due process concern, not an equality one. After all, even if the law denies all persons legal counsel, this law is still unconstitutional. Therefore, the above law is constitutionally suspect not because it violates one's right to equality but because it violates an individual's constitutional right to counsel. In other words, the true complaint against the above law is exhausted by the objection that it violates the individual's non-comparative right, and nothing of moral significance is added by characterizing it as an infringement of equality.

While I propose that common law Asian courts should all adopt the 'forbidden personal traits' model of equality, one must note at this juncture some significant points of difference between Hong Kong, Singapore, and Malaysia. While the Hong Kong Basic Law is silent on the grounds of discrimination presumptively prohibited, its statutory Bill of Rights Ordinance expressly prohibits discrimination on the grounds of race, colour, sex, language, religion, political, or other opinion, national or social origin, property, or birth.[71] As for Singapore, aside from the general equal protection clause enshrined under Article 12(1), Article 12(2) of its Constitution proceeds by expressly prohibiting discrimination against Singapore citizens only on the grounds of religion, race, descent, or place of birth.[72] In Malaysia, besides its general equal protection clause enshrined under Article 8(1), Article 8(2) of its Constitution also bans discrimination against Malaysians on the grounds of religion, race, gender, descent, or place of birth;[73] one must note though that, notwithstanding Article 12(1) and 12(2), Article 153 of the Malaysia Constitution expressly permits for state affirmative action to protect the special position of the Malays of Peninsular Malaysia and the indigenous people of Sabah and Sarawak.

Although the respective jurisdictions expressly prohibit different types of discrimination, courts, in determining whether the general equal protection clause is violated, should not confine their inquiry to only personal characteristics that are explicitly proscribed in their jurisdictions.

[71] Bill of Rights Ordinance (Cap 383), Article 22.

[72] Article 12(2) of the Singapore Constitution reads: 'Except as expressly authorized by this Constitution, there shall be no discrimination against citizens of Singapore on the ground only of religion, race, descent or place of birth in any law or in the appointment to any office or employment under a public authority or in the administration of any law relating to the acquisition, holding or disposition of property or the establishing or carrying on of any trade, business, profession, vocation or employment.'

[73] Article 8(2) of the Malaysia Constitution reads: 'Except as expressly authorized by this Constitution, there shall be no discrimination against citizens on the ground only of religion, race, descent, gender or place of birth in any law or in the appointment to any office or employment under a public authority or in the administration of any law relating to the acquisition, holding or disposition of property or the establishing or carrying on of any trade, business, profession, vocation or employment.'

With regard to Hong Kong, the equal protection clause was deliberately drafted in ambiguous, open-textured language, and no specific bases of discrimination are explicitly defined or articulated. The framers' choice to adopt a broad principle of equality must thus be respected, and judges are free to recognize specific grounds of non-discrimination that take into account Hong Kong's international obligations under the International Covenant on Civil and Political Rights.[74]

As for Malaysia and Singapore, though the Constitutions expressly bar certain grounds of state discrimination, these specific enumerated grounds should be viewed as constitutional supplements to the general equal protection clauses and should not be perceived as constitutional limits on the interpretive scope of the equal protection clauses. Fortunately, the latter approach has also never been the judicial practices in Malaysia or Singapore.[75] More importantly, if the latter approach was correct, the inclusion of the general equal protection clauses would be wholly tautologous and unnecessary. After all, if the judicial inquiry in Malaysia and Singapore is confined to eliminating discrimination only on the basis of those stipulated grounds, the enactment of the general equal protection clauses would serve no analytical purpose and their inclusion in the constitutions would simply amount to mere surplusage. Logically, this cannot be the intent of the constitutional framers, nor is there any historical evidence available to support such a view.

Nevertheless, while I agree that these Asian courts could recognize grounds of discrimination that are not enumerated but analogous to those characteristics expressly proscribed in their specific jurisdictions, for example age or sexual orientation, as *prima facie* forbidden, I would argue that the courts should openly recognize these 'analogous' grounds *only* when a constitutional challenge is brought against a legislative classification that differentiates on that particular prohibited basis. This is preferable to a 'maximalist'[76] approach where the courts recognize at one

[74] Article 39 of the Hong Kong Basic Law reads: 'The provisions of the International Covenant on Civil and Political Rights, the International Covenant on Economic, Social and Cultural Rights, and international labour conventions as applied to Hong Kong shall remain in force and shall be implemented through the laws of the Hong Kong Special Administrative Region. The rights and freedoms enjoyed by Hong Kong residents shall not be restricted unless as prescribed by law. Such restrictions shall not contravene the provisions of the preceding paragraph of this Article.'

[75] The Singapore Court of Appeal in *Lim Meng Suang* in fact held that Article 12(2) of the Singapore Constitution, which enshrines the enumerated grounds of discrimination, operates 'in addition to the "reasonable classification" test'. *Lim Meng Suang* (n 24) at [90].

[76] Cass Sunstein, *One Case at a Time: Judicial Minimalism on the Supreme Court* (Cambridge, Harvard University Press 1999) 9–10. Sunstein views maximalist judges as those who set out broad rules and also give ambitious theoretical justifications for the outcomes they reach.

go all the personal traits that they would view as presumptively suspect. Professor Cass Sunstein has argued in favour of minimalistic and narrow judicial rulings when courts have to rule on a 'constitutional issue of high complexity about which many people feel deeply and on which the nation is divided (on moral or other grounds)';[77] to this end, the common law courts in Asia should avoid taking on the legislature's (or the citizenry's) deeply held moral commitments unless it is necessary for resolving the dispute before them. In this way, minimalistic rulings are also dialogic so far as they increase space for democratic deliberation on other legislative practices not at issue that also disadvantage persons on the basis of historical stereotypes or prejudices. By staying its hand and allowing the citizenry to continue to offer their competing views about equality's mandate until a legal dispute over a particular traits-based statutory differentiation presents itself in court, the judiciary also avoids any potential backlash that may occur if it prematurely expresses views on controversies that are not ripe for adjudication. This is especially important for equality claims where moral evolution takes place over time and the judiciary's 'constructive uses of silence'[78] can minimize conflict and allow the citizenry's views to shift and accommodate changing facts and/or values.[79] As observed by Jeff King, this strategy of judicial incrementalism is in fact a regular feature of the common law as '(r)easoning by analogy, following precedent, and deciding cases on narrow grounds are all familiar tools of the common law judge'.[80]

D. 'Fundamental Rights' Model

The 'fundamental rights' version of equality is a judicial model where there is a presumptive violation of equal protection when the state distinguishes between persons on any legislative basis that affects one individual/group's ability to exercise a constitutional right.

This strand of 'equal protection' had also surfaced in the American decision of *Police Department v Mosley*[81] when the United States Supreme Court invalidated a city ordinance, which banned picketing near a school in session unless it was the picketing of any school involved in a labour dispute, on the

[77] Ibid. 5.

[78] Cass Sunstein, *Legal Reasoning and Political Conflict* (New York, Oxford University Press 1996) 39.

[79] Ibid. 41.

[80] Jeff King, 'Institutional Approaches to Judicial Restraint' (2008) 28 *Oxford Journal of Legal Studies* 409, 429.

[81] 408 US 92 (1972) (United States Supreme Court).

ground that the equal protection clause was violated. This judicial resort to the equality clause has been criticized for being legally flawed as the city's legislative distinction on the basis of the subject matter of the picketing in essence offended American free speech principles, and any reference to equal protection was thus unnecessary.[82]

Within common law Asia, this judicial model of equality was also applied in the Malaysian Federal Court decision of *Sivarasa* as discussed above;[83] and, with respect, the judicial reliance on the equal protection clause therein was equally gratuitous. The central issue in *Sivarasa* was whether the lawyer's constitutional right of association was infringed upon when the state barred members of Parliament or office-holders in any political party from concurrently running for office in the governing council of the Bar. The court should not instead conceptualize in equal protection terms the very issue posed by a line drawn on the basis of the denial of a non-comparative constitutional right. The issue ought to be resolved solely in terms of the non-comparative constitutional right that had *prima facie* been abridged. As astutely observed by Professor Michael Perry:

> Equal protection is not a catchall norm to be invoked whenever government makes impermissible distinctions between classes of persons, a principle so indeterminate as to be vacuous. Like other constitutional norms and principles, equal protection serves a distinctive function in our constitutional jurisprudence; the principle of equal protection forbids government to impose a negative signification on morally irrelevant factors, in particular personal traits. The distinctive character of that function ought not to be obscured by crowding every imaginable sort of claim into the equal protection clause.[84]

III. Justifying Equality Infringements

In the above sections of my chapter, I have defended the 'forbidden personal traits' model of substantive equality as the only logical, meaningful, and judicially manageable model of equality that courts should apply. Nevertheless, it is also accepted that, like all contesting and competing rights, the right to equality is not absolute and can be justifiably limited by the state.

The proportionality doctrine has emerged in most rights-based democracies in the West as the lynchpin judicial test for courts to determine whether

[82] Michael Perry, 'Modern Equal Protection: A Conceptualisation and Appraisal' (1979) 79 *Columbia Law Review* 1023, 1076.

[83] *Sivarasa Rasiah* (n 40).

[84] Perry (n 82) 1082–3.

a *prima facie* violation of the right to equality can nonetheless be justified and sustained.[85] This proportionality inquiry has equally been accepted as good law in Hong Kong.

The Hong Kong CFA in *Yau Yuk Lung* formulated its version of the proportionality analysis as follows and examined three cumulative factors in deciding whether a legislative infringement of the right to equality was justified:

(1) The difference in treatment must pursue a legitimate aim. For any aim to be legitimate, a genuine need for such difference must be established.
(2) The difference in treatment must be rationally connected to the legitimate aim.
(3) The difference in treatment must be no more than is necessary to accomplish the legitimate aim.[86]

There are many benefits that follow from this proportionality inquiry to rights-infractions.

First, the onus of demonstrating that this rights-violation is justified rests with the state. This creates a 'culture of justification'[87] whereby the state is always required to provide reasoned arguments for the exercise of its powers. Secondly, this three-part inquiry is structured such that the courts are provided with tangible, concrete questions that they seek legislative answers to when determining the law's constitutionality.[88] The transparent, explicit nature of this inquiry also constrains the judiciary as it limits the factors the courts can consider in assessing the legality of the legislative action.[89]

Nevertheless, while the proportionality inquiry may provide courts with the structural mechanism to review the propriety of legislative/administrative action, the standard of review that courts should adopt remains unsettled. This is so as scholars have recognized two general limitations to judicial review. First, it is recognized that, vis-à-vis the legislature, the judiciary lacks democratic legitimacy.[90] Since judges are less accountable to the electorate, the judicial forum may not be the most appropriate institution to resolve

[85] *R v Oakes* [1986] 3 SCR 103 (Supreme Court of Canada); *Huang v Secretary of State for the Home Department* [2007] UKHL 11 (HL); *Sunday Times v UK* (1979–80) 2 EHRR 245 (European Court of Human Rights).

[86] *Yau Yuk Lung* (n 29) [26].

[87] Murray Hunt, 'Sovereignty's Blight: Why Contemporary Public Law Needs the Concept of "Due Deference"' in Nicholas Bamforth & Peter Leyland (eds), *Public Law in a Multi-Layered Constitution* (Oxford, Hart Publishing 2003) 340.

[88] Paul Craig, *Administrative Law* (6th edn, London, Sweet & Maxwell 2008) 637.

[89] Aileen Kavanagh, *Constitutional Review under the UK Human Rights Act* (Cambridge, Cambridge University Press 2009) 255.

[90] Jeremy Waldron, *Law and Disagreement* (Oxford, Oxford University Press 2001).

societal disputes concerning the contested application of competing rights. Second, on certain issues concerning resource allocation, fiscal planning, and national security, it is generally recognized that the political branches of government have more information, experience, and skills to assess the consequences of particular decisions and resolve such questions correctly,[91] and therefore the judiciary may be institutionally less competent to decide whether the legislative/administrative limitations are constitutionally reasonable or right. These twin concerns about the court's intrinsic limitations have led to a demand for judicial deference in public law where courts are encouraged to assign weight to the primary determinations of the political branches and exercise restraint when they review legislative/administrative decisions.[92]

Nevertheless, the extent to which this doctrine of deference should play within the proportionality analysis is subject to much academic disagreement, and it is to this debate that I now turn. Julian Rivers has argued that the proportionality analysis should be conceived as a variable standard of review, 'which requires the seriousness of prima facie rights-infringement to be matched by decreasing judicial deference and restraint'.[93] Aileen Kavanagh agrees with this contextual approach to deference.[94] Nevertheless, for Kavanagh, the severity of the rights-derogation is only an important factor judges should consider;[95] courts should also consider their institutional competence/expertise, democratic legitimacy and prudential concerns in assessing a particular issue when deciding upon the level of deference they should accord the political branches.[96] Professor Jeffrey Jowell accepts that courts may defer to the political branches on grounds of relative institutional competence, but he argues against any judicial deference on the ground that the legislature is a democratically more legitimate decision-making body.[97] Professor Trevor Allan, on the other hand, does not reject the idea of judicial deference per se; while he believes that courts may take into account 'questions of constitutional propriety and judicial restraint [that] are internal to the ordinary judicial process',[98] he refutes Kavanagh's

[91] Aileen Kavanagh, 'Deference or Defiance? The Limits of the Judicial Role in Constitutional Adjudication' in G Huscroft (ed), *Expounding the Constitution: Essays in Constitutional Theory* (Cambridge, Cambridge University Press 2008) 184, 193–9.

[92] Aileen Kavanagh, 'Defending deference in public law and constitutional theory' (2010) 126 *Law Quarterly Review* 222, 223.

[93] Julian Rivers, 'Proportionality and Variable Intensity of Review' (2006) 65 *Cambridge Law Journal* 174, 177.

[94] See also Alison Young, 'In Defence of Due Deference' (2009) 72 *Modern Law Review* 554.

[95] Kavanagh, 'Defending deference in public law and constitutional theory' (n 92) 226.

[96] Kavanagh, 'Deference or Defiance?' (n 91) 192.

[97] Jeffrey Jowell, 'Judicial Deference: Civility, Servility or Institutional Capacity?' [2003] *Public Law* 592, 596.

[98] Trevor Allan, 'Judicial Deference and Judicial Review: Legal Doctrine and Legal Theory' (2011) 127 *Law Quarterly Review* 96, 100.

suggestion that deference may be defended on prudential grounds where courts may consider whether 'a particular judicial decision would produce a backlash in society; whether society is ready for the legal change; whether it might be counterproductive to introduce it at this particular time; and whether the elected branches of government would then move to curtail the powers of the courts as a result'.[99]

In general, I agree with Kavanagh that judges should take into account their relative institutional competence/expertise and any democratic legitimacy or prudential concerns when deciding upon the level of deference that they should accord the political branches. Nevertheless, one must note that for Kavanagh, a judge has to discharge two obligations when engaging in constitutional adjudication. First, he or she has to carry out a substantive evaluation of the legal merits; and second, he or she has to consider questions of relative institutional competence, expertise, and legitimacy vis-à-vis the elected branches of government.[100] This bifurcated approach is however premised on the assumption that the two judicial inquiries are essentially always separate and distinct; and to this extent, I would part company with Kavanagh's analysis.

After all, during constitutional adjudication, judges labour under conditions of epistemic uncertainty that can be empirical and/or moral in nature. Judges may be unsure whether they have the necessary expertise or training to factually evaluate certain polycentric legislative measures and/or they may be uncertain whether their normative disagreements with certain legislative goals are actually morally correct. These dual uncertainties thus bear on how a judge may assess the intrinsic merits of a rights-dispute and a judge must thus integrate the above concerns within his or her internal substantive evaluation of the legal merits to arrive at the best possible outcome in the case before him or her, and should not embark on a substantive evaluation independent of the institutional inquiry into the court's epistemic competence.

However, Professor Allan may be mistaken to assume that prudential concerns have no place in this judicial calculus. He argues that judicial moves to placate a hostile legislature are a form of subterfuge, which is inconsistent with the fundamental judicial duty to impartially administer justice in each case according to law.[101] Nevertheless, this view is premised too on an assumption that judges are infallible in their moral deliberations; whenever judges unwillingly submit to legislative whims, they must be consciously subverting

[99] Kavanagh, 'Deference or Defiance?' (n 91) 205.
[100] Kavanagh, 'Defending deference in public law and constitutional theory' (n 92) 231.
[101] Allan (n 98).

the rule of law. But if we take the view that judges are capable of committing moral blunders, and that they are conscious of their own fallibilities, we may agree that judges, when deciding upon highly contested moral dilemmas, should take into account any strongly held views of the legislature (or the electorate), as it is equally plausible that in the long run these legislative views may prove to be the normatively correct ones. Therefore, to this extent, the prudential concerns raised by Kavanagh dovetail with the argument for judicial deference on the ground of the legislature's relative democratic legitimacy in resolving contested applications of competing rights/interests.[102]

Furthermore, while courts are granted a constitutional mandate to interpret rights, and they should discharge this democratic duty faithfully, there may be exceptional cases in which a particular law reform may create widespread upheaval in society that courts may prefer to secure some consensus or support from the elected branches of government before they so act. This should not be viewed as a form of judicial abdication as Jowell has argued,[103] but instead as a candid recognition that judges must sometimes 'refrain from putting right an injustice contained in primary legislation, if to do so would cause more harm than good'.[104] This prudential concern is accentuated in parts of common law Asia where dominant-party politics prevail; where the semi-permanent government, as discussed in Chapter 4, is able to overrule the courts by constitutional or extra-constitutional means, judges may prefer to stay their hand. Some may argue that justice should prevail, even if the heavens fall. But if the heavens do fall, would the constitutional polity in question and the claimant in particular be better off?

In view of my foregoing discussion on judicial deference, I would now explain how the proportionality inquiry (so far as it is applied to equality rights-infringements) can be applied in a manner that reflects my concerns discussed above. To this end, the doctrinal rules that courts observe or apply must seek to minimize the costs of erroneous decisions and the costs of operating under those legal rules.[105]

[102] See Young (n 94) 579. One must note that Allan himself has accepted that there are situations when judges should defer to the political branches of government on democratic grounds. See Trevor Allan, 'Human Rights and Judicial Review: A Critique of "Due Deference" ' (2006) 65 *Cambridge Law Journal* 671.

[103] Jeffrey Jowell, 'Judicial Deference and Human Rights: A Question of Competence' in Paul Craig & Richard Rawlings (eds), *Law and Administration in Europe: Essays in Honour of Carol Harlow* (Oxford, Oxford University Press 2003) 67, 80.

[104] Aileen Kavanagh, 'Judicial Restraint in the Pursuit of Justice' (2010) 60 *University of Toronto Law Journal* 23, 31.

[105] See Paul Horwitz, 'Three Faces of Deference' (2008) 83 *Notre Dame Law Review* 1061, 1091; David Strauss, 'The Ubiquity of Prophylactic Rules' (1988) 55 *University of Chicago Law Review* 190, 193.

Essentially, I would argue that the common law Asian courts should develop a 'sliding scale' of review to determine whether the equality infringement in question is justified. This sliding scale would permit courts to subject different categories/types of personal traits-differentiation to varying standards of judicial scrutiny. For example, all the common law courts in Asia may decide to subject any gender-based legislative differentiation to the strictest level of judicial scrutiny.[106]

On the other hand, with regard to sexual orientation discrimination, courts in different jurisdictions may decide to diverge on the standard of review they adopt. In Hong Kong, the courts should continue to subject legislative differentiations on the ground of sexual orientation to strict scrutiny, as this standard of review has become an accepted judicial practice. Common law courts in Singapore and Malaysia on the other hand might, for prudential and democracy legitimacy concerns, prefer to subject this ground of discrimination to rational basis review at the outset, and heighten the standard of review when the legislature (and the electorate) is less adverse to such a legal change.[107]

Julian Rivers has also advocated a sliding scale of review for rights-infringement. However, for Rivers, the intensity of judicial review depends solely on how substantial a right-limitation is, as judicially conceived.[108] While the severity of a right-infringement on the aggrieved should be a very significant consideration when courts decide the intensity of its review, one must note that a judicial focus on this factor alone would lead courts to neglect the very epistemic deficits that judges suffer from when they make this substantive determination in the first place. After all, it is equally plausible that the legislature (or the electorate) may normatively disagree vigorously with this judicial determination of a substantial rights-derogation. Alternatively, with regard to decisions with significant 'allocative impact',[109]

[106] Strict scrutiny is justified as the governments in all three jurisdictions have all openly recognized that gender discrimination is a *prima facie* forbidden basis for legislative differentiation. Malaysia amended Article 8(2) of its Constitution in 2001 to expressly prohibit gender discrimination. As for Hong Kong, gender discrimination is expressly prohibited under the Bill of Rights Ordinance and the Sex Discrimination Ordinance. While gender discrimination is not expressly prohibited under Article 12(2) of the Singapore Constitution, the Singapore government has expressed its view that the principle of gender equality is implicitly entrenched under Article 12(1), the general equal protection clause. See CEDAW Committee, Fourth Periodic State Report: Singapore (3 April 2009) CEDAW/C/SGP/4, at para E.1.

[107] One may note that private consensual sexual intercourse between men remains a crime both in Singapore and Malaysia. With regard to Singapore, the government in 2007 undertook not to actively enforce this law against consenting adults, though it also refused to formally repeal the legislation.

[108] Julian Rivers, 'Proportionality and Variable Intensity of Review' (2006) 65 *Cambridge Law Journal* 174, 205–6.

[109] Jeff King, 'The Justiciability of Resource Allocation' (2007) 70 *Modern Law Review* 197.

the courts may simply not have the requisite expertise or training to assess whether the legislative allocative decision is reasonable.

One strategy to minimize the epistemic deficits that courts suffer from when they make substantive determinations of rights-derogation in discrimination cases is for judges to subject different types of personal traits-differentiations to varying standards of review. Legislative differentiations on prohibited bases that, by common accord, are deemed socially repugnant would require the most rigorous justification. On the other hand, differentiations on grounds where the polity is in a state of moral evolution should only, for now, attract rational review. This multi-tiered approach to the prohibited bases of differentiations would naturally vary both between jurisdictions and over time.[110] The greater the degree of epistemic uncertainty, the more judicial restraint may be required.[111]

Nevertheless, one may conceive of situations where a form of legislative differentiation may be perceived to be particularly morally odious to the polity at large, for example gender-based classification, and may thus justify heightened judicial review, but these distinctions may equally have significant allocative impact and trigger empirical epistemic uncertainties for which judges are ill-equipped to assess accurately on a strict-scrutiny basis. The strategy to overcome this conundrum is not for courts to abandon the use of strict scrutiny altogether. Instead, judges should merely evaluate what Tom Hickman terms the 'relative proportionality' of the legislative measure chosen over the other viable alternatives.[112] The court herein would require the state to justify its choice of choosing one legislative measure over a less intrusive alternative when such viable legislative alternatives are presented by the aggrieved. The chosen legislative measure would only be deemed disproportionate when the court identifies a significant and considerable imbalance, in light of the legislative alternatives, between the additional impact of the chosen measure on the aggrieved and its additional benefits on society. This strategy thus minimizes the error costs that judges might incur when courts engage in what has been termed an 'overall balance'[113] or 'narrow proportionality'[114] test, which requires the judiciary to measure the costs in

[110] Sandra Fredman, 'From Deference to Democracy: the role of Equality under the Human Rights Act 1998' (2006) 122 *Law Quarterly Review* 53, 76.

[111] Kavanagh, 'Defending deference in public law and constitutional theory' (n 92) 223, 235.

[112] Tom Hickman, 'The Substance and Structure of Proportionality' [2008] *Public Law* 694, 712.

[113] Alan Brady, *Proportionality and Deference under the UK Human Rights Act* (Cambridge, Cambridge University Press 2012) 7.

[114] Mark Elliott, 'Proportionality and Deference: The Importance of a Structured Approach' in Forsyth, Elliott, Jhaveri, Ramsden & Hill, *Effective Judicial Review: A Cornerstone of Good Governance* (Oxford, Oxford University Press 2010).

maintaining adherence to fundamental rights more generally with the benefits of the measure in terms of the communitarian interests that are actually fulfilled.[115] Equally, it avoids any error costs that might result from the implementation of *prima facie* morally odious legislative differentiations that are under-scrutinized by the courts merely because any such judicial intervention would have significant allocative impact on the political branches of government.

On the other hand, prudence may counsel in favour of judicial restraint when courts are faced with legislative differentiations on grounds where the polity is in a state of moral flux. This, however, does not mean that such cases are non-justiciable, and that courts should abdicate their responsibility from intervening. Instead, courts, in such situations, should merely adopt a posture of deference and uphold the impugned legislation so long as there is a rational basis for the legislative decision. This posture of judicial deference is especially justified in situations where the 'personal traits' differentiation is not widely perceived by the polity at large to be morally odious, for example differential treatments against out-of-state residents, *and* the consequences of any judicial intervention in favour of the aggrieved would have 'damaging or disruptive implications for an economic strategy where priorities are set in light of the overall picture and specialist expertise'.[116]

The judicial use of rational basis review, a dialogic sub-constitutional doctrine that I have discussed in Chapter 5, is premised on the understanding that we should not equate 'the scope of a constitutional norm as coterminous with the scope of its judicial enforcement'.[117] Due to institutional constraints and democratic concerns, judges may not want to exhaust the full content of a constitutional norm so that the political branches of the government may, on their own, flesh out the conceptual boundaries of that implicated right. Rational basis review is a dialogic device that does precisely that; so far as the judiciary under-enforces the Constitution against public officials, the government is given a substantially freer hand to determine what is (or is not) constitutional state action. Democratic or prudential considerations must never be determinative of how courts should decide cases. But one must also recognize that a richer conception of the substantive rule of law would not only legitimatize a role for courts to impose legal limits on the political branches, it would also provide a constitutional space for the democratic branches of government to build upon or disagree with the judicial conception of rights.[118]

[115] Hickman (n 112) 711.

[116] Kavanagh, *Constitutional Review Under the UK Human Rights Act* (n 92) 223.

[117] Lawrence Sagar, *Justice in Plainclothes: A Theory of American Constitutional Practice* (New Haven, Yale University Press 2006) 86.

[118] Hunt (n 87) 350.

Where courts have independently decided to apply rational basis review over certain legislative or executive actions, they are, in effect, granting significant latitude to the political branches to pursue the constitutional course of action they want. This conception of 'deference as respect'[119] underscores the judicial sensitivity to the role that the elected branches of government can play in the determination of rights in any legal system, such that an inter-branch dialogic model of rights-protection can ensue.

This traits-based sliding scale of review is not wholly novel for it is reminiscent of the legal developments in the United States. The United States Supreme Court has adopted a three-tier approach under its equal protection clause: race-based classifications attract strict scrutiny,[120] gender-based distinctions require 'an exceeding persuasive justification',[121] while legislative differentiations on the ground of sexual orientation attract, for now, rational review.[122] This traits-based approach is arguably also accepted as good law in the United Kingdom where legislative differentiations on the ground of race, caste, gender, and sexual orientation are subject to 'intense'[123] or 'careful'[124] scrutiny, while statutory distinctions on the basis of age, ability, education, and occupation are 'very much a matter for the democratically elected branches of government'.[125]

Furthermore, this traits-based sliding scale of review is essentially what the Hong Kong judiciary is implicitly already applying. In *Fok Chun Wa*, the CFA held that with regard to unequal treatment on the basis of one's 'race, colour, gender, sexual orientation, religion, politics or social origin',[126] courts will subject the 'relevant legislation or decision to a particularly severe scrutiny'[127] as '[t]hey are fundamental societal values'.[128] Nevertheless, the Chief Justice of Hong Kong went on to opine when a less rigorous mode of judicial scrutiny may be warranted:

[119] David Dyzenhaus, 'The Politics of Deference: Judicial Review and Democracy' in M Taggart (ed), *The Province of Administrative Law* (Oxford, Hart Publishing 1997) 286.

[120] *Adarand Constructors, Inc v Peña* 515 US 200 (1995) (United States Supreme Court).

[121] *United States v Virginia* 518 US 515 (1996) (United States Supreme Court).

[122] *Romer v Evans* 517 US 620 (1996) (United States Supreme Court).

[123] *Ghaidan v Godin-Mendoza* [2004] 2 AC 557 (HL) [19].

[124] *Carson v Secretary of State for Work and Pensions* [2006] 1 AC 173 (HL) [16].

[125] Ibid. [126] *Fok Chun Wa* (n 67) [76]. [127] Ibid. [78].

[128] Ibid. [77]. One must note that while the Hong Kong Court of Final Appeal in *Secretary for Justice v Yau Yuk Lung* was right to subject the legislative differentiation on the basis of sexual orientation to strict scrutiny, this law would also have been invalidated on rational basis review. On the facts, the Hong Kong government could not provide any justifications to explain why the impugned statute did not also criminalize public acts of heterosexual conduct nor could it explain why public acts of homosexual conduct could not be as effectively prosecuted under the common law, as was the case for similar heterosexual acts.

On the other hand, where other characteristics or status which do not relate to such notions or values are involved, and here I would include residence status, the courts will hesitate much more before interfering; in other words, more lee-way is given to the Executive, Legislature or other authorities.[129]

Therefore, on the facts, the CFA applied rational basis review and held that the Hong Kong government's denial of non-residents to subsidized obstetric care at public hospitals was 'entirely within the spectrum of reasonableness'[130] for it was 'comprehensible and rational'[131] to distinguish between persons on the basis of their residency status in the disbursements of public funds.

Rational basis review does not mean, however, that any impugned statutory provision or bye-law is immune from judicial invalidation. In *Kong Yun Ming v Director of Social Welfare*,[132] the Hong Kong Court of Appeal, on the basis of rational review, invalidated a governmental rule that required a person to have resided in Hong Kong for at least one year immediately before his or her application for public social welfare assistance. It is noteworthy that this one-year requirement was neither discussed nor proposed by the governmental task force specially convened to review the social welfare scheme in Hong Kong, and the only justification that the government could provide for this one-year rule was that it was seeking to exclude persons who had lived outside from Hong Kong for a long time from applying for social welfare. But, as noted by the Court of Appeal, the one-year measure was one that caught within its net those who had not been absent for a long time 'within any *sensible* meaning of that phrase in the context of this issue',[133] especially since 'no evidence of any analysis or recognition'[134] of the impact of this rule was adduced in court. This one-year rule was thus rightly invalidated on the basis of rational review. After all, under an epistemically based rule of deference, deferees (or institutions that are deferred to) should also be obliged to reason in good faith and thoughtfully towards their conclusions. As observed by Professor Paul Horwitz, '[a] conclusion that is reached in haste, or carelessly, or without serious consideration of the complexity of the question, is hardly one that partakes of the quality of epistemic authority that is the basis for judicial deference'.[135]

Although the 'forbidden personal traits' model of equality coupled with a sliding scale of review is only accepted as good law in Hong Kong within common law Asia, the judicial adoption of this model of equality would not pose too disruptive a legal change in Singapore and Malaysia as this new

[129] Ibid. [77]. [130] Ibid. [90]. [131] Ibid. [92].
[132] [2012] HKEC 229 (Hong Kong Court of Appeal). [133] Ibid. [166].
[134] Ibid. [168]. [135] Horwitz (n 105) 1101–2.

approach would not cast doubt on the correctness of the recent past decisions, discussed above, reached by their appellate courts.

With regard to the Malaysia Federal Court decision of *Danaharta Urus v Kekatong*,[136] the impugned statutory provision, which barred the courts from granting an injunction against the nation's asset management company, did not distinguish between individuals on the basis of any personal traits, and the constitutional right to equality should not have been engaged at all. Similarly, in the Malaysia Court of Appeal decision of *Public Prosecutor v Harmenderpall Singh*,[137] the disparate treatment between persons charged for reckless driving and those charged for reckless driving resulting in death did not differentiate between individuals on the basis of their personal traits, and the right of equality was thus again not engaged. In the same vein, the constitutional challenge in *Sivarasa Rasiah v Badan Peguam Malaysia*[138] against a legislative provision, which barred lawyers from serving on the governing body of the Malaysian Bar if they were either members of Parliament or office-holders in any political party, would not implicate the right to equality as the statute did not distinguish between individuals on the basis of their personal characteristics. In all of the above three Malaysian decisions, the applicants were not distinguished on the basis of their personal traits and hence their right to equality was thus not even *prima facie* infringed; there was thus no need for the state to demonstrate how the impugned measures were proportionate on that basis.

Turning to Singapore, the extraterritorial anti-corruption penal provision that applied only to Singaporean citizens was also rightly upheld by the Court of Appeal in *Public Prosecutor v Taw Cheng Kong*.[139] Even though there was a differential treatment on the basis of one's citizenship, this measure was proportionate as the government was merely seeking to suppress corruption in Singapore while observing 'the comity of nations'[140] that argued against the regulation of the subjects of other sovereign powers' outside one's jurisdiction. Furthermore, some deference was also rightly accorded to the political branches as this measure implicated the conduct of inter-state foreign affairs, for which courts have limited expertise in general, and the law disadvantaged their own citizens, that is the political majority, and the measure thus did not evince any legislative disrespect for individuals that are historically subjected to stereotype and/or prejudice in Singapore. As for *Yong Vui Kong v Public Prosecutor*,[141] the legislative measure that imposed the mandatory death sentence on persons that traffic more than 15g of a type of controlled

[136] *Danaharta Urus* (n 2).
[137] *Harmenderpall Singh* (n 13).
[138] *Sivarasa Rasiah* (n 40).
[139] *Taw Cheng Kong* (n 17).
[140] Ibid. [71].
[141] *Yong Vui Kong* (n 21).

drug did not violate a person's right to equality as this statutory differentia did not distinguish between individuals on the basis of a personal trait. The sheer draconian nature of the mandatory death penalty certainly poses due process concerns in Singapore; but the constitutional infraction at issue is certainly not an equal protection one.

On the other hand, turning to the gay rights decision in *Lim Meng Suang*,[142] the Singapore Court of Appeal should have struck down the impugned law as an unjustified statutory measure that differentiated on the basis of one's sexual orientation, but it could have done so by merely applying the sub-constitutional technique of rational basis review. If a judicial result achieves nothing more than public backlash against gay couples, such a decision would be positively harmful to the interests that are seeking to be protected in the first place.[143] Therefore, it would be prudent and dialogic for the court not to expound, in the first instance, on whether the Singapore Parliament was constitutionally permitted to criminalize same-sex sexual activity in general. Instead, the court should focus on one significant feature of Section 377A: sexual relations between women are not criminalized. Any prescribed legislative differentia does not need to be the most effective method of achieving the object of the law in question, but if the statutory differentia in question is so under-inclusive that a huge segment of persons that should, pursuant to that legislative object, be targeted was legislatively omitted, one can very reasonably argue that the law is irrational. If the object of Section 377A is to display the state's moral opprobrium against homosexuality, the legislative omission in Singapore to equally criminalize sexual relations between women, a significant proportion of homosexual activity, would surely suggest that there is no rational connection between the statutory differentia sought to be drawn and the object of the law. Therefore, even if the Singapore Court of Appeal had applied rational review, Section 377A could have been deemed a violation of equal protection. In this way, the ruling is minimalistic as the court is not refuting, in the first instance, the legitimacy of the country's (regressive) views on homosexuality; the court would be merely questioning the rationality of the method by which the state is seeking to achieve its aim. The ruling is also dialogic as the court is not entrenching a 'maximalist' constitutional rule that forbids the criminalization of all consensual same-sex sexual conduct; therefore, the government would retain the statutory option of passing an ordinary legislation to criminalize same-sex intimacy between women if it so chooses; but as such a legislative reply is highly unlikely in Singapore where the government has been trying to avoid

[142] *Lim Meng Suang* (n 24). [143] Kavanagh (n 104) 33.

doing anything on this issue altogether,[144] this judicial decision would still have been a victory for gay rights, albeit writ small.

IV. Conclusion

The formal model of equality requires all persons within the same legislative class to be treated equally, but it provides no substantive moral criteria to assess the propriety of any statutory differentiations such that all forms of legislative classifications are arguably constitutionally permissible, regardless of how irrational or offensive they may be. The rational connection model, as commonly applied, is not much better. It generally only scrutinizes the nexus between the object of the law and the legislative classifications, but it also does not question the validity of the legislative objective itself. Furthermore, the courts can either sustain or reject the rationality of the legislation by merely manipulating the level of abstraction of the legislative object (judicially discerned) in deciding whether there is a rational connection between the legislative class and the said object. The 'fundamental rights' model of equality, on the other hand, deems all legislative distinctions that affect an individual's ability to exercise a constitutional right *prima facie* invalid, but in so doing, equal protection becomes so indeterminate a constitutional principle that it becomes vacuous and devoid of any distinct substantive meaning. In the final analysis, the 'forbidden personal traits' model of equality where courts would restrict presumptively forbidden differentiating descriptors to personal traits, that is personal characteristics for which individuals with these traits have been historically subjected to stereotype and/or prejudice, serves as the only logical, meaningful, and judicially manageable model of equality for common law Asia.

Furthermore, I have argued that these Asian common law courts should develop a 'sliding scale' of review to determine whether the equality infringement in question is justified. This sliding scale would permit courts to subject different categories/types of personal traits-differentiation to varying standards of judicial scrutiny, and the standard of review may differ over time and space.

A variable standard of review rightfully acknowledges that judges labour under conditions of epistemic uncertainty during constitutional adjudication that can be empirical and/or moral in nature. Where courts are unsure

[144] See Lynette Chua, 'Pragmatic Resistance, Law, and Social Movements in Authoritarian States: The Case of Gay Collective Action in Singapore' (2012) 46(4) *Law & Society Review* 713.

whether they have the necessary expertise to assess factually the correctness of polycentric legislative measures and/or they are uncertain whether their normative disagreements with certain legislative objectives are morally correct, the application of the sub-constitutional dialogic device of rational basis review grants significant latitude to the political branches to make these constitutional determinations. This deferential standard of review leaves room for the political branches to make independent contributions to the discourse on rights and a constitutional dialogue thus ensues. This sliding scale of review thus recognizes that the judicial conception of individual rights should not always trump the legislative determination of collective welfare, and that the judicial role is 'not privileged above common politics but is one institutional method of problem solving acting in concert with other institutions'.[145]

[145] King (n 80) 441.

9

Right to Due Process

Most human rights instruments in the world include some form of constitutional guarantee against arbitrary state action. In its varied modes, this due process constitutional clause seeks to constrain and limit the government's ability to deprive a person of his or her life or liberty with the use of penal sanctions.

Within the common law Asia jurisdictions under consideration, it is noteworthy that their courts of final resort do not share the same judicial understanding of what the constitutional right to due process entails or requires. In fact, a survey of the case law in Hong Kong, Malaysia, and Singapore reveals four distinct judicial models of due process. Interestingly, even within each jurisdiction, the courts are not consistent in upholding a particular model of criminal due process. One must note, at the outset, that my discussion on constitutional due process primarily examines the judicially determined constitutional limits on the state's ability to deprive an individual of his or her life, or to incarcerate him or her, as this has been the focus of the case law.

First, we may observe a formal model of due process. This model merely requires the state deprivation in question to be authorized by law; the judiciary will examine whether the state action is in compliance with the law of the land as duly enacted by the legislative/executive branch but it will not further question whether the impugned law in question is substantively or procedurally fair. Second, the originalist model imposes both substantive and procedural limits on state action, but the courts would only invalidate legislative action that would be considered arbitrary as originally understood by the framers of their constitutions. Third, the adjudicatory model of due process protects only an individual's substantive and/or procedural interests within the criminal adjudicatory process. According to this third model, the courts are only concerned about ensuring the reliability and integrity of the guilt determining process, and they would not further examine whether the statutory offences in question (and the constituent elements of the crime) or the legislatively prescribed sentences are substantively fair. Finally, the substantive model of due process imposes substantive constraints on the principles of *mens rea* such that the state can generally only impose penal sanctions on persons who are morally blameworthy for their conduct[1] and will also insist upon some proportionality between the punishment imposed and the offender's degree of moral culpability.

One must note at the outset that, even within the same jurisdiction, the Asian territorial courts do not always observe the same model of due process. Nevertheless, it is fair to state that a line of Malaysian[2] and Singaporean[3] decisions subscribes to the formal model; the Singapore appellate courts have currently endorsed the originalist approach;[4] the adjudicatory model encapsulates the general trend of the Malaysian judiciary;[5] and finally, Hong Kong is most aligned with the substantive model.[6]

In this chapter, I shall advance the following central claim: the substantive model of due process represents the only meaningful and normatively defensible constitutional standard of due process for courts in these Asian jurisdictions to apply. Section I of this chapter begins with a survey of the four models of criminal due process as exemplified by case law. Section II proceeds by arguing why, apart from the substantive model, the other three judicial models of due process are inherently defective as constitutional safeguards against arbitrary state action. Section III concludes by examining how these Asian common law courts can advance a substantive understanding of due process with the use of several dialogic sub-constitutional doctrines that I had discussed in Chapter 5, and they include the enforcement of procedural constitutional rules, common law rights that herein take the form of clear-statement rules, and/or delayed declarations of invalidity. As highlighted in Chapter 4, where the political branches of government in these authoritarian regimes are able to constitutionally (or extra-constitutionally) rein in activist courts without facing the same enforcement and bargaining costs that ruling parties in liberal democracies have to grapple with, the judicial use of

[1] Victor Ramraj, 'Four Models of Due Process' (2004) 2 *International Journal of Constitutional Law* 492, 493. One may note that Ramraj's four models of due process are as follows: the formal model; the procedural model; the procedural-privacy model; and the substantive model. The originalist and the adjudicatory models I examine are absent from his discussion.

[2] *Pihak Berkuasa Negeri Sabah v Sugumar Balakrishnan* [2002] 3 MLJ 72 (Federal Court of Malaysia).

[3] *Mohammad Faizal bin Sabtu v PP* [2012] SGHC 163 (High Court of Singapore).

[4] *Yong Vui Kong v PP* [2010] SGCA 20 (Singapore Court of Appeal).

[5] *Lee Kwan Woh v PP* [2009] 5 MLJ 301 (Federal Court of Malaysia); *Shamim Reza bin Abdul Samad v* PP [2011] 1 MLJ 471 (Federal Court of Malaysia).

[6] *Lau Cheong v HKSAR* [2002] 2 HKLRD 612 (Hong Kong Court of Final Appeal); *So Wai Lun v HKSAR* [2006] 3 HKLRD 394 (Hong Kong Court of Final Appeal).

these sub-constitutional doctrines can open up *statutory* pathways for the lawmakers to re-instate their original views or legislate on comparable matters.

I. Overview of the Four Models of Due Process

Section I maps out the four models of due process that are applied by the appellate courts in Malaysia, Singapore, and Hong Kong when they interpret the general due process clauses enshrined in their respective Constitutions. At the outset, it may be useful to restate the respective constitutional clauses that guard against arbitrary state deprivations of the citizenry's life or liberty.

Malaysia: 'No person shall be deprived of his life or personal liberty save in accordance with law.'[7]

Hong Kong: 'No Hong Kong resident shall be subjected to arbitrary or unlawful arrest, detention or imprisonment... [A]rbitrary or unlawful deprivation of the life of any resident shall be prohibited.'[8]

Singapore: 'No person shall be deprived of his life or personal liberty save in accordance with law.'[9]

This section of my chapter focusses on how the territorial courts have interpreted their respective general due process clauses and, in particular, how they have sought to constrain the ability of the state to impose penal sanctions on the citizenry. One may also note, at the outset, that while the precise texts of the various due process clauses may differ across the jurisdictions under study, the phraseology of the constitutional clauses do not, by themselves, mandate any jurisdiction to observe any particular model of due process. The constitutional meaning of what is 'arbitrary' in Hong Kong or is 'in accordance with law' in Malaysia and Singapore is not self-evident and would require judicial interpretation and exposition. In other words, there is sufficient textual ambiguity in each of the enshrined due process clauses for the respective courts to adopt any of the four interpretive models. Given that the territorial courts have a normative choice to make in this regard, it is only by differentiating between these four judicial models of due process that we can better appreciate the interpretive options available to the courts in each jurisdiction, such that we can understand more fully the rationale for preferring one model over another, as I shall elaborate upon in Section II of this chapter.

[7] Malaysia Constitution, Article 5(1). [8] Hong Kong Basic Law, Article 28.
[9] Singapore Constitution, Article 9(1).

A. Formal Model

According to the formal model of due process, any legislative enactment that deprives the citizenry of their lives or liberty would be constitutionally valid so long as the impugned deprivation is authorized by a duly enacted law.[10] The courts herein would only ensure that the state has complied with the laws of the land; the judiciary would not further inquire into whether the process by which this deprivation takes place or whether the substance of the offence is fair and reasonable.

This formal model of due process was endorsed by the Federal Court of Malaysia in *Pihak Berkuasa Negeri Sabah v Sugumar Balakrishnan*.[11] On the facts, the applicant's entry permit to the Malaysian State of Sabah was cancelled by Sabah's Director of Immigration. Furthermore, the Immigration Act stated that the Director did not need to provide the applicant with an opportunity to be heard before his permit was cancelled and an ouster clause further provided that there 'shall be no judicial review in any court of any act done or any decision made'[12] by the Director under the Act except in regard to any question relating to compliance with any procedural requirement of this Act. Specifically, the applicant argued that the legislative abrogation of the right to a hearing and the statutory exclusion of judicial review violated his right to due process as protected under Article 5(1) of the Malaysian Constitution. The Federal Court unanimously disagreed. In particular, Justice Mohamed Dzaiddin opined as follows:

> It is clear . . . that the constitutional rights as guaranteed under art 5(1) of the Federal Constitution can be taken away in accordance with law. Hence, s 59 of the Act, which removes the audi alteram partem rule, which was duly enacted by Parliament, is valid and constitutional.[13]

According to the Federal Court, since the state deprivation in question had been expressly authorized by legislation that was duly enacted by Parliament, 'it is not permissible for our courts to intervene and disturb a statutorily unreviewable decision on the basis of a new amorphous and wide ranging concept of substantive unfairness'.[14]

In the same vein, the Singapore High Court in the Magistracy Appeal of *Mohammad Faizal bin Sabtu v Public Prosecutor*[15] has equally endorsed this formal understanding of the constitutional right to due process. On the facts, the accused argued, *inter alia*, that the legislative imposition of a minimum

[10] Ramraj (n 1) 496. [11] *Sugumar* (n 2).
[12] Immigration Act (Act 155), s 59(A). [13] *Sugumar* (n 2) [84]. [14] Ibid. [34].
[15] *Mohammad Faizal bin Sabtu v PP* [2012] SGHC 163 (High Court of Singapore).

mandatory sentence of caning coupled with five years' imprisonment, where the offender was a repeat consumer of specified drugs, was manifestly excessive and disproportionate, such that the punishment was not 'in accordance with law' for the purpose of Article 9(1) of the Singapore Constitution. Chief Justice Chan of Singapore flatly disagreed:

> The principle of proportionality, as a principle of law (as opposed to a principle of good government), has no application to the legislative power to prescribe punishments... The courts must impose the legislatively prescribed sentence on an offender even if it offends the principle of proportionality.[16]

Citing with approval a pre-Human Rights Act extra-curial observation of Lord Bingham of Cornhill, the learned Chief Justice agreed with his Lordship that any statutory restriction of the sentencing discretion of judges is a 'political question—a question of what is beneficial for the polity—not a constitutional question'.[17]

According to this formal conception of the rule of law, the judiciary would not pass judgment on the content of the legislation. This is the prerogative of the political branches of government. The judiciary's role during constitutional adjudication is thus confined to ensuring that there is some publicly accessible, clear, and prospectively authorized formal rule that sanctions the impugned state action in question; the courts would do nothing further regardless of how unfair or unjust the impugned law might be.[18]

B. Originalist Model

According to the originalist model of due process, the courts would pass judgment on the content of legislative action, but it would only invalidate statutes that would be considered arbitrary as originally understood by the framers of their Constitutions.

This model of due process was endorsed by the Singapore Court of Appeal in *Yong Vui Kong v Public Prosecutor*.[19] On the facts, the accused was convicted of trafficking 47.27g of diamorphine, a controlled drug, by the High Court of Singapore and was sentenced to death under the Misuse of Drugs Act.[20] On appeal, the accused argued that his sentence, that is the mandatory nature of the death penalty (hereinafter MDP) as prescribed by the

16 Ibid. [60].
17 Tom Bingham, 'The Courts and the Constitution' (1996) 7 *King's College Law Journal* 12, 25.
18 Ramraj (n 1) 497.
19 *Yong Vui Kong* (n 4).
20 Misuse of Drugs Act (Cap 185).

impugned statute, infringed upon Article 9(1) of the Singapore Constitution as the expression 'law' enshrined under Article 9(1) excluded inhuman forms of punishment; and accordingly, he could not be statutorily deprived of his life in this manner.

Specifically, counsel for the accused had sought to ask the court to follow a series of Privy Council decisions from the Caribbean States,[21] where the Law Lords in the United Kingdom had overturned the MDP imposed by the respective state legislations. Nevertheless, the Court of Appeal flatly rejected their applicability as these foreign decisions involved Constitutions which expressly prohibited inhuman punishments whilst 'the Singapore Constitution does not contain any express prohibition against inhuman punishment'[22] and 'it would not be appropriate for [judges] to legislate new rights into the Singapore Constitution under the guise of interpreting existing constitutional provisions'.[23]

According to the Chief Justice for the unanimous court, Singapore's due process clause was based on its equivalent in the 1963 Malaysian Federal Constitution,[24] which was likewise based on the 1957 Malayan Constitution drafted pursuant to the advice of the Federation of Malayan Constitutional Commission chaired by Lord Reid (Reid Commission). In the Chief Justice's opinion, the fact that the Reid Commission did not recommend in favour of an express prohibition against inhuman punishment despite its inclusion in the European Convention on Human Rights—an instrument that applied in all the British colonies (including Singapore and Malaysia) prior to independence, clearly illustrated that this omission was deliberate and not due to ignorance or oversight.[25] Furthermore, the Chief Justice noted that the Singapore Government, in 1969, had unambiguously rejected a proposal by Singapore's Constitutional Commission[26] to initiate a constitutional amendment that would have expressly prohibited the state imposition of inhuman punishment. Therefore, according to the Court of Appeal, it was 'not legitimate for this court to read into Art 9(1) a constitutional right which was decisively rejected by the Government in 1969, especially given the historical context in which that

[21] See *Reyes v The Queen* [2002] 2 AC 235 (Privy Council); *Fox v The Queen* [2002] 2 AC 284 (Privy Council); *R v Hughes* [2002] 2 AC 259 (Privy Council).

[22] *Yong Vui Kong* (n 4) [60].

[23] Ibid. [59].

[24] Singapore became a constituent state of Malaysia in 1963 and gained full independence as a sovereign republic in 1965.

[25] *Yong Vui Kong* (n 4) [62].

[26] The Singapore Constitutional Commission was tasked by the Singapore government in 1966 to make recommendations on constitutional changes that might be necessary to protect the rights of minorities in Singapore.

right was rejected'.[27] Ergo, the Court of Appeal was espousing an originalist understanding of the Singapore Constitution and would in turn only invalidate 'legislation of so absurd or arbitrary a nature that it could not possibly have been contemplated by our [Singapore's] constitutional framers as being "law" when they crafted the constitutional provisions protecting fundamental liberties'.[28]

The originalist model of due process presents itself as a perceived resolution to the tension between constitutionalism and democracy. So far as courts only implement the original understanding of the Constitution, judges would be adjudicating in a democratically legitimate way as they are merely enforcing the original meaning of the constitutional text that was duly enacted by the people via their representatives.[29] It is thus believed that originalism, as a mode of constitutional interpretation, can best promote predictability and also prevent illegitimate constitutional change under the guise of judicial interpretation.[30]

C. Adjudicative Model

Pursuant to the adjudicative model, the purpose of the due process clause is to ensure the accuracy and integrity of the process by which the guilt of the accused is judicially determined. This model would impose constraints on the legislature or the executive if they seek to dispense with any procedures that are deemed essential to the conduct of a fair trial. Nevertheless, the substantive and procedural interests that this model protects relate solely to the accused's interests in the adjudicative process; the court is only interested in ensuring that the accused has received a fair trial; it would thus appear that the courts would not further inquire into whether it is normatively fair for the legislature to criminalize certain conduct or impose certain types of punishments.

This model of due process was first conceived by the Federal Court of Malaysia in *Lee Kwan Woh v Public Prosecutor*.[31] According to Justice Gopal

[27] *Yong Vui Kong* (n 4) [72].

[28] *Yong Vui Kong* (n 4) [16].

[29] Aileen Kavanagh, 'Original Intention, Enacted Text, and Constitutional Interpretation' (2002) 47 *American Journal of Jurisprudence* 255, 261

[30] See Robert Bork, *The Tempting of America: The Political Seduction of the Law* (New York, Free Press 1990) 143–60; Antonin Scalia, 'Common Law Courts in a Civil Law System: The Role of the United States Federal Courts in Interpreting the Constitution and Laws' in Amy Gutmann (ed), *A Matter of Interpretation* (Princeton, Princeton University Press 1997) 17.

[31] *Lee Kwan Woh v PP* [2009] 5 MLJ 301 (Federal Court of Malaysia).

Sri Ram for the unanimous court, the fundamental right guaranteed by Article 5(1) of the Malaysian Constitution mandated that the state deprivation in question be 'fair both in point of procedure and substance'.[32] More importantly, he opined as follows:

> [W]hen the principle is applied to a criminal case, what it means is that an accused has a constitutionally guaranteed right to receive a fair trial by an impartial tribunal and to have a just decision on the facts.[33]

On the facts, the accused was convicted of drug trafficking but the trial court had denied him the opportunity of submitting that he had no case to answer at the close of the prosecution's case. According to the Federal Court, this denial deprived the accused of his implied right to a fair trial guaranteed under Article 5(1). Presumably, this would have warranted a re-trial; but on the facts, the Federal Court also decided that the trial judge had 'clearly erred in the way'[34] he appreciated the evidence and the conviction was quashed.

Subsequently in *Shamim Reza v Public Prosecutor*,[35] the Federal Court of Malaysia fleshed out the parameters of this fundamental right to a fair trial. In particular, the court opined that the right to a fair trial would include the right to be represented by competent counsel. More importantly, the court so observed:

> [T]he incompetence of counsel in the conduct of a defence in a criminal trial is a ground on which a conviction may be quashed provided that (i) such incompetence must be flagrant in the circumstances of the given case; and (ii) it must have deprived the accused of a fair trial thereby occasioning a miscarriage of justice.

On the facts, the conviction in question was affirmed as there was no display of flagrant incompetence on the part of the defence counsel.

The adjudicative model of due process therefore safeguards the substantive and procedural rights of the accused so far as it ensures that the guilt determination process would be fair. Nevertheless, so far as his or her due process rights are confined within the adjudicative context, he or she would have no judicial recourse if the essence of his or her complaint is that it is constitutionally impermissible for the legislature to criminalize a particular conduct or mete out a particular punishment for a crime. In other words, the substantive criminal law and its accompanying statutory sentences would be beyond judicial reproach.

[32] Ibid. [18]. [33] Ibid. [34] Ibid. [30].
[35] *Shamim Reza v Public Prosecutor* [2011] 1 MLJ 471 (Federal Court of Malaysia).

D. Substantive Model

The substantive model of due process safeguards not only the rights of the accused within the adjudicative context but it also inquires into the substance of the criminal law, that is it mandates the presence of fault or moral culpability as a precondition to criminal liability and insists that the punishment imposed on an offender must be sufficiently proportionate to his or her degree of moral blameworthiness.[36]

Within common law Asia, Hong Kong is the only jurisdiction that has come close to embodying this substantive ideal of due process. In *Lau Cheong v HKSAR*,[37] the Court of Final Appeal (CFA) was asked to decide whether the imposition of a mandatory life sentence on the accused convicted of murder violated his right against arbitrary imprisonment as protected under Article 28 of the Basic Law. Notably, the CFA observed as follows:

> [A] term of imprisonment lawfully ordered may nonetheless be "arbitrary". It follows that such arbitrariness may reside in the substantive rules of criminal liability whose breach led to the imprisonment ordered.[38]

In particular, the CFA emphasized that Article 28 would also prohibit laws that are 'sufficiently disproportionate to justify describing the law as "arbitrary"—a disproportion so great as to reduce the law virtually to something capricious, unreasoned or without reasonable cause'.[39] Nevertheless, on the facts, the CFA upheld the constitutionality of the mandatory life sentence for convicted murderers, in view of the gravity of the crime and the fact that the legislature had concurrently provided for a statutory regime for the individualized review of each sentence even after its mandatory imposition, such that an independent board had the power to recommend conversion of such life sentences to fixed terms or to direct conditional releases in appropriate cases.[40]

Nonetheless, subsequently in *So Wai Lun v HKSAR*,[41] the CFA was unwilling to fully embrace this substantive conception of due process. On the facts, the accused argued that the statutory crime of unlawful intercourse with a girl under the age of 16 was arbitrary and thus unconstitutional as the legislature had dispensed with a *mens rea* requirement for the offence to be established. The CFA was however unwilling to accept that due process concerns would invalidate the legislative prerogative to introduce absolute offences.

[36] Ramraj (n 1) 502.
[37] *Lau Cheong v HKSAR* [2002] 2 HKLRD 612 (Hong Kong Court of Final Appeal).
[38] *Lau Cheong* (n 37) [42]. [39] Ibid. [112]. [40] Ibid. [125].
[41] *So Wai Lun v HKSAR* [2006] 3 HKLRD 394 (Hong Kong Court of Final Appeal).

According to Bokhary and Chan PJJ for the CFA:

> Where the legislature has enacted an absolute offence, the judiciary will not strike down the offence merely on the basis of a view that it would be preferable for the offence to admit of a defence of belief or reasonable belief.[42]

Therefore, while the Hong Kong courts are willing to demand that the legislature provide for sentences that are proportionate to the crime, the judiciary would not subject the statutory standard of criminal fault to constitutional scrutiny.

II. Evaluating the Four Models

A. Formal Model

According to the formal model of due process, the constitutional restraint against arbitrary state action merely requires the government to comply with the laws of the land. The citizenry is afforded whatever rights the legislature has conferred upon them; the judiciary is unconcerned with whether these laws are in themselves fair, just, or reasonable.

This positivistic conception of due process would guard against any unauthorized abuse of power by the executive or administrative officials. But in all the above jurisdictions we have surveyed, it would be highly exceptional for the state to deprive a person of his or her liberty without acting upon some legislative basis for its actions. If this understanding of due process is sustained, the scope of judicial review for an alleged infringement of due process rights would be significantly narrowed and severely curtailed as courts would now merely exercise 'a limited form of judicial review based on the concept of legality'.[43]

We would now turn and examine the reasons advanced by the Malaysian and Singaporean judges for upholding this model of due process. In *Sugumar Balakrishnan*, with reference to the ouster clause that excluded judicial review over the impugned immigration legislation, the Federal Court observed as follows:

> In our view, Parliament having excluded judicial review under the Act, it is not permissible for our courts to intervene and disturb a statutorily unreviewable decision on the basis of a new amorphous and wide ranging concept of substantive unfairness as a separate ground of judicial review.

42 *So Wai Lun* (n 41) [37].

43 *Sugumar* (n 2) 514.

In the same vein, the Chief Justice of Singapore in *Mohammad Faizal* was adamant that the 'courts must impose the legislatively prescribed sentence on an offender even if it offends the principle of proportionality'[44] as, according to the learned judge, the desirability of mandatory sentences is a 'political question—a question of what is beneficial for the polity—not a constitutional question'.[45]

In the above-mentioned instances, the judges seemed to have forgotten that in a regime with constitutional review, even if Parliament has sought to oust judicial review statutorily or impose a certain punishment for specified offences, the courts, as arbiters of the Constitution, are constitutionally free to invalidate these legislations if they are deemed inconsistent with a constitutionally enshrined fundamental right. Therefore, it is no answer for the courts to prize the legislative prerogative to enact laws and impose punishments above judicial review when Parliamentary supremacy is no longer accepted as the constitutional arrangement of the day. To this extent, the learned Chief Justice of Singapore is misguided to have endorsed Lord Bingham's pre-UK Human Rights Act extra-curial observation on the non-reviewability of statutory sentences.

Furthermore, with respect to Singapore specifically, while its Constitution permits the state to deprive a person of his or her liberty in 'accordance with law', the term 'law' provided in Article 9(1) of the Constitution is not confined to the legislation passed by Parliament. In fact, Article 2(1) of the Singapore Constitution expressly defines the term 'law' to also include 'the common law in so far as it is in operation in Singapore and any custom or usage having the force of law in Singapore'. Since the Singapore Constitution expressly provides that an individual may not be incarcerated unless his or her deprivation is both authorized by legislation and/or common law principles, it is thus textually open to the Singapore judiciary via the Article 9(1) due process clause to develop and apply a body of constitutional common law which trumps statutory provisions that infringe upon this fundamental liberty.

Finally, if the constitutional due process safeguards in Singapore and Malaysia merely require the state deprivation of life and liberty in question to be authorized by any statute enacted in a formally valid way, the entrenchment of a Constitution as a safeguard against majoritarian excesses, in the words of Lord Diplock on behalf of the Privy Council on an appeal from Singapore in *Ong Ah Chuan v Public Prosecutor*, 'would be little better than a mockery'.[46]

[44] *Mohammad Faizal bin Sabtu* (n 3) [60]. [45] Ibid.

[46] *Ong Ah Chuan v PP* [1979–80] SLR 710 (Privy Council of Singapore) [26].

B. Originalist Model

Pursuant to the originalist model of due process, the judiciary would only invalidate any legislation that is considered arbitrary as originally understood by the framers of the Singapore Constitution.

This brand of originalism has been termed 'hard originalism'[47] and it is largely defended by scholars who seek to transform constitutional law into a system of rules such that judicial review becomes more democratic by virtue of its connection to the past judgments of the constitutional framers; and consequently, judicial discretion is also fettered and legal predictability enhanced by this judicial turn to history.[48] Originalists often caution that if judges are allowed to stray from the original understanding of the Constitution, they will be given a free rein to amend the Constitution; and judges who are non-elected officials would be imposing norms that the people have not accepted through their democratically elected representatives.[49]

However, the espousal of 'hard originalism' as the preferred theory of constitutional adjudication in Singapore by the Court of Appeal in *Yong Vui Kong* is not unproblematic, and it is to these reasons we now turn.

First, the constitutional text of Singapore's Fundamental Liberties Clauses, of which the due process clause is one of them, was not deliberated upon by a Constituent Assembly of the independent state in question. Instead, upon gaining independence from Malaysia in 1965, Singapore simply made most Fundamental Liberties provisions found in the Malaysia Federal Constitution applicable in Singapore via the Republic of Singapore Independence Act.[50] Certainly, the fact that the legislature of a newly

[47] Cass Sunstein, *Legal Reasoning and Political Conflict* (New York, Oxford University Press 1996) 173.

[48] Robert Bork, *The Tempting of America: The Political Seduction of the Law* (New York, Free Press 1990) 143–60; Antonin Scalia, 'Common Law Courts in a Civil Law System: The Role of the United States Federal Courts in Interpreting the Constitution and Laws' in Amy Gutmann (ed), *A Matter of Interpretation* (Princeton, Princeton University Press 1997) 17. For an insightful discussion on originalism, see also Vicki Jackson, *Constitutional Engagement in a Transnational Era* (Oxford, Oxford University Press 2010) 20–2, and Vicki Jackson & Jamal Greene, 'Constitutional Interpretation in Comparative Perspectives: Comparing Judges or Courts?' in Tom Ginsburg & Rosalind Dixon (eds) *Comparative Constitutional Law* (Cheltenham, Edward Elgar, 2011) 599.

[49] Antonin Scalia, 'Commentary' (1996) 40 *Saint Louis University Law Journal* 1119; Antonin Scalia & Bryan Garner, *Reading Law: The Interpretation of Legal Texts* (St Paul, Thomson West 2012) 88.

[50] For example, the Singapore Parliament deliberately omitted to include Article 13 of the Malaysian federal Constitution which guarantees the right to property and guarantees adequate compensation for any state deprivation of this right. See Tan & Thio, *Constitutional Law in Malaysia and Singapore* (Singapore, LexisNexis 2010) 74; Kevin YL Tan, 'State and Institution Building through the Singapore Constitution 1965–2005' in Thio & Tan (eds), *Evolution of a Revolution: Forty Years of the Singapore Constitution* (New York, Routledge 2009) 50, 54.

sovereign republic consciously adopted those provisions conferred upon these Singaporean liberties a legal life of their own. But the mere enactment of the law alone does not provide us with a clue as to what was the original meaning the framers attached to those provisions they adopted. Furthermore, since the Singapore constitutional framers did not deliberate upon the phraseology of the Fundamental Liberties Clauses, but merely imported them as a matter of expedience from Malaysia, one does wonder whether it is even possible to discern the original meaning they attached to those provisions adopted from Malaysia.[51] At best, one can try to discern the original intent of those framers (and the members on the Reid Constitutional Commission) when Malaysia's Constitution was drafted and adopted, but it would be a very curious state of affairs for Singaporean judges in modern independent Singapore to give effect to and be fettered by the original intent of another nation state's constitutional framers.[52]

Second, the Court of Appeal in *Yong Vui Kong*'s application of this originalist mode of interpretation is also problematic. The Chief Justice was unwilling to accept that Singapore's due process clause could be interpreted to include an implied general prohibition against inhuman punishment as the Singapore Government had in 1969 unambiguously rejected a proposal by a Constitutional Commission to amend the Constitution and provide for such an express right. However, one must remember that the Fundamental Liberties Clauses of the Singapore Constitution came into effect in 1965 soon after Singapore's independence. Hence, it is unclear, even on an originalist understanding of the Singapore Constitution, whether it was legitimate for the court to discern the original intent of the constitutional framers in 1965, when they imported the applicable Fundamental Liberties Clauses from Malaysia, from a Parliamentary decision taken four years later to reject a proposal to provide for an express prohibition against inhuman punishment.

Third, even if a common practice, for example the death penalty, was accepted at the time the constitutional provisions were adopted, this does not establish the fact that the framers intended to constitutionalize that convention for subsequent generations to obey. It is equally possible that the framers had given little thought to that issue or preferred to allow future generations to decide the issue for themselves. This interpretation is also more consistent with a textual reading of the constitutional provisions. The

[51] It is also debatable whether one can even ascertain a single collective intent of a large group of constitutional drafters and/or ratifiers, each of whom may have different intentions. See Paul Brest, 'The Misconceived Quest for the Original Understanding' (1980) 60 *Boston University Law Review* 204, 209–22.

[52] For a fuller discussion of this case, see Yap Po Jen, 'Constitutionalising Capital Crimes: Judicial Virtue or Originalism Sin?' [2011] *Singapore Journal of Legal Studies* 281.

Singapore Framers, like framers of other national Constitutions, have used both specific and broad provisions within the constitutional text, thus indicating that separate clauses should be interpreted at different levels of generality. Where the framers wanted the constitutional clauses to be read strictly, they used highly specific and particular words. For example, a member of the Singapore Parliament must be 'of the age of 21 years or above'.[53] The Constitution does not say that a Member of Parliament must be of sufficient maturity in age. The Singapore Parliament, unless sooner dissolved, shall continue for five years from the date of its first sitting and shall then stand dissolved.[54] The Constitution does not say that the Singapore Parliament, unless sooner dissolved, shall continue for a reasonable period of years and shall then stand dissolved. Given that the framers had intentionally left the constitutional provisions enshrining terms like 'in accordance with law' or 'equal protection' ambiguously worded, fully comprehending that the language was not specific and could be interpreted in various ways, the choice to adopt a broader principle must thus be respected. After all, if a prohibition's reach is restricted to the practices that were thought to fall foul of the Constitution at the time the provisions were adopted, it would leave no room for the reasoned adjudication of practices that scientific and technological advancements or changed socio-economic circumstances may bring.[55] Thus, such broadly phrased constitutional clauses have to embody abstract principles rather than merely just encapsulate and enshrine historical practices.

As Professor Jack Balkin has observed:

> [Constitutional adopters] choose vague standards or abstract principles because they want to channel political judgment but delegate the task of construction and application to future generations.[56]

Fidelity to the Constitution requires judges to pay credence to the framers' choice of rules and/or standards in the bill of rights. The Singapore Court of Appeal's decision to shackle the Constitution to the framers' original specific application of the text at the time of enactment, when they had deliberately chosen vague, open-textured language, may indeed be inconsistent with the framers' original intent of enacting an enduring instrument with constitutional standards and spaces that allow future generations of lawmakers and judges to design as appropriate to their evolving circumstances.

[53] Singapore Constitution, Article 44(2)(b). [54] Ibid. Article 65(4).

[55] Mark D Greenberg & Harry Litman, 'The Meaning of Original Meaning' (1998) 86 *Georgetown Law Journal* 569, 580.

[56] Jack Balkin, 'Nine Perspectives on Living Originalism' [2012] *University of Illinois Law Review* 815, 817.

This more nuanced understanding of originalism has been termed 'framework' originalism[57] or 'expressed intent' originalism.[58] Herein, courts would only give effect to the intent of the framers which is 'manifest in the text itself';[59] where the constitutional text does not explicitly specify or prohibit a certain course of conduct, the judges are free to flesh out the constitutional framework so long as the judicial developments are consistent with the text so enacted. This constitutional liberty granted by the framers to the judiciary, the primary institutional interpreter of the Constitution, is for the Singapore Courts to exercise judiciously and not to reject categorically.

C. Adjudicative Model

According to the adjudicatory model of due process, the court would ensure that an individual receives a fair trial before he or she is convicted of the offence for which he or she is charged. This adjudicatory understanding of due process is significant so far as it contributes to the accuracy and integrity of the dispute-settling procedures. So far as the accused is presented with an adequate opportunity to present his or her case through the assistance of counsel before a fair and impartial tribunal, and involuntary confessions or inadmissible evidence elicited as a result of police malpractices may be judicially excluded, the citizenry at large would also have confidence in a legal system that insures the reliability and integrity of the guilt determination process. As observed by Professor Sanford Kadish, the essential values upheld by the accommodation of these interests are that 'the guilty be punished with sufficient consistency to serve the social functions of the criminal law; that the freedom of the individual responsibly to govern his social behaviour and the respect for individual decency be preserved'.[60]

Nevertheless, so far as the Malaysian courts in *Lee Kwan Woh* and *Shamim Reza* have confined criminal due process to the requirement that an accused must receive a fair trial by an impartial tribunal, the judiciary appears to be focussing only on the substantive and procedural interests of the accused within the adjudicatory context, and it would not further examine the propriety of the substance of the criminal law and its corresponding sentencing regime. If so, as Professor Henry Hart once facetiously observed, 'a crime is

[57] Jack M Balkin, 'Framework Originalism and the Living Constitution' (2009) 103 *Northwestern University Law Review* 549.

[58] Aileen Kavanagh, 'Original Intention, Enacted Text, and Constitutional Interpretation' (2002) 47 *American Journal of Jurisprudence* 255.

[59] Ibid. 283.

[60] Sanford H Kadish, 'Methodology and Criteria in Due Process Adjudication—A Survey and Criticism' (1957) 66 *Yale Law Journal* 319, 349.

anything which is called a crime, and a criminal penalty is simply the penalty provided for doing anything which has been given that name'.[61] This development, I argue, should give us some pause for concern.

First, the normative distinction between the substantive criminal law and the process-related rules is unclear. After all, process-related rules are often just a measure of how much the substantive entitlements are worth and of what we are willing to sacrifice to see a given goal attained.[62] Equally, the procedure one uses determines how much substance is achieved by the state. Unless one takes the view that courts should abandon 'process-related' review altogether, to be consistent, there is no reason why the judiciary should not equally engage in the substantive review of penal sanctions as well.

Second, one does wonder why the Constitution should protect against retail-level deprivation of due process rights (fair trial rights) but not against wholesale deprivations by the legislature via the use of the substantive criminal law.[63] If the reasons we observe the adjudicatory model of due process are that we want to maximize the reliability of the guilt determination process and preserve the intrinsic dignity of the individual, surely both concerns would also be undermined if the court does not further examine whether the individual is morally culpable or blameworthy to warrant the penal sanctions imposed on him or her. As argued by Claire Finkelstein, 'a theory of crime will become judicially idle unless it can also provide a way of identifying constraints on the kinds of criminal statutes legislatures may draft'.[64]

If we abandon a positivistic understanding of crime and punishment and allow for the judicial oversight of the elements of criminal offences and their corresponding sentences, two fundamental constraints on the legislative imposition of penal sanctions would come into play. The first concerns the culpability of the offender. The actor of the crime should have the requisite *mens rea* in the commission of the offence;[65] and typically, the imposition of liability without fault should be confined to regulatory offences. Second, even where the essential elements of criminal liability are established, there must be some limits on the severity of the punishments that the legislature

[61] Henry M Hart, 'The Aims of the Criminal Law' (1958) 23 *Law and Contemporary Problems* 401, 404.

[62] Frank Easterbrook, 'Substance and Due Process' [1982] *Supreme Court Review* 85, 112–13.

[63] Larry Alexander, 'Are Procedural Rights Derivative Substantive Rights?' (1998) 17 *Law & Philosophy* 19, 27.

[64] Claire Finkelstein, 'Positivism and the Notion of an Offence' (2000) 88 *California Law Review* 335, 336.

[65] Professor Herbert Wechsler in designing the United States Model Penal Code has categorized the different types of *mens rea* as follows: (1) 'purpose', denoting the actor's conscious objective; (2) 'knowledge', meaning awareness; (3) 'recklessness', referring to the conscious creation of risk; and (4) 'negligence', indicating inadvertent risk creation.

may impose, that is the severity of the penal punishment must be proportionate to the seriousness of the crime. So far as we accept that the judiciary has a constitutional role in placing limits on the substance of the criminal law, the right to due process would no longer be merely a constitutional imprimatur for the legislative judgment on the propriety of statutory offences and the concomitant sentences, but a means by which the judiciary can have a discourse with the legislature on crime, culpability, and punishment.

D. Substantive Model

Pursuant to the substantive model of due process, besides ensuring an individual's right to a fair trial, the courts will also insist generally upon the presence of criminal fault as a prerequisite to the imposition of penal liability, and demand for some proportionality between the punishment imposed and the offender's degree of moral blameworthiness.

Within the common law Asian jurisdictions under discussion, Hong Kong is the only territory that has come close to fulfilling this conception of due process. In *Lau Cheong v HKSAR*,[66] the Hong Kong Court of Final Appeal (CFA) accepted that 'arbitrariness may reside in the substantive rules of criminal liability'[67] and that 'arbitrariness is not excluded merely because detention is pursuant to lawful procedures'.[68] Therefore, the Article 28 due process clause would equally prohibit laws that are 'sufficiently disproportionate to justify describing the law as "arbitrary"—a disproportion so great as to reduce the law virtually to something capricious, unreasoned or without reasonable cause'.[69]

What is however unfortunate is that the CFA has refused to acknowledge that the constitutional right to due process would equally impose a minimum standard of criminal fault for penal liability to attach. In *So Wai Lun v HKSAR*,[70] the CFA was unwilling to accept that due process concerns could invalidate the legislative choice to dispense with a *mens rea* requirement for the offence of unlawful sexual intercourse with a minor to be established. This holding is problematic on two counts and it is to them that we now turn.

First, so far as the Hong Kong legislature has attempted to cast the burden of proving a particular defence on the accused, the Hong Kong courts have almost always 'read down' the statutory presumption as an evidential burden of production, so as to vindicate his or her right to be presumed innocent until proven guilty.[71] Therefore, if the Legislative Council had attempted to

[66] [2002] 2 HKLRD 612 (Hong Kong Court of Final Appeal). [67] Ibid. [42].
[68] Ibid. [43]. [69] *Lau Cheong* (n 66) [112]. [70] *So Wai Lun* (n 41).
[71] *HKSAR v Hung Chan Wa* [2006] 3 HKLRD 841 (Hong Kong Court of Final Appeal).

enact a defence of reasonable belief, but had cast the burden of proof on the accused, the CFA would almost surely have decided that this presumption falls foul of the Basic Law. If so, as observed by Professor Michael Hor, this would create an anomalous situation whereby the 'Legislature may not cast the burden of proof on the accused with respect to, say, *mens rea*, but it may do away with it entirely'.[72]

Secondly, on normative grounds, it is both unfair and inefficacious for the state to sanction a person's conduct without reference to the actor's state of mind. As Professor Herbert Packer rightly observed:

> It is inefficacious because conduct unaccompanied by an awareness of the factors making it criminal does not mark the actor as one who needs to be subjected to punishment in order to deter him or others from behaving similarly in the future, nor does it single him out as a socially dangerous individual who needs to be incapacitated or reformed. It is unjust because the actor is subjected to the stigma of a criminal conviction without being morally blameworthy. Consequently, on either a preventive or a retributive theory of criminal punishment, the criminal sanction is inappropriate in the absence of mens rea.[73]

Arguably, some might take the view that the imposition of absolute liability would spur an individual to the exercise of extreme diligence. This was indeed the view advanced by the CFA in *So Wai Lun*. As Bokhary and Chan PJJ argued in their joint judgment, the imposition of absolute liability would encourage people to 'avoid what may be unlawful and steering well away from the line between legality and illegality';[74] on the facts, this would add materially to the protection of young girls against predatory men. But if this line of argument is taken to its logical conclusion, one must also accept that the punishment of adult family members of the principal offender as accessories to the crime would have a theoretical tendency to prevent the said crime, as persons could be incited to intense watchfulness over the conduct of their family members.[75] Surely, the CFA would not also consider this statutory course of action constitutional?

The imposition of liability without fault may be constitutionally acceptable where one is concerned with regulatory offences that have relatively minor penalties attached. However, where the offence carries 'serious sanctions and

[72] Michael Hor, 'Criminal Due Process in Hong Kong and Singapore: A Mutual Challenge' (2007) 37 *Hong Kong Law Journal* 65.

[73] Herbert Packer, 'Mens Rea and the Supreme Court' [1962] *Supreme Court Review* 107, 109.

[74] *So Wai Lun* (n 41) [39].

[75] Clarence E Laylin & Alonzo H Tuttle, 'Due Process and Punishment' (1921–22) 20 *Michigan Law Review* 614, 632.

the stigma of official condemnation',[76] liability should be reserved for persons who are morally blameworthy to some degree, that is the offender must at the very least have been negligent in allowing the prohibited act to occur. Where the individual could not have discovered, even if he or she had exercised reasonable care, the illegal nature of the activities for which he or she is engaged, the moral force of the criminal law would be undermined and his or her right to due process violated by the incarceration.

III. Dialogic Tools to Implementing Substantive Due Process

In the earlier sections, I have argued that the substantive model of due process is the only logical and meaningful safeguard against arbitrary state action. Accordingly, the judiciary should not only ensure that an individual receives a fair trial before he or she is convicted of the offence he or she is charged with, the courts should also generally insist upon the presence of criminal fault as a precondition to the imposition of penal liability, and demand for some proportionality between the statutory punishment imposed and the offender's degree of moral culpability.

Nevertheless, in this section of my chapter, I shall endeavour to show how common law courts in Asia can apply some of the dialogic sub-constitutional tools, which I first discussed in Chapter 5, when observing this substantive conception of due process, such that the legislature is not excluded or side-lined in the constitutional discourse on criminal law and procedure. As we have examined in Chapter 4, the exercise of dialogic or weaker forms of judicial review may be more appropriate when strong governments, like those found in common law Asia, are able to respond to unpopular constitutional rulings by ousting constitutional review or even the judges. When courts are uncertain about how the political branches of government may react to an adverse ruling, it may be prudent for judges to vindicate rights in a cautious and dialogical fashion. After all, unlike courts that are situated in de-centralized and fragmented political systems, these Asian judges are unable to deliver activist rulings with impunity.[77]

[76] John Jeffries & Paul Stephan III, 'Defences, Presumptions, and the Burden of Proof in the Criminal Law' (1979) 88 *Yale Law Journal* 1371, 1374.

[77] Eric Ip, 'The Evolution of Constitutional Adjudication in the Chinese Special Administrative Regions: Theory and Evidence' (2013) 61 *American Journal of Comparative Law* 799, 805.

A. Procedural Constitutional Rules

The first dialogic tool at the court's disposal is the judicial use of procedural constitutional rules. Where the impugned statute is invalidated because there has been a procedural constitutional irregularity, a channel for dialogue between the courts and the legislature remains open as lawmakers retain the right to pursue the same substantive goals again after complying with the constitutional procedures judicially conceived. One such example would be the Federal Court of Malaysia decision in *Lee Kwan Woh v Public Prosecutor* earlier discussed.[78] In that case, Gopal Sri Ram FCJ gave an expansive reading of Article 5(1) to include 'a constitutionally guaranteed right to receive a fair trial'.[79] On the facts, the trial judge denied the accused the opportunity of submitting that he had no case to answer at the close of the prosecution's case; and according to the Federal Court, this irregularity violated the implied constitutional right to a fair trial provided under Article 5(1). This decision is noteworthy on two counts. First, the Federal Court had adopted a robust and extra-textual reading of the enshrined constitutional liberties by recognizing an implied right to a fair trial when the Malaysian Constitution does not expressly provide for this. Second, this activist judicial stance can nevertheless be considered dialogic so far as the state is not deprived of the right to prosecute and incarcerate an offender for any substantive offence it seeks to criminalize; the same substantive ends can still be pursued after the state complies with the judicially imposed procedural constitutional rule.

Therefore, in the Malaysian decision of *Pihak Berkuasa Negeri Sabah v Sugumar Balakrishnan*,[80] the Federal Court should have also imposed procedural constitutional rules to vindicate the substantive conception of due process. So far as the Immigration Act expressly ousted judicial review, the court could have required the state to justify why such limits on the applicant's right to due process were fair and reasonable. In other words, the government would have to show how this limit was proportionate.

In this regard, the Hong Kong CFA's decision in *Solicitor v Law Society*[81] may be of particular relevance. In that case, the applicant challenged the constitutionality of the Legal Practitioners Ordinance[82] so far as it barred any appeals against decisions of the Solicitors Disciplinary Tribunal to the CFA. Notwithstanding the statutory ouster of the court's jurisdiction, the CFA observed as follows:

[78] *Lee Kwan Woh* (n 31). [79] *Lee Kwan Woh* (n 31).
[80] *Sugumar Balakrishnan* (n 2).
[81] (2003) 6 HKCFAR 570 (Hong Kong Court of Final Appeal).
[82] Legal Practitioners Ordinance (Cap 159).

The legislature in providing for appeals in statutes may limit recourse to the Court for final adjudication and thus, may limit its power of final adjudication to appeals permitted by such statutes. But limitation cannot be imposed arbitrarily by the legislature. The limitation imposed must pursue a legitimate purpose and there must be reasonable proportionality between the limitation and the purpose sought to be achieved. These dual requirements will be referred to collectively as the proportionality test.[83]

In applying the proportionality test to a particular limitation, the CFA would ascertain the purpose of the limitation and matters such as 'the subject-matter of the dispute, whether it concerns fact or law, whether it relates to substantive rights and obligations or only procedural matters, what is at stake, the need for speedy resolution, and the cost implications of dispute resolution'.[84] When considering whether the limitation is reasonably proportionate to the legitimate purpose, the courts will also examine the nature and extent of the limitation.

In such circumstances, the imposition of the proportionality doctrine herein serves two ends. First, it forces the government to reveal some of its privately held information on why the impugned ouster clause is necessary; by raising the legislative enactment costs of such ouster clauses, the judiciary is also increasing the credibility of the government's assertion that it has a sufficiently strong public interest in the legislation to justify the rights-derogation.[85] Second, even if the courts eventually mandate review over the Immigration Act, this is a procedural imposition which merely serves as a judicial brake on legislative excesses that may transpire when lawmakers are negligent or when they act in haste. Such dialogic rules leave room for the legislature and the executive to effectuate their substantive goals through alternate procedures such that the re-formulated policies adhere more closely to fundamental constitutional norms. In imposing such a procedural constitutional rule, judges are not expressing any views on the normative content of the impugned penal legislation; they are merely seeking to examine the adequacy of the decision-making process and realize certain process values that would enhance the transparency and legitimacy of the state action. Therefore, as I have discussed in Chapter 5, this sub-constitutional technique is dialogic as the judiciary is not precluding the legislature from achieving the primary statutory aims of the impugned penal legislation in question; the lawmakers are still empowered to legislate on the same substantive matter after enhancing the quality of their deliberative *process*.

[83] *Solicitor v Law Society* (n 81) [31]. [84] Ibid. [33].

[85] Matthew Stephenson, 'The Price of Public Action: Constitutional Doctrine and the Judicial Manipulation of Legislative Enactment Costs' (2008) 118 *Yale Law Journal* 2, 15.

B. Common Law Clear-Statement Rules

The second dialogic sub-constitutional tool available to the courts would be the judicial enforcement of common law rights that herein take the form of clear-statement rules. This method of dialogue is most suitable when courts are seeking to vindicate a normative conception of culpability within the substantive criminal law. In other words, the courts need not entrench, at the outset, the inclusion of a *mens rea* requirement for all penal offences; instead, the judiciary could, as a rule of construction, construe all crimes as 'requiring scienter when the legislature is silent as to intent'.[86]

This approach was indeed available to the Hong Kong CFA in *So Wai Lun*. On the facts, Section 124(1) of the Crimes Ordinance[87] criminalizes unlawful sexual intercourse with a girl under the age of 16, but it is noteworthy that this offence-creating provision is actually silent on *mens rea*. Therefore, it would be open to the CFA, in the absence of any express legislative statement on this matter,[88] to afford the accused the opportunity of disproving *mens rea*, that is to adduce evidence that he genuinely and reasonably believed that his sexual partner was at least 16 years old. Interestingly, the judicial recognition of a defence of reasonable mistaken belief is indeed the standard course taken by the Singapore courts where the offence-creating penal provision is silent on *mens rea*.[89] One must however note that for sexual offences relating to the unlawful intercourse with minors, Section 377D of the Singapore Penal Code[90] expressly rules out the applicability of the defence of 'reasonable mistaken belief' where the accused is 21 years of age (or older) at the time of the alleged offence. Therefore, the Hong Kong CFA could equally impose a similar clear-statement rule such that if the Hong Kong legislature wants to remove the accused person's defence of reasonable belief in any particular circumstance, the legislature must state so in explicit terms, as Singapore has done.

[86] Finkelstein (n 64) 337.

[87] Crimes Ordinance (Cap 200), Section 124.

[88] In the Court of Appeal decision of *HKSAR v So Wai Lun*, [2005] 1 HKLRD 443, the court held that legislative history of Section 124(1) of the Crimes Ordinance 'clearly shows that the reasonable belief defence has been expressly repealed in Hong Kong'. But one must note that the repeal of the reasonable belief defence took place in 1897 vis-à-vis the Section 5 of the Protection of Women and Girls Ordinance, a predecessor legislative provision of the current Section 124(1). It is thus not self-evident nor was there any legislative history to indicate that the legislature that had enacted Section 124(1) of the Crimes Ordinance in its current form had also deliberately chosen to abolish a reasonable belief defence, especially since the prior change in legislation took place over a century ago and in relation to a statute that had been changed several times since then.

[89] See *Tan Khee Wan Iris v PP* [1995] 2 SLR 63 (High Court of Singapore); *M V Balakrishnan v PP* [1998] SGHC 416 (High Court of Singapore).

[90] Penal Code (Cap 224), Section 377D.

Arguably, the Hong Kong CFA has begun to reconsider its stance on the imposition of absolute liability.[91] In *Kulemesin v HKSAR*,[92] the CFA held that where the offence-creating penal provisions are silent or ambiguous as to the *mens rea*, 'the more serious the offence in terms of penalty and social obloquy, the less likely it is that the presumption of *mens rea* will be held to have been supplanted'. For regulatory offences, the CFA would be more willing to accept that the presumption of *mens rea* has been displaced, and the accused could be required to establish that he or she has a reasonable belief defence. However, where a serious offence carrying severe penalties is involved, a reverse onus may also be regarded as making 'excessive inroads into both the presumption of *mens rea* and the constitutionally protected presumption of innocence'.[93] In such cases, the CFA held that the following alternative regime on *mens rea* may apply:

> The prosecution need not set out to prove mens rea, but if there is evidence capable of raising a reasonable doubt that the defendant may have acted or omitted to act in the honest and reasonable belief that the circumstances or likely consequences of his conduct were such that, if true, liability would not attach, he must be acquitted unless the prosecution proves beyond reasonable doubt the absence of such exculpatory belief or that there were no reasonable grounds for such belief.[94]

By construing an ambiguous statute in ways that advance substantive values of due process, the judiciary would be actively promoting its vision of what the constitution requires. Yet, such constitutionally inspired common law clear-statement rules are dialogic and modest in nature as they leave space for the legislature to respond in disagreement, if it so chooses, and remove the due diligence defence in express terms. So far as the lawmakers are forced to debate openly when seeking a statutory reversal, the level of public attention drawn to the debates would only enhance the transparency and quality of the legislative deliberation. This rule is thus democracy-enhancing as the legislature is forced to determine explicitly whether it wants to sacrifice a specified

[91] See also Johannes Chan, 'Constitutional Protection of the Right to be Presumed Innocent and the Right Against Self-Incrimination: The Hong Kong Experience', (2013) 25 *Singapore Academy of Law Journal* 69.

[92] (2013) 16 HKCFAR 195.

[93] Ibid. at [89].

[94] Ibid. at [83]. On the facts, the CFA held that a presumption of *mens rea* would be construed to apply to Section 72 of the Shipping and Port Control Ordinance (Cap 313), such that if the defendant is able to rely on evidence which, if unrebutted, raises a reasonable doubt as to whether a reasonable excuse exists for his conduct and the resultant endangerment of the safety of any person upon any vessel or in the sea, he is entitled to be acquitted unless at the end of the day, the prosecution establishes beyond reasonable doubt that no such excuse exists or that the excuse relied on is not reasonable.

constitutional value in pursuit of a regulatory objective.[95] Furthermore, by deciding this matter via common law principles, the court can avoid, at the outset, the need to resolve the harder constitutional question of whether a minimum standard of criminal fault is constitutionally required. This display of judicial minimalism and moderation leaves room for the legislature to engage in the common enterprise of human rights advancement, and the court's institutional legitimacy, vis-à-vis the other branches of government and the public at large, is also preserved.

C. Delayed Declarations of Invalidity

Even when courts deem certain statutory punishments grossly disproportionate and excessive, thereby violating the proportionality limb of the substantive model of due process, judges can still engage in dialogic review so far as they utilize the sub-constitutional tool of delayed declarations of invalidity, instead of specific injunctions, as the constitutional remedy of choice.

Within common law Asia, as discussed in Chapter 5, Hong Kong is the only jurisdiction where the courts have applied this particular sub-constitutional technique. But one must note that the suspension order is neither expressly provided for in the Hong Kong Basic Law nor in the Canadian Constitution, the jurisdiction in which this remedy was first conceived. In *Koo Sze Yiu & another v Chief Executive of Hong Kong*,[96] the Hong Kong CFA expressly held that this judicial power to suspend the operation of a declaration arose from the inherent jurisdiction of the courts and was 'concomitant of the power to make the declaration in the first place'.[97] The judicial recognition of such a constitutional remedy should thus also be open to the Malaysia and Singapore judiciary, especially since a suspension order, in lieu of an immediate invalidation of legislation, not only provides latitude to the government in deciding how best to respond to the court's decision, but also gives time to the legislature to devise corrective legislation while the default statutory framework is preserved. Certainly, as I have acknowledged in Chapter 5, of the six sub-constitutional tools that I have discussed, delayed declarations of

[95] John Manning, 'Clear Statement Rules and the Constitution' (2010) 110 *Columbia Law Review* 399, 402.

[96] [2006] 3 HKLRD 45 (Hong Kong Court of Final Appeal). One may note that the majority on the Supreme Court of the United Kingdom in *Ahmed & Ors v HM Treasury (No 2)* [2010] 2 AC 534, acknowledged the Hong Kong Court of Final Appeal decision in *Koo Sze Yiu* but nonetheless refused to suspend the operation of their judgment that had quashed various asset-freezing subsidiary legislation. See Christopher Forsyth, 'The Rock and the Sand: Jurisdiction and Remedial Discretion', (2013) 18 *Judicial Review* 360.

[97] *Yong Vui Kong* (n 4) [35].

invalidity would be the most 'robust' tool in the judges' sub-constitutional arsenal; but so far as the legislature is still provided with the opportunity and flexibility to choose from an array of statutory options when rectifying the flawed law, parliamentarians are still given significant discretion and space to craft their considered response to the judicial determination, and inter-branch dialogue can still ensue.

With reference to the impugned mandatory nature of the capital punishment at issue in the Singapore decision of *Yong Vui Kong*, the Court of Appeal could have granted a suspension order on the facts. In a spirit of judicial minimalism, it would not be necessary for the court to declare that all mandatory death sentences are cruel and inhuman forms of punishments, and are thus unconstitutional. Such a maximalist ruling would surely trigger a constitutional amendment in Singapore, as the government is absolutely convinced that the retention of the mandatory death sentence would deter a substantial number of drug traffickers from entering the country.[98]

Instead, the court could simply have focussed on the specific due process concerns raised by the impugned statutory provision, which had legislatively imposed the mandatory death penalty on offenders who had trafficked more than a modest 15g of diamorphine. It is noteworthy that in *Yong Vui Kong*, the Court of Appeal had acknowledged that the mandatory death penalty, coupled with the 15g statutory differentia, had precluded the courts from considering the circumstances in which the offence came to be committed, withheld from the public information on the type of offenders who were more likely to re-offend, and denied the court the opportunity of distinguishing between different cases of drug trafficking,[99] all of which suggested 'possible reasons for expanding the differentia to take into account something more than just merely the quantity of controlled drugs trafficked'.[100] In view of this finding, the court should have declared that the statutory imposition of the mandatory death sentence for all offenders who trafficked a modest 15g (or more) of diamorphine was an arbitrary, disproportionate, and grossly excessive measure to be considered 'in accordance with law' under Article 9(1) of the Singapore Constitution. Coupled with this minimalist ruling that does not pre-emptively strike out all mandatory death sentences in Singapore, the Court of Appeal could also have further suspended the immediate application of its declaration of invalidity so that the government could be given an opportunity to deliberate between a range of statutory options available

[98] See Michael Hor, 'Singapore's Death Penalty—The Beginning of the End?' in Roger Hood & Surya Deva (eds), *Confronting Capital Punishment in Asia: Human Rights, Politics and Public Opinion* (Oxford, Oxford University Press 2013) 141.

[99] *Yong Vui Kong* (n 4) [113]. [100] Ibid.

when responding to the court's ruling. Such a decision would be dialogic as the Singapore government is given the constitutional space and discretion to re-assess independently the appropriate volume/type of drugs trafficked, and the degree of the offender's culpability, for the mandatory death sentence to be triggered.

Indeed, even though the judiciary on the facts did not force the government's hand, this case caused sufficient disquiet among the public for the government to review the use of the death penalty in Singapore. Upon the conclusion of this review in July 2012, the government decided that capital punishment would no longer be mandatory in drug trafficking cases where the offender has only played the role of a courier, and where he or she has either substantially cooperated with Singapore's Central Narcotics Bureau upon arrest, or has a mental disability which substantially impairs his or her appreciation of the gravity of the act.[101] All drug offenders on death row, including the accused in *Yong Vui Kong,* were considered for re-sentencing under the amended new legislation passed in late 2012.[102]

A suspended declaration of invalidity gives Parliament, rather than the judiciary, the opportunity to make the initial selection on how best to address the due process concerns, among those competing alternatives at hand, such that due deference is paid to the primacy of the Parliament's lawmaking prerogative.[103] This suspension order may force the lawmakers to re-evaluate a piece of legislation at a time, and within time limits, not of its choosing. But such a dialogic ruling would have allowed lawmakers to retain a very broad range of discretion to determine the scope of the statutory punishment deemed appropriate as the courts do not mandate the specifics of the legislative sequel. As a result, the suspension of a declaration of invalidity remains a crucial instrument of 'remedial dialogue'[104] between the courts and the legislature.

IV. Conclusion

The formal model of due process emaciates the judicial role in constitutional review so far as it requires the courts to focus only on a formalistic notion

[101] 'Singapore completes review of mandatory death sentence' Channel News Asia (9 July 2012); www.channelnewsasia.com/stories/singaporelocalnews/view/1212485/1/.html

[102] Misuse of Drugs Act (Cap 185), Section 33B. In particular, Yong Vui Kong was re-sentenced to life imprisonment in November 2013.

[103] See Bruce Ryder, 'Suspending the Charter' (2003) 21 *Supreme Court Law Review* (2d) 267, 275.

[104] See Kent Roach, 'Remedial Consensus and Dialogue under the Charter: General Declarations and Delayed Declarations of Invalidity' (2002) 35 *University of British Columbia Law Review* 211.

of legality that is divorced of any normative vision of what the rule of law entails. The originalist model includes within the adjudicatory framework a normative dimension; but if this normative vision of due process is shackled to the framers' original expected specific applications of the constitutional text at the time of its enactment, it would fly in the face of the framers' deliberate choice of using open-textured language to produce an enduring constitutional instrument for posterity to design as appropriate to their evolving circumstances. The adjudicatory understanding of due process is vital as it contributes to the accuracy and integrity of the dispute-settling procedures. But any judicial efforts to maximize the reliability of the guilt determination process and preserve the intrinsic dignity of the individual would be undercut if the judiciary does not further scrutinize whether the individual is sufficiently morally blameworthy to warrant the penal sanctions imposed on him or her. Therefore, a substantive understanding of due process that also insists upon the presence of criminal fault as a precondition to the imposition of criminal liability, and the demand for some proportionality between the penal sanction imposed and the offender's degree of moral culpability, remains the only logical and meaningful constitutional safeguard of an individual's right to due process.

Nevertheless, in observing the substantive conception of due process, so far as courts can implement this with the use of dialogic sub-constitutional doctrines that include procedural constitutional rules, common law clear-statement rules, and delayed declarations of invalidity, the political branches of government can equally remain involved in this constitutional discourse on criminal law and procedure. By not side-lining or excluding any legislative response to the court's interpretive mandate, the judiciary is ultimately allowing the constitutional entity to become more vibrant, more stable, and more legitimate as all its stakeholders—judges, elected officials, and the people—are given a voice to forge a shared understanding of the Constitution.

10

Conclusion

In the foregoing chapters, I have argued how dialogic judicial review can reshape the constitutional landscape in common law Asia.

As I have explored in Chapter 2, legislators are vulnerable to electoral whims and they have every incentive to preserve their incumbency by dodging controversial but important human rights issues that do not sit well with a majority of their constituents. Indeed, as observed by Lord Hope of Craighead, governance by majority rule alone is imperfect as 'solving problems by placing the answers into pre-determined boxes can make prisoners of us all'.[1] On the other hand, while judges may be insulated from electoral pressures, the nature of litigation means that they will 'see only small parts of complex wholes'[2] and they rarely have the training or expertise to appreciate fully the systemic effects or collateral consequences of their decisions.

Therefore, dialogic review greatly attenuates the force of the counter-majoritarian difficulty by allowing the elected representatives of the people to harness the ordinary political process to respond to any perceived judicial errors.[3] Nevertheless, dialogic review remains a crucial constitutional tool for human rights advancement as it allows the courts to reverse the burdens of bureaucratic inertia such that the aggrieved minority may often obtain a tangible remedy in court until and unless the legislatures expressly respond in disagreement.[4] Dialogic review therefore partially overcomes the misaligned legislative incentives by raising the enactment costs of rights-infringing governmental actions and encouraging the government to openly debate and deliberate upon the genuine public benefit of the impugned laws in question.[5] In this way, Parliament

[1] David Hope, 'The Judges' Dilemma', (2009) 58 *International and Comparative Law Quarterly* 753, 755.

[2] Cass Sunstein, *Legal Reasoning and Political Conflict* (New York, Oxford University Press 1996) 177.

[3] Christine Bateup, 'The Dialogic Promise: Assessing the Normative Potential of Theories of Constitutional Dialogue' (2006) 71 *Brooklyn Law Review* 1109.

[4] See Kent Roach, 'Constitutional and Common Law Dialogues' (2001) 80 *Canadian Bar Review* 481.

[5] See Matthew Stephenson, 'The Price of Public Action: Constitutional Doctrine and the Judicial Manipulation of Legislative Enactment Costs' (2008) 118 *Yale Law Journal* 2.

is always able to uphold its original views so long as it is willing to pay the political price. Dialogic review thus fragments the political between the courts and politicians so that they can engage each other in a struggle to read society's competing moral maps.[6] At its core, dialogic judicial review creates a culture of justification whereby governments are required to offer reasoned explanations for rights-derogations.[7]

Dialogic review is democratic so far as it compels the legislature to justify, articulate, and take responsibility for its decisions to limit or depart from the judicial rules imposed by its courts. Courts may have been the catalyst of change, but herein they do not enforce a settlement of constitutional rights. So far as lawmakers do decide to override, via the ordinary political process, the judicial conception of rights, the courts would have fostered a deliberative democracy that encourages a wider societal debate on complex ethical and/or polycentric issues. By raising the enactment costs of statutory rights-derogations, but not foreclosing the democratic process from correcting any perceived judicial error, dialogic review associated with sub-constitutional rules takes into account both the cognitive limitations of judges and the misaligned incentives of lawmakers. Constitutional rights are vindicated but the error costs of mistaken judgments are equally lowered.

Dialogic review is also prudential. As highlighted in Chapters 3 and 4, all the common law Asian jurisdictions under study have been governed by the same ruling party/coalition since decolonization and this state of affairs will persist for the foreseeable future. So far as the judiciary consciously preserves the right of the legislature to disagree with the court's decision via the use of the ordinary political processes, such that an override via a constitutional amendment can be avoided, any strain on the inter-branch relations and any potential backlash from the dominant ruling government can equally be minimized. Professor Alexander Bickel has observed that 'no good society can be unprincipled',[8] but he was equally adamant that 'no viable society can be principle ridden'.[9] If we want to remain both a good and viable society, we must arrive at a compromise between 'our principles and the complex, murky, and often resistant reality on which these principles operate'.[10] Dialogic review thus acknowledges the institutional dilemmas and

[6] Danny Nicol, 'Law and Politics after the Human Rights Act' [2006] *Public Law* 722.

[7] See Moshe Cohen-Eliya & Iddo Porat, 'Proportionality and the Culture of Justification' (2011) 59 *American Journal of Comparative Law* 463.

[8] Alexander Bickel, *The Least Dangerous Branch: The Supreme Court at the Bar of Politics* (2nd edn, New Haven, Yale University Press 1986) 64.

[9] Ibid.

[10] Anthony T Kronman, 'Alexander Bickel's Philosophy of Prudence' (1985) 94 *Yale Law Journal* 1567.

prudential constraints faced by these Asian judges during adjudication. In striking this delicate balance between deference and disagreement, I have identified in Chapter 5 how these Asian courts can craft rights-based mediating rules via the judicial use of one or more of the sub-constitutional norms/doctrines: (1) provisional or advisory determinations in constitutional matters; (2) administrative review; (3) common law liberties or statutory rights that are reversible by the ordinary political process; (4) procedural constitutional rules; (5) rational basis review of legislative actions; and (6) delayed declarations of invalidity.

These sub-constitutional norms and practices allow a final constitutional settlement to remain in abeyance. In Chapter 6, I have illustrated how the courts can utilize common law and administrative doctrinal pathways to reshape the common law of defamation and contempt of court, and also the regulatory scope of state control over public demonstrations. Specifically, Singapore is an outlier in her protection of free speech, and I have thus argued how her courts can recognize the *Reynolds* privilege as a *common* law defence to an action in defamation and adopt the proportionality analysis in *administrative* law when reviewing any executive restrictions on public assemblies, as the Malaysian and Hong Kong courts have done.

In Chapter 7, I have argued for the courts to uphold a balancing model of religious liberty; nevertheless, I propose that this model can be observed in a dialogic fashion. For instance, I have argued that the Singapore courts merely needed to engage in *administrative* review, that is the observance of traditional *Wednesbury* orthodoxy, in the Jehovah's Witnesses cases and quash the ministerial ban on all publications by that religious group, and invalidate the administrative policy that required all teachers in public schools to sing the national anthem at the school's flag-raising ceremony. For Malaysia, the civil courts could impose a clear-statement rule, which requires that the religious courts be conferred express jurisdiction by a relevant state legislation to adjudicate over a matter that the state governments are constitutionally authorized to legislate on, before the secular courts would cede jurisdiction in favour of the syariah courts.

Chapter 8 maps out my reasons why courts should adopt a 'forbidden personal characteristics' judicial model of equality; nonetheless, I have also argued that the judiciary should assign different categories of traits-differentiation to varying standards of judicial scrutiny, and this sliding scale of review may also vary over time and space. With regard to sexual orientation discrimination in particular, courts in different jurisdictions may decide to diverge on the standard of review they adopt. In Hong Kong, the courts should continue to subject legislative differentiations on the ground of sexual orientation to strict scrutiny, as this standard of review has become an accepted judicial practice. Common law courts in Singapore and Malaysia on the other hand might, for prudential and democracy legitimacy concerns, prefer to subject this ground of discrimination to rational basis review at the outset, and heighten the standard of review when the legislature (and the electorate) is less adverse to such a legal change.

Finally, in Chapter 9, I have proposed that courts should observe a substantive conception of due process that generally insists upon the presence of criminal fault as a precondition to the imposition of penal liability, and demand for some proportionality between the statutory punishment imposed and the offender's degree of moral culpability. Nevertheless, this substantive vision of due process can be vindicated dialogically with the use of procedural constitutional rules, common law clear-statement rules, and delayed declarations of invalidity. For instance, where the Federal Court of Malaysia in *Lee Kwan Woh v Public Prosecutor*[11] gave an expansive reading of Article 5(1) to include 'a constitutionally guaranteed right to receive a fair trial',[12] this activist judicial stance remains dialogic as the state is not deprived of the right to prosecute and incarcerate an offender for any substantive offence it seeks to criminalize; the same substantive ends can still be pursued after the state complies with the judicially imposed procedural constitutional rule. Furthermore, I have argued that the Hong Kong judiciary should impose a *common law* clear-statement rule such that if the Hong Kong legislature seeks to create an absolute liability offence and remove the accused person's defence of reasonable belief in any particular circumstance, the legislature must state so in explicit terms, as Singapore has done. Finally, when faced with a due process challenge against the mandatory death penalty imposed on offenders who had been convicted of trafficking more than 15g of diamorphine, the Singapore Court of Appeal in *Yong Vui Kong v Public Prosecutor*,[13] when invalidating the impugned primary legislation, could issue a delayed declaration of invalidity. In this way the legislature is given time and space to determine the specifics of a legislative sequel; in turn, due deference is thus paid to the primacy of Parliament's lawmaking prerogative.

While each sub-constitutional tool, as discussed from Chapters 6 to 9, may be placed on a different point of a spectrum that measures the 'robustness' of the judicial review associated with its deployment, every one of them is dialogic in nature as each of them leaves legislative space, to varying degrees, for the lawmakers to respond actively, as opposed to merely passively yielding, to the judiciary's determination of rights.

[11] *Lee Kwan Woh* [2009] 5 MLJ 301 (Federal Court of Malaysia). [12] Ibid.
[13] *Yong Vui Kong v PP* [2010] SGCA 20 (Singapore Court of Appeal).

The false belief that either the legislature or the judiciary may singularly and sufficiently defend the constitutional values of a society imposes a burden that neither branch of government can bear. It sets up unrealistic expectations that only invite disappointments or even court disasters.[14] Indeed, as expressively observed by American judge Learned Hand, 'the spirit of liberty is that spirit which is not too sure that it is right'.[15]

Dialogic review allows courts to seek not for universal truths but to reach a 'reflective equilibrium'[16] between their bona fide considered judgments on rights and the legislative understandings of substantive justice. In seeking harmony between the settled expectations of the past and the evolving needs of a changing society, the judiciary must convene an enduring and continuous colloquy on rights with the political branches of government and the broader polity at large. In such a constitutional system, '[t]he Court is a leader of opinion, not a mere register of it, but it must lead opinion, not merely impose its own; and—the short of it is—it labours under the obligation to succeed'.[17] This dialogue between the coordinate branches of government should be viewed as a constitutional blessing, and not a bane, for it conjoins the best in both statecraft and adjudication.

[14] Neal E Devins & Louis Fisher, *The Democratic Constitution* (Oxford, Oxford University Press 2004) 239.

[15] Learned Hand, 'The Spirit of Liberty', in Learned Hand & Irving Dillard, *The Spirit of Liberty: Papers and Addresses of Learned Hand* (New York, Alfred A Knopf 1952) 189–90.

[16] John Rawls, *A Theory of Justice* (Cambridge, Harvard University Press 1999) 43.

[17] Bickel (n 8) 239.

Bibliography

BOOKS AND ARTICLES

Adil, Mohamed & Azam, Mohamed, 'Law and Apostasy and Freedom of Religion in Malaysia' (2007) 2(1)(6) *Asian Journal of Comparative Law* 23

Afonso da Silva, Virgilio, 'Comparing the Incommensurable: Constitutional Principles, Balancing and Rational Decision' (2011) 31 *Oxford Journal of Legal Studies* 273

Aleinikoff, T Alexander, 'Constitutional Law in the Age of Balancing' (1987) 96 *Yale Law Journal* 943

Alexander, Larry, 'Are Procedural Rights Derivative Substantive Rights?' (1998) 17 *Law & Philosophy* 19

Alexander, Larry & Schauer, Fredrick, 'On Extrajudicial Constitutional Interpretation' (1997) 110 *Harvard Law Review* 1359

Alexander, Larry & Schauer, Fredrick, 'Defending Judicial Supremacy: A Reply' (2000) 17 *Constitutional Commentary* 455

Allan, James, 'Bill of Rights and Judicial Power—a Liberal's Quandary' (1996) 16 *Oxford Journal of Legal Studies* 337

Allan, T R S, 'Parliamentary Sovereignty: Law, Politics, and Revolution' (1997) 113 *Law Quarterly Review* 443

Allan, T R S, *Constitutional Justice: A Liberal Theory of the Rule of Law* (Oxford, Oxford University Press 2001)

Allan, T R S, 'Human Rights and Judicial Review: A Critique of "Due Deference"' [2006] 65 *Cambridge Law Journal* 671

Allan, T R S, 'Judicial Deference and Judicial Review: Legal Doctrine and Legal Theory' (2011) 127 *Law Quarterly Review* 96

Balkin, Jack, 'Nine Perspectives on Living Originalism' [2012] *University of Illinois Law Review* 815

Barendt, Eric, *Freedom of Speech* (Oxford, Oxford University Press 2005)

Bateup, Christine, 'The Dialogic Promise: Assessing the Normative Potential of Theories of Constitutional Dialogue' (2006) 71 *Brooklyn Law Review* 1109

Bickel, Alexander, *The Least Dangerous Branch: The Supreme Court at the Bar of Politics* (2nd edn, New Haven, Yale University Press 1986)

Bingham, Tom, 'The Courts and the Constitution' (1996) 7 *King's College Law Journal* 12

Bork, Robert, *The Tempting of America: The Political Seduction of the Law* (New York, Free Press 1990)

Brabyn, Janice, 'The Fundamental Freedom of Assembly and Part II of the Public Order Ordinance' (2002) 32 *Hong Kong Law Journal* 271

Brady, Alan, *Proportionality and Deference under the UK Human Rights Act* (Cambridge, Cambridge University Press 2012)
Brest, Paul, 'The Misconceived Quest for the Original Understanding' (1980) 60 *Boston University Law Review* 204
Breyer, Stephen, *Active Liberty: Interpreting a Democratic Constitution* (New York, Oxford University Press 2008)
Butler, Petra, 'Human Rights and Parliamentary Sovereignty in New Zealand' (2004) 35 *Victoria University Law Review* 341
Chan, Cora, 'State Immunity: Reassessing the Boundaries of Judicial Autonomy in Hong Kong' [2012] *Public Law* 601
Chan, Johannes, 'Constitutional Protection of the Right to be Presumed Innocent and the Right Against Self-Incrimination: The Hong Kong Experience' (2013) 25 *Singapore Academy of Law Journal* 69
Chan, Johannes & Lim, CL, *The Law of the Hong Kong Constitution* (Hong Kong, Sweet & Maxwell 2011)
Chan, Sek Keong, 'Judicial Review—From Angst to Empathy' (2010) 22 *Singapore Academy of Law Journal* 469
Chemerinsky, Erwin, 'In Defence of Judicial Review: A Reply to Professor Kramer' (2004) 92 *California Law Review* 1013
Chen, Albert, 'From Colony to Special Administrative Region: Hong Kong's Constitutional Journey' in Raymond Wacks (ed), *The Future of the Law in Hong Kong* (Hong Kong, Oxford University Press 1989)
Chen, Albert, 'Ng Ka Ling and Article 158(3) of the Basic Law' (2002) 5 *Journal of Chinese and Comparative Law* 221
Chen, Albert, 'The Congo Case: Introduction' (2011) 41 *Hong Kong Law Journal* 369
Chen, Albert & Cheung, Anne, 'Debating the Rule of Law in Hong Kong' in Randall Peerenboom (ed), *Asian Discourses of Rule of Law* (London, Routledge 2004) 257
Chernack, Gregory S, 'The Clash of Two Worlds: Justice Robert H Jackson, Institutional Pragmatism, and Brown' (1999) 72 *Temple Law Review* 51
Chua, Lynette, 'Pragmatic Resistance, Law, and Social Movements in Authoritarian States: The Case of Gay Collective Action in Singapore' (2012) 46(4) *Law & Society Review* 713
Coenen, Dan T, 'A Constitution of Collaboration: Protecting Fundamental Values with Second-Look Rules of Interbranch Dialogue' (2001) 42 *William and Mary Law Review* 1578
Cohen-Eliya, Moshe & Porat, Iddo, 'Proportionality and the Culture of Justification' (2011) 59 *American Journal of Comparative Law* 463
Collins, Hugh, 'Discrimination, Equality and Social Inclusion' (2003) 66 *Modern Law Review* 43
Cottrell, Jill, 'Fair Comment, Judges and Politics in Hong Kong' (2003) 27 *Melbourne University Law Review* 33
Craig, Paul, *Administrative Law* (6th edn, London, Sweet & Maxwell 2008)
Craig, Paul, 'Proportionality, Rationality and Review' [2010] *New Zealand Law Review* 265

Debeljak, Julie, 'Parliamentary Sovereignty and Dialogue under the Victorian Charter of Human Rights and Responsibilities: Drawing the Line between Judicial Interpretation and Judicial Law-Making' (2007) 33 *Monash University Law Review* 9

Den Otter, Ronald, *Judicial Review in an Age of Moral Pluralism* (Cambridge, Cambridge University Press, 2009)

Devins, Neal E & Fisher, Louis, *The Democratic Constitution* (Oxford, Oxford University Press 2004)

Dixon, Rosalind, 'Creating Dialogue about Socioeconomic Rights: Strong-form versus Weak-form Judicial Review Revisited' (2007) 5 *International Journal of Constitutional Law* 391

Dixon, Rosalind, 'The Supreme Court of Canada, Charter Dialogue and Deference' (2009) 47 *Osgoode Hall Law Journal* 235

Dworkin, Ronald, *Taking Rights Seriously* (Cambridge, Harvard University Press 1977)

Dyzenhaus, David, 'The Politics of Deference: Judicial Review and Democracy' in M Taggart (ed), *The Province of Administrative Law* (Oxford, Hart Publishing 1997) 286

Easterbrook, Frank, 'Substance and Due Process' [1982] *Supreme Court Review* 85

Ekins, Richard, 'Judicial Supremacy and the Rule of Law' (2003) 119 *Law Quarterly Review* 127

Elliott, Mark, 'Proportionality and Deference: The Importance of a Structured Approach' in Forsyth, Elliott, Jhaveri, Ramsden & Hill, *Effective Judicial Review: A Cornerstone of Good Governance* (Oxford, Oxford University Press 2010)

Elliott, Mark and Forsyth, Christopher, 'The Rule of Law in Hong Kong: Immigrant Children, the Court of Final Appeal and the Standing Committee of the National People's Congress' (2000) 8 *Asia Pacific Law Review* 53

Eskridge, William, Jr & Frickey, Philip P, 'Quasi-Constitutional Law: Clear Statement Rules as Constitutional Lawmaking' (1992) 45 *Vanderbilt Law Review* 595

Ewing, Keith, 'Human Rights' in Peter Cane & Mark Tushnet (eds), *The Oxford Handbook of Legal Studies* (Oxford, Oxford University Press 2003)

Ewing, Keith & Gearty, Conor, 'Rocky Foundations for Labour's New Rights' (1997) 5 *European Human Rights Law Review* 146

Fallon, Richard, *Implementing the Constitution* (Cambridge, Harvard University Press 2001)

Fallon, Richard, 'Judicial Manageable Standards and Constitutional Meaning' (2006) 119 *Harvard Law Review* 1274

Fallon, Richard, 'The Core of an Uneasy Case for Judicial Review' (2008) 121 *Harvard Law Review* 1693

Feldman, David, 'Human Dignity as a Legal Value' [1999] *Public Law* 682

Fenwick, Helen, 'The Right to Protest, the Human Rights Act and the Margin of Appreciation' (1999) 62 *Modern Law Review* 491

Finkelstein, Claire, 'Positivism and the Notion of an Offence' (2000) 88 *California Law Review* 335
Forsyth, Christopher, 'The Rock and the Sand: Jurisdiction and Remedial Discretion' (2013) 18 *Judicial Review* 360
Fredman, Sandra, 'From Deference to Democracy: the role of Equality under the Human Rights Act 1998' (2006) 122 *Law Quarterly Review* 53
Friedman, Barry, 'Dialogue and Judicial Review' (1993) 91 *Michigan Law Review* 577
Fuller, Lon, 'The Forms and Limits of Adjudication' (1978) 92 *Harvard Law Review* 353
Gardbaum, Stephen, *The New Commonwealth Model of Constitutionalism: Theory and Practice* (Cambridge, Cambridge University Press 2013)
Ginsburg, Tom, *Judicial Review in New Democracies: Constitutional Courts in Asian Cases* (Cambridge, Cambridge University Press 2003)
Ghai, Yash, *Hong Kong's New Constitutional Order* (2nd edn, Hong Kong, Hong Kong University Press 1999)
Goldsworthy, Jeffrey, 'Homogenising Constitutions' (2003) 23 *Oxford Journal of Legal Studies* 483
Goldsworthy, Jeffrey, 'Judicial Review, Legislative Override, and Democracy' in Tom Campbell, Jeffrey Goldsworthy & Adrienne Stone (eds), *Protecting Human Rights: Instruments and Institutions* (Oxford, Oxford University Press 2003) 268
Greenawalt, Kent, *Religion and the Constitution* (Princeton, Princeton University Press 2006)
Greenberg, Mark D & Litman, Harry, 'The Meaning of Original Meaning' (1998) 86 *Georgetown Law Journal* 569
Greschner, Donna, 'Does Law Advance the Cause of Equality?' (2001) 27 *Queen's Law Journal* 299
Griffith, JAG, 'The Brave New World of Sir John Laws' (2000) 63 *Modern Law Review* 159
Gyorfi, Tamas, 'Between Common Law Constitutionalism and Procedural Democracy', (2013) 33 *Oxford Journal of Legal Studies* 317
Halsbury's Laws of England (4th edn, Reissue)
Hand, Learned, 'The Spirit of Liberty' in Learned Hand & Irving Dillard, *The Spirit of Liberty: Papers and Addresses of Learned Hand* (New York: Alfred A Knopf 1952) 189
Hand, Learned, *The Spirit of Liberty* (New York, Alfred A Knopf 1953)
Hand, Learned, *The Bill of Rights* (Cambridge, Harvard University Press 1958)
Harding, Andrew, 'The 1988 Constitutional Crisis in Malaysia' (1990) 39 *International and Comparative Law Quarterly* 57
Harding, Andrew, *Law, Government and the Constitution of Malaysia* (The Hague, Kluwer Law International 1996)
Harding, Andrew, *The Constitution of Malaysia: A Contextual Approach* (Oxford, Hart Publishing 2012)
Harel, Alon & Shinar, Adam, 'Between Judicial and Legislative Supremacy: A Cautious Defence of Constrained Judicial Review' (2012) 10 *International Journal of Constitutional Law* 950

Hart, Henry M, 'The Aims of the Criminal Law' (1958) 23 *Law and Contemporary Problems* 401

Hershkoff, Helen, '"Just Word": Common Law and the Enforcement of State Constitutional Social and Economic Rights' (2010) 62 *Stanford Law Review* 1521

Hickman, Tom, 'The Substance and Structure of Proportionality' [2008] *Public Law* 694

Hickman, Tom, 'Problems for Proportionality' [2010] *New Zealand Law Review* 303

Hickman, Tom, *Public Law after the Human Rights Act* (Oxford, Hart Publishing 2010)

Hirschl, Ran, *Constitutional Theocracy* (Cambridge, Harvard University Press 2010)

Hogg, Peter, *Constitutional Law of Canada* (4th edn, Scarborough, Carswell 1997)

Hogg, Peter & Bushell, Allison, 'The Charter Dialogue Between the Courts and Legislatures (Or Perhaps the Charter of Rights Isn't Such a Bad Thing After All)' (1997) 35 *Osgoode Hall Law Journal* 75

Hope, David, 'The Judges' Dilemma', (2009) 58 *International and Comparative Law Quarterly* 753

Hor, Michael, 'The Freedom of Speech and Defamation: JBJ v Lee Kuan Yew' [1992] *Singapore Journal of Legal Studies* 542

Hor, Michael, 'Law and Terror: Singapore Stories and Malaysian Dilemmas' in Michael Hor, Victor Ramraj & Kent Roach (eds), *Global Anti-Terrorism: Law and Policy* (Cambridge, Cambridge University Press 2005) 284

Hor, Michael, 'Criminal Due Process in Hong Kong and Singapore: A Mutual Challenge' (2007) 37 *Hong Kong Law Journal* 65

Hor, Michael, 'Criminal Justice in the Chan Court: Change, Contestation and Conservatism in the Court of Appeal' in Yeo Tiong Min, Hans Tjio, & Tang Hang Wu (eds), *SAL Conference 2011: Developments in Singapore Law between 2006 and 2010—Trends and Perspectives* (Singapore, Academy Publishing 2011) 147

Hor, Michael, 'Singapore's Death Penalty—The Beginning of the End?' in Roger Hood & Surya Deva (eds), *Confronting Capital Punishment in Asia: Human Rights, Politics and Public Opinion* (Oxford, Oxford University Press 2013) 141

Horwitz, Paul, 'Three Faces of Deference' (2008) 83 *Notre Dame Law Review* 1061

Huang-Thio, SM, 'Equal Protection and Rational Connection' [1963] *Public Law* 412

Huffman, James L, 'Advisory Opinions and Canadian Constitutional Development: The Supreme Court's Reference' (1990) 74 *Minnesota Law Review* 1251

Hunt, Murray, 'Sovereignty's Blight: Why Contemporary Public Law Needs the Concept of "Due Deference"' in Nicholas Bamforth & Peter Leyland (eds), *Public Law in a Multi-Layered Constitution* (Oxford, Hart Publishing 2003) 340

Ip, Eric, 'The Evolution of Constitutional Adjudication in the Chinese Special Administrative Regions: Theory and Evidence' (2013) 61 *American Journal of Comparative Law* 799

Jackson, Vicki, *Constitutional Engagement in a Transnational Era* (Oxford, Oxford University Press 2010)

Jackson, Vicki & Greene, Jamal, 'Constitutional Interpretation in Comparative Perspective: Comparing Judges or Courts?' in Tom Ginsburg & Rosalind Dixon (eds), *Comparative Constitutional Law* (Cheltenham, Edward Elgar 2011) 599

Jeffries, John & Stephan, Paul III, 'Defences, Presumptions, and Burden of Proof in the Criminal Law' (1979) 88 *Yale Law Journal* 1371

Jowell, Jeffrey, 'Judicial Deference and Human Rights: A Question of Competence' in Paul Craig & Richard Rawlings (eds), *Law and Administration in Europe: Essays in Honour of Carol Harlow* (Oxford, Oxford University Press 2003) 67

Jowell, Jeffrey, 'Judicial Deference: Servility, Civility or Institutional Capacity?' [2003] *Public Law* 592

Jowell, Jeffrey, 'Parliamentary Sovereignty under the New Constitutional Hypothesis' [2006] *Public Law* 562

Kadish, Sanford H, 'Methodology and Criteria in Due Process Adjudication—A Survey and Criticism' (1957) 66 *Yale Law Journal* 319

Kavanagh, Aileen, 'Original Intention, Enacted Text, and Constitutional Interpretation' (2002) 47 *American Journal of Jurisprudence* 255

Kavanagh, Aileen, 'Participation and Judicial Review: A Reply to Jeremy Waldron' (2003) 22(5) *Law and Philosophy* 451

Kavanagh, Aileen, 'Deference or Defiance? The Limits of the Judicial Role in Constitutional Adjudication' in G Huscroft (ed), *Expounding the Constitution: Essays in Constitutional Theory* (Cambridge, Cambridge University Press 2008) 184

Kavanagh, Aileen, *Constitutional Review under the UK Human Rights Act* (Cambridge, Cambridge University Press 2009)

Kavanagh, Aileen, 'Defending Defence in Public Law and Constitutional Theory' (2010) 126 *Law Quarterly Review* 222

Kavanagh, Aileen, 'Judicial Restraint in the Pursuit of Justice' (2010) 60 *University of Toronto Law Journal* 23

Kavanagh, Aileen, 'Reasoning about Proportionality under the Human Rights Act 1998: Outcomes, Substance and Process' (2014) 130 *Law Quarterly Review* 235

Kenyon, Andrew & Ang, Hean Leng, 'Reynolds Privilege, Common Law Defamation and Malaysia' [2010] *Singapore Journal of Legal Studies* 256

King, Jeff, 'The Justiciability of Resource Allocation' (2007) 70 *Modern Law Review* 197

King, Jeff, 'Institutional Approaches to Judicial Restraint' (2008) 28 *Oxford Journal of Legal Studies* 409

Kronman, Anthony T, 'Alexander Bickel's Philosophy of Prudence' (1985) 94 *Yale Law Journal* 1567

Kyritsis, Dimitrios, 'Representation and Waldron's Objection to Judicial Review' (2006) 26 *Oxford Journal of Legal Studies* 733

Kyritsis, Dimitrios, 'Constitutional Review in Representative Democracy' (2012) 32 *Oxford Journal of Legal Studies* 297

Kyritsis, Dimitrios, 'Proportionality as a Constitutional Doctrine' (2014) 34 *Oxford Journal of Legal Studies* 395
Laws, John, 'Law and Democracy' [1995] *Public Law* 72
Laws, John, 'The Constitution: Morals and Rights' [1996] *Public Law* 622
Laylin, Clarence E & Tuttle, Alonzo H, 'Due Process and Punishment' (1921–1922) 20 *Michigan Law Review* 614
Lee, HP, *Constitutional Conflicts in Contemporary Malaysia* (Kuala Lumpur, Oxford University Press 1995)
Lewis, Philip, *Gatley on Libel and Slander* (London, Sweet & Maxwell, 1981)
Lo, Sonny, *Competing Chinese Political Visions* (Santa Barbara, Praeger 2010)
Luban, David, 'Incommensurable Values, Rational Choice, and Moral Absolutes' (1990) 38 *Cleveland State Law Review* 65
Ma, Ngok, 'Political Parties and Elections' 131–32 in Lam, Lui, Wong, & Holliday (eds), *Contemporary Hong Kong Politics: Governance in the Post-1997 Era* (Hong Kong, Hong Kong University Press 2007) 117
Manning John, 'Clear Statement Rules and the Constitution' (2010) 110 *Columbia Law Review* 399
Marican, Pawancheek, 'Murtad (Apostasy) and Art 121(1A) of the Federal Constitution' [1998] 2 MLJ lxxvii
Marshall, Geoffrey, *Constitutional Theory* (Oxford, Clarendon Press 1971)
Masterman, R M W, 'Interpretations, Declarations and Dialogue: Rights protection under the Human Rights Act and Victorian Charter of Human Rights and Responsibilities' [2009] *Public Law* 112
Masterman, R M W, *The Separation of Powers in the Contemporary Constitution: Judicial Competence and Independence in the United Kingdom* (Cambridge, Cambridge University Press 2011)
McDonald, Leighton, 'New Directions in the Australian Bill of Rights Debate' [2004] *Public Law* 22
McDonald, Leighton, 'Rights, "Dialogue" and Democratic Objections to Judicial Review' (2004) 32 *Federal Law Review* 1
Meiklejohn, Alexander, *Free Speech and its Relation to Self-Government* (New York, Harper Brothers 1948)
Metzger, Gillian E, 'Ordinary Administrative Law as Constitutional Common Law' (2010) 110 *Columbia Law Review* 479
Metzger, Gillian E, 'Embracing Administrative Common Law' (2012) 80 *George Washington Law Review* 1293
Mill, John Stuart, *On Liberty*, ed. Elizabeth Rapaport (1st edn, Indianapolis, Hackett Publishing Company 1859)
Milmo, Patrick & Rogers, W V H, *Gatley on Libel and Slander* (9th edn, London, Sweet & Maxwell 1998)
Moller, Kai, 'Proportionality: Challenging the Critics' (2012) 10 *International Journal of Constitutional Law* 709
Monaghan, Henry, 'Foreword: Constitutional Common Law' (1975) 89 *Harvard Law Review* 1

Moon, Richard, *The Constitutional Protection of Freedom of Expression* (Toronto, University of Toronto Press 2000)

Morton, F L, 'Dialogue or Monologue? A Reply to Hogg and Thornton' [April 1999] *Policy Options* 23

Nicol, Danny, 'Law and Politics after the Human Rights Act', [2006] *Public Law* 722

Packer, Herbert, 'Mens Rea and the Supreme Court' [1962] *Supreme Court Review* 107

Perry, Michael, 'Modern Equal Protection: A Conceptualisation and Appraisal' (1979) 79 *Columbia Law Review* 1023

Perry, Michael, 'Protecting Human Rights in a Democracy: What Role for the Courts?' (2003) 38 *Wake Forest Law Review* 635

Peters, Christopher J, 'Assessing the New Minimalism' (2000) 100 *Columbia Law Review* 1454

Posner, Richard, *How Judges Think?* (Cambridge, Harvard University Press 2008)

Post, Robert, 'The Social Foundations of Defamation Law: Reputation and the Constitution' (1986) 74 *California Law Review* 691

Rajah, Jothie, *Authoritarian Rule of Law: Legislation, Discourse and Legitimacy in Singapore* (Cambridge, Cambridge University Press 2012)

Ramraj, Victor, 'Four Models of Due Process' (2004) 2 *International Journal of Constitutional Law* 492

Ramraj, Victor & Yap, Po Jen, 'Singapore' in Gerhard Robbers (ed), *Encyclopedia of World Constitutions* (New York, Facts on File 2007) 817

Rawls, John, *A Theory of Justice* (Cambridge, Harvard University Press 1999)

Raz, Joseph, *Ethics in the Public Domain: Essays in the Morality of Law and Politics* (Oxford, Clarendon Press 1994)

Raz, Joseph, 'Free Expression and Personal Identification' in Wil Waluchow (ed), *Free Expression: Essays in Law and Philosophy* (Oxford, Clarendon Press 1994) 13

Raz, Joseph, 'Disagreement in Politics' (1998) 43 *American Journal of Jurisprudence* 25

Redish, Martin, 'The Value of Free Speech' (1982) 130 *University of Pennsylvania Law Review* 591

Rivers, Julian, 'Proportionality and variable intensity of Review' (2006) 65 *Cambridge Law Journal* 174

Roach, Kent, 'Constitutional and Common Law Dialogues' (2001) 80 *Canadian Bar Review* 481

Roach, Kent, *The Supreme Court on Trial: Judicial Activism or Democratic Dialogue* (Toronto, Irwin Law 2001)

Roach, Kent, 'Remedial Consensus and Dialogue under the Charter: General Declarations and Delayed Declarations of Invalidity' (2002) 35 *University of British Columbia Law Review* 211

Roach, Kent, 'Dialogic Judicial Review and its Critics' (2004) 23 *Supreme Court Law Review* 49

Roach, Kent, 'A Dialogue about Principle and a Principled Dialogue: Justice Iacobucci's Substantive Approach to Dialogue' (2007) 57 *University of Toronto Law Journal* 499

Roosevelt, Kermit, 'Constitutional Calcification: How the Law Becomes What the Court Does' (2005) 91 *Virginia Law Review* 1649

Ryder, Bruce, 'Suspending the Charter' (2003) 21 *Supreme Court Law Review* (2d) 267

Sadurski, Wojciech, *Freedom of Speech and its Limits* (Dordrecht, Kluwer 1999)

Sadurski, Wojciech, 'Judicial Review and the Protection of Constitutional Rights' (2002) 22 *Oxford Journal of Legal Studies* 275

Sagar, Lawrence, *Justice in Plainclothes: A Theory of American Constitutional Practice* (New Haven, Yale University Press 2006)

Scalia, Antonin, 'Commentary' (1996) 40 *Saint Louis University Law Journal* 1119

Scalia, Antonin, 'Common Law Courts in a Civil Law System: The Role of the United States Federal Courts in Interpreting the Constitution and Laws' in Amy Gutmann (ed), *A Matter of Interpretation* (Princeton, Princeton University Press 1997) 17

Scalia, Antonin & Garner, Bryan, *Reading Law: The Interpretation of Legal Texts* (St. Paul, Thomson West 2012)

Scanlon, Thomas, 'A Theory of Freedom of Expression' (1972) 1 *Philosophy and Public Affairs* 204

Schauer, Frederick, *Free Speech: A Philosophical Enquiry* (Cambridge, Cambridge University Press 1982)

Schrock, Thomas S & Welsh, Robert C, 'Reconsidering the Constitutional Common Law' (1978) 91 *Harvard Law Review* 1117

Sheridan & Groves, *The Constitution of Malaysia* (4th edn, Singapore, Malayan Law Journal 1987)

Shin, Patrick, 'The Substantive Principle of Equal Treatment' (2009) 15(2) *Legal Theory* 149

Stephenson, Matthew, 'The Price of Public Action: Constitutional Doctrine and the Judicial Manipulation of Legislative Enactment Costs' (2008) 118 *Yale Law Journal* 2

Stephenson, Scott, 'Constitutional Reengineering: Dialogue's Migration from Canada to Australia' (2013) 11 *International Journal of Constitutional Law* 870

Strauss, David, 'The Ubiquity of Prophylactic Rules' (1988) 5 *University of Chicago Law Review* 190

Suffian, Mohammed, *An Introduction to the Constitution of Malaysia* (Kuala Lumpur, Di-chetak di-Jabatan Chetak 1972)

Sunstein, Cass, *Legal Reasoning and Political Conflict* (New York, Oxford University Press 1996)

Sunstein, Cass, *One Case at A Time: Judicial Minimalism on the Supreme Court* (Cambridge, Harvard University Press 1999)

Sunstein, Cass, *A Constitution of Many Minds: Why the Founding Document Doesn't Mean what it Meant Before* (Princeton, Princeton University Press 2009)

Sunstein, Cass, 'Nondelegation Canons' (2009) 67 *University of Chicago Law Review* 315

Swede, Richard, 'One Territory—Three Systems? The Hong Kong Bill of Rights' (1995) 44 *International and Comparative Law Quarterly* 358

Sweet, Alec Stone & Mathews, Jud, 'Proportionality Balancing and Global Constitutionalism' (2008) 47 *Columbia Journal of Transnational Law* 72

Tan & Thio, *Constitutional Law in Malaysia and Singapore* (Singapore, LexisNexis 2010)

Tan, David, 'The Reynolds Privilege in a Neo-Confucianist Communitarian Democracy: Reinvigorating Freedom of Political Communication in Singapore' [2011] *Singapore Journal of Legal Studies* 456

Tan, Kevin, 'The Presidency in Singapore: Constitutional Developments' in Tan & Lam, *Managing Political Change in Singapore: The Elected Presidency* (New York, Routledge 1997)

Tan, Kevin, 'A Short Legal and Constitutional History of Singapore' in Kevin Tan (ed), *The Singapore Legal System* (Singapore, National University of Singapore Press 1999) 26

Tan, Kevin, 'State and Institution Building through the Singapore Constitution 1965–2005' in Thio & Tan (eds), *Evolution of a Revolution: Forty Years of the Singapore Constitution* (New York, Routledge 2009) 50

Tey, Tsun Hang, 'Confining the Freedom of the Press in Singapore: A "Pragmatic" Press for "Nation Building"?' (2008) 30 *Human Rights Quarterly* 876

Tey, Tsun Hang, 'Singapore's jurisprudence of Political Defamation and its Triple-Whammy Impact on Political Speech' [2008] *Public Law* 452

Thio, Li-ann, 'The Secular Trumps the Sacred: Constitutional Issues Arising from *Colin Chan* v *Public Prosecutor*' (1995) 16 *Singapore Law Review* 26

Thio, Li-ann, 'An "i" for an "I"?—Singapore's Communitarian Model of Constitutional Adjudication' (1997) 27 *Hong Kong Law Journal* 152

Thio, Li-ann, 'Trends in Constitutional Interpretation: Oppugning *Ong*, Awakening *Arumugam*?' [1997] *Singapore Journal of Legal Studies* 240

Thio, Li-ann, 'Lex Rex or Rex Lex? Competing Conceptions of the Rule of Law in Singapore' (2002) 20 *UCLA Pacific Basin Law Journal* 1

Thio, Li-ann, 'Apostasy and Religious Freedom: Constitutional Issues Arising from the *Lina Joy* Litigation' (2006) 2 *Malayan Law Journal* 1

Thio, Li-ann, 'Jurisdictional Imbroglio: Civil and Religious Courts, Turf Wars and Article 121(1A) of the Federal Constitution' in Andrew Harding & H P Lee (eds), *Constitutional Landmarks in Malaysia: 1957–2007* (Kuala Lumpur, LexisNexis 2007)

Thio, Li-ann, 'Singapore: (S)electing the President—Diluting Democracy?' (2007) 5 *International Journal of Constitutional Law* 526

Thio, Li-ann, 'Courting Religion: The Judge Between Caesar and God in Asian Courts' [2009] *Singapore Journal of Legal Studies* 52

Thio, Li-ann, *A Treatise on Singapore Constitutional Law* (Singapore, Academy Publishing 2012)

Thio, Li-ann, 'Between Apology and Apogee, Autochthony: The "Rule of Law" Beyond the Rules of Law in Singapore' [2012] *Singapore Journal of Legal Studies* 269

Thio, Li-ann & Neo, Jaclyn, 'Religious Dress in Schools: the Serban controversy in Malaysia' (2006) 55 *International and Comparative Law Quarterly* 671

Tremblay, Luc B, 'The Legitimacy of Judicial Review: The Limits of Dialogue Between Courts and Legislatures' (2005) 3 *International Journal of Constitutional Law* 617

Trindade, FA, 'The Removal of the Malaysian Judges' (1990) 106 *Law Quarterly Review* 51

Trindade, FA, 'Malice and the Defence of Fair Comment' (2001) 117 *Law Quarterly Review* 169

Tsakyrakis, Stavros, 'Proportionality: An Assault on Human Rights?' (2009) 7 *International Journal of Constitutional Law* 468

Tushnet, Mark, 'Policy Distortion and Democratic Debilitation: Comparative Illumination of the Countermajoritarian Difficulty' (1995) 94 *Michigan Law Review* 245

Tushnet, Mark, *Taking the Constitution Away From the Courts* (Princeton, Princeton University Press 1999)

Tushnet, Mark, 'Subconstitutional Constitutional Law: Supplement, Sham or Substitute?' (2001) 42 *William and Mary Law Review* 1871

Tushnet, Mark, 'New Forms of Judicial Review and the Persistence of Rights and Democracy-Based Worries' (2003) 38 *Wake Forest Law Review* 813

Tushnet, Mark, 'Weak Form Judicial Review and "Core" Civil Liberties' (2006) 41 *Harvard Civil Rights-Civil Liberties Law Review* 1

Tushnet, Mark, 'Dialogic Judicial Review' (2008) 61 *Arkansas Law Review* 205

Tushnet, Mark, 'How Different Are Waldron and Fallon's Core Cases For and Against Judicial Review' (2010) 30 *Oxford Journal of Legal Studies* 49

Tussman, Joseph & tenBroek, Jacobus, 'The Equal Protection of the Laws' (1949) 37 *California Law Review* 341

Vermeule, Adrian, *Law and the Limits of Reason* (Oxford, Oxford University Press 2008)

Vile, MJC, *Constitutionalism and the Separation of Powers* (Oxford, Clarendon Press 1967)

Wade, William & Forsyth, Christopher, *Administrative Law* (10th edn, Oxford, Oxford University Press 2009)

Waldron, Jeremy, 'A Right-Based Critique of Constitutional Rights' (1993) 13 *Oxford Journal of Legal Studies* 18

Waldron, Jeremy, *Law and Disagreement* (Oxford, Clarendon Press 1999)

Waldron, Jeremy, *Law and Disagreement* (Oxford, Oxford University Press 2001)

Waldron, Jeremy, 'The Core of the Case Against Judicial Review' (2006) 115 *Yale Law Journal* 1346

Weiler, Paul, 'Rights and Judges in a Democracy: A New Canadian Version' (1984) 18 *Journal of Law Reform* 51

Wellington, Harry, 'On Freedom of Expression' (1979) 88 *Yale Law Journal* 1105

Westen, Peter, 'The Empty Idea of Equality' (1982) 95 *Harvard Law Review* 537
Yap, Po Jen, '10 Years of the Basic Law: The Rise, Retreat and Resurgence of Judicial Power' (2007) 36 *Common Law World Review* 166
Yap, Po Jen, 'Constitutionalising Capital Crimes: Judicial Virtue or Originalism Sin?' [2011] *Singapore Journal of Legal Studies* 281
Yap, Po Jen, 'Defending Dialogue' [2012] *Public Law* 527
Yap, Po Jen, 'Section 377A and Equal Protection in Singapore—Back to 1938?' (2013) 25 *Singapore Academy of Law Journal* 630
Yatim, Rais, 'The Road to Merdeka' in Andrew Harding & HP Lee (eds), *Constitutional Landmarks in Malaysia: The First Fifty Years 1957–2007* (Kuala Lumpur, LexisNexis 2007)
Young, Alison, 'In Defence of Due Deference' (2009) 72(4) *Modern Law Review* 554
Young, Alison, *Parliamentary Sovereignty and the Human Rights Act* (Oxford, Hart Publishing 2009)
Young, Ernest, 'Constitutional Avoidance, Resistance Norms, and the Preservation of Judicial Review' (2000) 78 *Texas Law Review* 1549
Young, Simon & Law, Anthony, 'Privileged to Vote: Inequalities and Anomalies of the FC System' in Christine Loh (ed), *Functional Constituencies: A Unique Feature of the Hong Kong Legislative Council* (Hong Kong, Hong Kong University Press 2006) 59
'Legislative Purpose, Rationality, and Equal Protection' (1972) 82 *Yale Law Journal* 123

GOVERNMENT PUBLICATIONS

CEDAW Committee, Fourth Periodic State Report: Singapore (3 April 2009) CEDAW/C/SGP/4
Parliament of Singapore, *Shared Values* (White Paper, Paper Cmd 1, 1991)
Report of the Tribunal Established under Article 125(3) and (4) of the Federal Constitution: Re: YAA Tun Dato' Hj Mohammed Salleh Abas, (7 July 1988)
Report of the Tribunal Established under Article 125(3) and (4) of the Federal Constitution: Re: YB Tan Sri Wan Suleiman, (23 September 1988)

Index

absolute liability, 212, 217, 226
actus reus, 125–7
administrative review, 4, 80, 88, 104, 135, 225 See sub-constitutional review
  in Hong Kong, 90
  in Malaysia, 91–2
  in Singapore, 89–91, 156–9
advisory review, 4, 80, 104, See sub-constitutional review
  in Canada, 86
  in Hong Kong, 87–8
  in Malaysia, 87
  in Singapore, 87
  in UK, 86–7
Alexander, Larry, 3, 8, 17–8, 210
Allan, James, 13
Allan, T.R.S., 3, 8, 19–20, 182–4
Anwar Ibrahim, 73, 113
apostasy, 150–1, 153, 155–6, See Syariah courts, See freedom of religion

Balkin, Jack, 208
Bickel, Alexander, 2, 8, 224
Bokhary, Kemal, 64, 66, 102, 204, 212

capital punishment, 219–20
Chan, Johannes, 31, 217
Chan, Sek Keong, 77, 90, 199–200, 205, 207
Chen, Albert, 31, 63, 65, 88
clear-statement rules, 79, 81, 92, 159, 196, 216–7, 221, 226, See common law liberties
Coenen, Dan, 79, 81
common law clear-statement rules. See clear-statement rules, See common law liberties
common law liberties, 4, 80, 104, 218, 225, See sub-constitutional review
  in Hong Kong, 94, 216–7
  in Malaysia, 153–6, 159
  in Singapore, 93–4
common law review, 135, See common law liberties
Condorcet Jury Theorem, 15
constitutional dialogue, 2, 3, 30, 101, 105, 162, 193
constitutionalism, 17, 27, 77–8, 93, 201
contempt of court, 110, 127–8, 225
  categories of, 122
  in Hong Kong, 124–6
  in Malaysia, 126
  in Singapore, 122–4
counter-majoritarian difficulty, 8, 223, See judicial review
covert surveillance, 101
Craig, Paul, 134, 181, 184
criminal law, 46, 54, 82, 133, 202–3, 209–11, 213, 216, 221
culpability, 196, 203, 210, 213, 216, 220–1, 226
culture of justification, 181, 224

declaration of incompatibility, 7, 86
defamation, 136
  fair comment defence, 94, 112–3
  in Hong Kong, 94, 110–3, 118
  in Malaysia, 113–5
  in Singapore, 115–22
  Lange defence, 113–5
  qualified privilege. See Lange defence, See *Reynolds* defence
  reputational interest, 110
  Reynolds defence, 110–2, 114–22
  Reynolds privilege, 225, See *Reynolds* defence
delayed declarations of invalidity, 4, 80, 104–5, 196, 221, 225–6, See sub-constitutional review
  in Hong Kong, 101–3, 218
  in Singapore, 218–20
democratic accountability, 106, 109
democratic legitimacy, 135, 181–4
dialogic review, 2, 3, 8, 31, 78, 80, 86, 93, 96, 101, 104, 109, 159, 213, 218, 223–4, 227
  in Canada, 7
  in Hong Kong, 95
  in New Zealand, 7
  in United Kingdom, 7
  justification of, 23–7
  the advantage of, 22
  the premise of, 22
dialogic tools, 78, 100, 110, 140, 214
differential treatment, 165, 168, 170, 175, 187, 190, See right to equality

discrimination, 103, 167–8, 175–8, 185–6, 225, See right to equality
Dixon, Rosalind, 24, 27, 206
due process, 4, 21, 177, 191, 226
  adjudicative model, 195, 201–2, 209–11, 221
  formal model, 195, 198–9, 204–5, 220–1
  in Hong Kong, 96, 196–7, 203–4, 211–2, 216–8
  in Malaysia, 47, 196–8, 201–2, 204, 209, 214
  in Singapore, 54, 196–7, 199–201, 205–8, 218–20
  originalist model, 195, 199–201, 206–9, 221
  substantive model, 195–6, 203–4, 211–3, 221
Dworkin, Ronald, 28, 174

Elliott, Mark, 63–4, 186
equal protection clause, 161, 163, 169, 171, 173, 177–8, 180, 185, 188, See right to equality
Eskridge, William, 79, 81, 84
European Court of Human Rights, 95, 115–6, 175, 181
extraterritorial criminal liability, 99

Fairuz, Ahmad, 73, 151
Fallon, Richard, 10–11, 83, 174
Forsyth, Christopher, 63–4, 89, 218
free speech, 180, 225, See freedom of expression
freedom of expression, 4, 17, 107–8, 127, 133, 135
  in Hong Kong, 39, 94–5, 109, 111
  in Malaysia, 46, 109
  in Singapore, 54, 109, 115, 119
freedom of religion, 4
  balancing model of, 140, 143–4, 147–52, 159, 225
  categorization model of, 140, 142–3, 145–7, 158–9
  formal model of, 140–1, 144–5, 158
  in Hong Kong, 39, 139, 142, 145–7
  in Malaysia, 46, 139, 143–4, 150–6, 159
  in Singapore, 54, 139, 141–2, 144–6, 156–9
freedom of religious belief, 139, 142, See freedom of religion
Frickey, Philip, 79, 81, 84
Fuller, Lon, 134

Gardbaum, Stephen, 28
Ghai, Yash, 31, 65
Ginsburg, Tom, 77, 206

Hand, Learned, 19, 227
hard originalism, 206–8, See originalist model, due process
Hickman, Tom, 1, 7–8, 135, 186
Hirschl, Ran, 154
homosexuality, 113, 167–8, 188, 191, 260, See right to equality
Hong Kong
  Chief Executive, 37–8, 90, 101
  Constitutional Amendment Procedure of, 40
  constitutional history of, 31–3
  Fundamental Rights in, 38–40
  judiciary, 38, 59, 88, 90, 125, 133, 226
  Legislative Council, 34–7, 98, 103
  Provisional Legislative Council, 35, 39, 59
  relationship with Chinese Authorities, 33–4, 60, 66
  right of abode, 40, 58–9, 61–5
Hor, Michael, 75, 77, 120, 212, 219
Horwitz, Paul, 189
House of Lords, 110–1, 114, 122, 167

institutional competence, 83–4, 134, 182–3
institutional legitimacy, 106, 218
International Covenant on Civil and Political Rights, 39, 59, 95, 167, 178

Jowell, Jeffrey, 3, 8, 19–20, 182, 184
judicial deference, 26–7, 99, 105, 182, 184, 187, 189, See rational basis review
judicial incrementalism, 179
judicial minimalism, 2, 92, 106, 109, 218–9
judicial restraint, 162, 182, 186–7
judicial review
  dialogic form of, 4, See dialogic review
  dialogic model of, 24, 27, 29, 85, See dialogic review
  strong-form review, 2, 9, 11, 14, 25
  weak-form review, 2, 25, 88
judicial supremacy, 3, 8, 28–9, 31, 85
  critiques of, 17–21

Kavanagh, Aileen, 1, 11–2, 14, 97, 99, 181–4, 201, 209
King, Jeff, 121, 136, 179, 185
Kyritsis, Dimitrios, 12–4, 104, 106

Laws, John, 19–20
Lee, Kuan Yew, 49, 115, 117

legislative intervention, 103, 106, 109
legislative supremacy, 3, 8, 20, 28
arguments in favour of, 9–10
critics of, 10–6
Li, Andrew, 59, 66, 94, 113, 176
Lord Bingham of Cornhill, 111, 199, 205
Lord David Hope of Craighead, 223
Lord Diplock, 127, 205
Lord Donald Nicholls of Birkenhead, 111–4, 122

Ma, Geoffrey, 66, 188
majoritarian excesses, 205
Malaysia
Conference of Rulers, 43–4, 47
constitutional amendment procedure of, 47–8
constitutional history of, 40–2
fundamental liberties, 46–7
judiciary, 44–6, 68, 73, 91, 133, 150
King, 43–5, 68–70, 87
Parliament, 42–3, 47
Prime Minister, 43, 45, 67–70, 72–3
Reid Commission, 41, 200
mandatory death penalty, 166, 191, 219, 226, See capital punishment
Mason, Anthony Frank, 102
Menon, Sundaresh, 77
mens rea, 125–7, 196, 203, 210–2, 216–7
Metzger, Gillian, 89, 93, 136, 156
Mill, John Stuart, 107
minimalist rulings, 2, 110, 179, 191, 219, See judicial minimalism
Monaghan, Henry, 79–80

national security, 74–6, 91, 134, 145, 157, 182

Omar, Abdul Hamid, 69–70, 126

Packer, Herbert, 212
Parliamentary sovereignty, 19
Perry, Michael, 180
Privy Council, 45, 53, 111, 125, 200, 205
procedural constitutional rules, 4, 80, 96, 104, 196, 221, See sub-constitutional review
in Hong Kong, 97–8, 214–5
in Malaysia, 97, 214
proportionality analysis, 83, 131, 133–4, 181–2, 225
proportionality doctrine, 83, 130, 134–5, 180, 215, See proportionality analysis
proportionality inquiry, 181, 184, See proportionality analysis
proportionality review. See proportionality analysis
public assemblies, 110, 128–35, 225, See right to assemble
public order (ordre public), 98, 131, See right to assemble

rational basis review, 4, 80, 104, 163, 187–9, See sub-constitutional review
in Hong Kong, 100
in Singapore, 99–100
rational classification test, 166, 173
rational connection test, 165–6, 173–4, See rational classification test
Rawls, John, 174, 227
reasonable classification test. See rational classification test
resource allocation, 182
Reynolds defence. See defamation
Ribeiro, Roberto, 95
right to assemble, 128, 134–5
in Hong Kong, 39, 95, 131–2
in Malaysia, 46, 132–3
in Singapore, 54, 129–31
right to equality, 4, 20–1
forbidden personal characteristics model, 161, 167–8, 174–9, 192, 225
formal model, 161, 163–4, 169–71, 192
fundamental rights model, 161, 168–9, 179–80, 192
in Hong Kong, 39, 95, 163, 167–8, 176–8, 181, 188, 189
in Malaysia, 46, 162–5, 168–70, 177–8, 180, 190
in Singapore, 54, 99, 163, 165–6, 172–3, 177–8, 190–2
rational connection model, 161, 164–6, 171–3, 192
right to fair trial, 201, 210–1, 213, See due process
in Malaysia, 97, 202, 209, 214, 226
right to free expression. See freedom of expression
right to marriage, 103
right to privacy, 39, 94
right to vote, 34–5
of prisoners, 102–3
Rivers, Julian, 83, 134, 182, 185
Roach, Kent, 24, 27, 75, 93, 101, 220, 223
rule of law, 14, 17–21, 27, 74, 159, 171, 184, 187, 199, 221

Schauer, Frederick, 3, 8, 17–8, 109, 121
Schrock, Thomas, 80–4

separation of powers, 82, 92
sexual orientation discrimination, 185, 225, See discrimination
Singapore
  basic structure of the Constitution, 76
  constitution history of, 48–50
  constitutional amendment procedure of, 55
  fundamental liberties, 54–5
  judiciary, 53, 75–6, 89, 120, 133, 218, 220
  Parliament, 50–1, 54, 75–6, 87, 159, 191, 207–8
  President, 52–4, 74–6, 87, 89
  Prime Minister, 51–2, 54–5
Sino-British Joint Declaration, 32, 59–60
sliding scale of review, 162, 185, 188–9, 192–3, 225
social welfare, 11, 21, 40, 63, 100, 134
Sri Ram, Gopal, 91–2, 97, 132, 201–2, 214
Standing Committee of the National People's Congress, 38, 40, 57, 59–66, 78, 88
statutory' rights interpretation, 93, 104, See sub-constitutional review
  in Hong Kong, 94–6
sub-constitutional doctrines, 80, 84, 86, 103, 136, 159, 196, 221, See sub-constitutional review
sub-constitutional review, 4, 79, 159, See dialogic review
  critiques of, 81–5
  justifications of, 82–5
  types of, 80
sub-constitutional tools, 79, 105, 110, 135, 152, 163, 213, 218, See sub-constitutional review
sub-constitutionalism, 80–5, See sub-constitutional review
Sunstein, Cass, 2, 92, 106, 109, 153, 179, 206, 223
Supreme Court of Canada, 24, 86, 101, 147, 167–8, 171, 174, 181
Syariah courts, 45–6, 139–40, 150–2, 153–6, 225

temporary suspension order, 101–3, See delayed declarations of invalidity
Thio, Li-ann, 52, 74, 77, 109, 119, 143, 145–6, 151, 155
transsexual marriage, 103, See right to marriage
Tsakyrakis, Stavros, 147, 149
Tun Salleh, 45, 58, 66, 68–71, 126
Tushnet, Mark, 2, 10, 17, 22–5, 80, 84

United States Constitution, 79–80
United States Supreme Court, 2, 28, 79–81, 107, 115–6, 149, 179, 188

Vermeule, Adrian, 3, 8, 14–6

Wacks, Raymond, 31
Waldron, Jeremy, 3, 8, 181
  critiques of his arguments, 10–6
  on legislative supremacy, 9–10
Wednesbury review, 135, 158, 225
Wee, Chong Jin, 74, 76
Welch, Robert, 80–4

Yong, Pung How, 76–7, 141–2, 144–5
Young, Alison, 1, 7, 8, 99, 182, 184